RAJIV GANDHI

RAJIV GANDHI
SON OF A DYNASTY

— • —

NICHOLAS NUGENT

BBC BOOKS

Published by BBC Books,
a division of BBC Enterprises Limited,
Woodlands, 80 Wood Lane, London W12 0TT

First published 1990

© Nicholas Nugent 1990

ISBN 0 563 36007 0

Set in 11/13pt Sabon

Printed and bound in Great Britain by
Butler & Tanner Ltd, Frome
Jacket printed by Belmont Press, Northampton

Photographic Acknowledgments

1 & 2 *Sunday*, Calcutta, 3 Camera Press; 4 Mela Ram & Sons,
Dehra Dun; 5 Goyal Studios, Dehra Dun; 6, 7 & 8 Dilsher Virk;
9 Subha News Agency, Madras; 10 *India Today*, Delhi; 11
Camera Press; 12 Rex Features; 113 Camera Press; 14 *Sunday*,
Calcutta; 15 Rex Features; 16 *Sunday*, Calcutta; 17 Rex Features;
18 Associated Press; 19 *India Today*, Delhi; 20 *Sunday*,
Calcutta; 21 *India Today*, Delhi; 22 Rex Features; 23 *Sunday*,
Calcutta; 24 Rex Features; 25 *Sunday*, Calcutta; 26 *India Today*,
Delhi; 27, 28 & 29 *Sunday*, Calcutta.

Contents

Nehru-Gandhi Family Tree

Motilal Nehru　=　Swarup Rani
1861–1931　　*1869–1938*

Jawaharlal Nehru　=　Kamala
1889–1964　　*1899–1936*

Indira Nehru　= Feroze Gandhi
1917–1984　　*1912–1960*

Rajiv Gandhi　= Sonia Maino　　　　Sanjay Gandhi = Maneka Anand
1944–　　*1946–*　　　　　*1946–1980*　　*1956–*

Rahul　　Priyanka　　　　　Feroze Varun
1970　　*1972*　　　　　*1980*

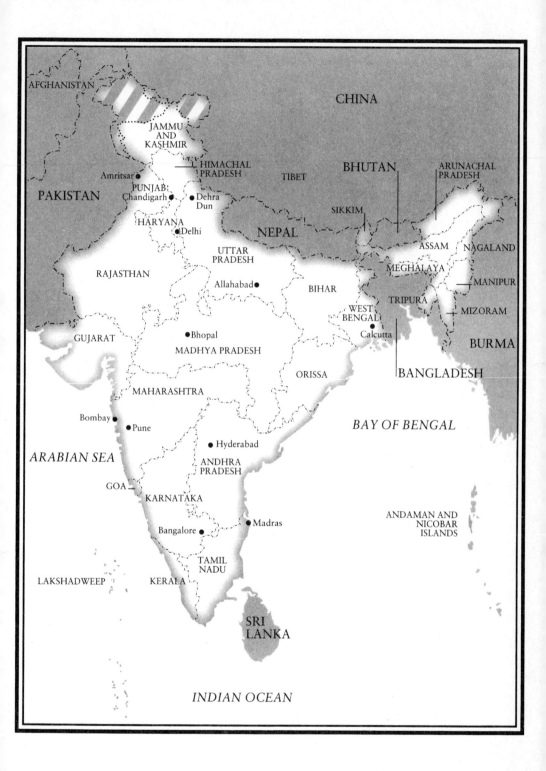

The Workings of India's Democracy

India's constitution is modelled on the British pattern of parliamentary democracy, which gives a central role to the prime minister. The major differences between the systems are that in India the constitution rather than Parliament is supreme; also, as a republic, India has an elected president as head of state, rather than a monarch. The president is elected to serve for five years by an electoral college consisting of the members of both houses of Parliament and of all state legislative assemblies. On election, the president takes up residence in Rashtrapati Bhawan, the grand pink sandstone palace in New Delhi which was formerly the residence of the British viceroys of India. The president's most important task is to select and administer the oath of office to a prime minister. Since the prime minister is answerable to the House of the People, or *Lok Sabha*, the president is bound to select someone he believes can command the majority support of that house.

Once the prime minister has been sworn in, the constitution obliges the president to follow his advice, and that of his ministers. It is the prime minister who, for all practical purposes, rules India as head of government, though the constitution vests executive power in the president. The prime minister's power depends on his retaining majority support in the *Lok Sabha* and, implicitly, in his own party too. Theoretically, the president can dismiss the prime minister since constitutionally the latter holds office 'during the pleasure of the president'.

The prime minister rules through the two houses of Parliament; the round Parliament House is adjacent to Rashtrapati Bhawan and the Secretariat, demonstrating the close links between the institutions of government. Members of the *Lok Sabha*, the House of the People, are elected at intervals which must not exceed five years. At the 1989 elections, nearly 500 million voters from the age of eighteen upwards were entitled to cast their vote to fill the 545 seats, making India easily the world's largest democracy with universal adult suffrage. Most candidates contested on behalf of one of the many political parties.

Unlike the *Lok Sabha,* the *Rajya Sabha,* or Council of States, is never dissolved. Most of its 244 members are elected, for a six-year term, by members of state legislative assemblies, and take up their seats as representatives of that state. One third of *Rajya Sabha* members step down every second year. Before a bill can become law, it has to be passed by both houses of Parliament, and must also receive the presidential assent.

Though India is not a true federation, the constitution vests considerable power in state governments. Some powers are specifically allocated to state governments, some are reserved to central government whilst others are shared between them. Each of the twenty-five states has a legislative assembly, which also has a five-year tenure. In addition, some states have a second house; a legislative council. The elected leader of the majority party or alliance generally becomes that state's chief minister, an office he or she holds at the pleasure of the state governor. The governor is appointed by the central government, and exercises a role in relation to the state similar to that of the president in relation to the nation.

The power of the central government to dismiss a state government and take over control of that state by declaring what is known as 'President's Rule' is one of the more controversial provisions of the constitution, and one which has frequently been applied. States like Punjab, Jammu and Kashmir and Assam have been ruled by central government over prolonged periods as a result of this procedure.

Apart from the executive and legislature, India also has an independent judiciary based on a system of courts and statute law, though the courts also apply personal, or religious, law side by side with statute law. India's armed forces, the fourth largest in the world, are subject to political control and have never shown any inclination to take power, unlike the armed forces in neighbouring Pakistan and Bangladesh.

Preface

The main inspiration for this book came from sitting in the gallery of the Indian Parliament in early 1987 watching and listening to the stormy debates arising from the events described in chapters nine and ten, and from covering the Allahabad by-election a year later. I felt these experiences gave me a right to attempt to chronicle the events as they were confronted by their key player. It helps, of course, that I have myself shared some of the experiences of Rajiv Gandhi's earlier life – Doon School, Cambridge and the thrill of learning to fly – and have been visiting India for more than half its independent life. Nor do I make any apologies, by way of explanation as to how this book came about, for my own fascination with the political process of the world's largest democracy.

There are many people to whom I owe thanks. Rajiv Gandhi was kind enough to share memories with me, as were many other participants in his story, for I have tried to base my account as much on oral as on written sources. I am not acknowledging individually those to whom I spoke, but thank them collectively for their recollections and opinions. My appreciation goes also to friends and colleagues who have been kind enough to read parts of the text and to make suggestions, though responsibility for the accuracy of anything I have written is, of course, my own. My especial thanks for help in this and other respects go to Mark Tully, Satish Jacob, Shernaz Italia and the staff of the BBC Delhi Bureau, to Arthur Goodhart, Subash Chakravarti, Rita Manchanda, Derek Brown, Jim Manor, Jasvinder Singh, Rahul Bedi, to my colleagues in the BBC Eastern Service for coping with my absences, and for similar reasons, as well as for her proof-reading expertise, to my wife, Xuan.

In my mind's eye, I have three contrasting images of Rajiv Gandhi, all of them acquired within the space of one month in late 1985. There was Rajiv Gandhi the international statesman, attired in dark blue 'Nehru-collared' suit, standing by the side of Mrs Thatcher outside 10 Downing Street on his first visit to Britain as Prime Minister. Three weeks later at Delhi airport, I saw him descend from the aircraft that had taken him and Sonia to London, the Caribbean, the United Nations and Moscow. Dressed in *kurta pyjama,* he appeared every inch the Indian politician. A week later I was present at Doon School when Rajiv arrived by helicopter as chief guest at the school's golden jubilee celebrations. Wearing his old boys' blazer and tie, it was easy to think of him as a slightly balding schoolboy. This was the most relaxed of the three images: the Rajiv Gandhi amongst his old classmates. There is yet another Rajiv Gandhi that few outsiders see: the very private man at home with Sonia, the children and their five dogs, a home whose doors are rarely opened to political colleagues, and where he enjoys the nearest his bodyguards allow to a private life. I have tried to portray all these.

Nicholas Nugent

LONDON, AUGUST 1990

CHAPTER ONE

Greatness Thrust Upon Him

It was the last day of October 1984. There was a pre-electoral atmosphere in Delhi. The prime minister, Indira Gandhi, knew she must call a general election within two months; possibly she had already chosen a date. That morning she was taking a break from campaigning and from the regular audience, or *darshan,* that Indian prime ministers give to people with petitions or grievances to present. Instead she was to give a television interview to Peter Ustinov. The camera was in place at the adjoining office as Mrs Gandhi, wearing a bright saffron-coloured sari, set out from her residence at about 9.12 a.m.

As Mrs Gandhi reached the boundary between her home, 1 Safdarjung Road, and her office, 1 Akbar Road, the first of more than twenty shots rang out. The prime minister fell to the ground immediately as shots were repeatedly fired at her. It was all so sudden that she already lay dying before soldiers of the Indo-Tibetan Border Police in their hut a short distance away reacted. Behind the intense security of the prime ministerial compound, India's prime minister had been shot dead by two members of her own bodyguard.

The men who shot Mrs Gandhi were both Sikhs, members of the warrior race from the north-western state of Punjab. Sikhism is a religion which emerged in the early sixteenth century. Its founder, Guru Nanak, disliked the polytheism of India's majority faith, Hinduism, as well as the rigid hierarchy of its castes. The faith that he founded aimed to blend some aspects of both Hinduism and Islam whilst leaving aside what he considered to be their less savoury aspects.

In recent years, some Sikhs have protested at what they consider to be the pre-eminence of Hinduism in India, constitutionally a secular state. As a small community numbering a mere 12 million in a land of over 800 million, Sikhs have some reason to feel paranoid towards the much more numerous Hindus, even though the influence of Sikhs in business, the armed forces and government has regularly been much greater than their numbers would suggest. Some Sikhs feel so strongly that their community has been relegated to an inferior status that they want Punjab and surrounding areas, where Sikhs predominate, to break away from India and become a separate nation called Khalistan, 'the land of the pure'.

When Sikh bodyguards opened fire on Mrs Gandhi, nobody was in any doubt that Sikh grievances lay behind the assassination. Less than five months earlier, in an effort to quell the violence that was afflicting Punjab and neighbouring states as a result of Sikh agitation, Mrs Gandhi had ordered the army into Sikhism's holiest shrine, the Golden Temple at Amritsar. It was the most difficult decision of Mrs Gandhi's sixteen years in power. The objective was to flush out Jarnail Singh Bhindranwale, an extremist Sikh leader who had taken refuge from the authorities inside the temple compound after being implicated in various violent crimes. From inside the compound, where he was surrounded by heavily armed followers, Bhindranwale planned and co-ordinated the killing of Hindus in the state in a bloodthirsty pursuit of Sikh separatist demands.

Operation Blue Star turned out to be a clumsy and bungled operation in which several hundred soldiers and pilgrims, as well as Bhindranwale and his followers, died. Worse still, even in the eyes of Sikhs who were not supporters of Bhindranwale's agitation, parts of the temple compound and its holy centrepiece, the Akal Takht – to which Sikh pilgrims come from around the world to pay their respect – were brutally violated and damaged. Operation Blue Star created a sense of rage amongst Sikhs with many vowing that Mrs Gandhi would pay for this action with her life. Security measures around the prime minister were increased and units of the elite commando force, the Indo-Tibetan Border Police, were brought in to provide a security cordon around her home. Because of their reputation as fighting men, there are lots of Sikhs in many Indian army regiments. After Operation Blue Star, it was an elementary precaution to entrust Mrs Gandhi's security to a para-military force that had a high reputation for efficiency and contained no Sikhs. It became increasingly difficult to gain access to the prime minister, though she still maintained the long-established routine of receiving security-checked members of the public at her morning *darshan*.

There were plans to remove Sikhs from the corps of bodyguards who surrounded the prime minister at all times, but Mrs Gandhi herself is said to have rejected this. So, two Sikhs – Beant Singh, who had been several years in the prime minister's service and had accompanied her on visits abroad, and the more recently recruited Satwant Singh – were on duty that fateful October morning. The subsequent commission of enquiry into the assassination was to hear that Satwant Singh had swapped duties so that he could be on the same shift as his fellow Sikh. Mrs Gandhi's son, Rajiv, who lived along with his family in the same house as his mother, was later to tell an interviewer he had wondered at the behaviour of Satwant Singh a couple of times, and had even asked for him to be removed from the inner security cordon on one occasion.[1] But nothing about the two men on that morning aroused the suspicion of Mrs Gandhi's security officer or her special assistant, R. K. Dhawan, both of whom were with her as she made her way to the interview.

Later, testimony was to be given that Beant Singh and Satwant Singh met regularly at Delhi's best-known *gurudwara,* or Sikh temple, Bangla Sahib. It was here, according to the claims of witnesses, that the conspiracy was hatched as the two men met with other disaffected Sikhs. Beant Singh was the leader, with Satwant Singh the accomplice – a reluctant one according to some accounts. Their precise relationship, and how they had planned the assassination, will remain a matter of conjecture, as Beant Singh was shot dead by Indo-Tibetan police moments after the shooting. The official enquiry concluded that there had been a conspiracy, and even pointed a finger of suspicion at Mrs Gandhi's much trusted aide, R. K. Dhawan. It suggested he had deliberately rearranged the timing of the television interview, and had countermanded orders that Sikhs be removed from the prime minister's bodyguard after Operation Blue Star. When the enquiry report was eventually published, after first being suppressed, the evidence for a conspiracy was seen to be slender. Nonetheless, Satwant Singh and another alleged conspirator were tried and hanged more than four years later.

After the shooting, the fatally wounded and unconscious Mrs Gandhi was carried to a car by R. K. Dhawan, helped by Mrs Gandhi's daughter-in-law, Sonia. The car bearing the prime minister raced the three miles to Delhi's foremost medical academy, the All India Institute

---

[1] Interview with M. J. Akbar in *Sunday,* 10–16 March 1985, quoted in *Amritsar,* Tully and Jacob.

of Medical Sciences. It is likely Mrs Gandhi was already dead on arrival, but doctors laboured in the operating theatre to revive her. She was given continuous blood transfusions, although they probably realised at an early point that their efforts were in vain. Those around Mrs Gandhi were then left with the awesome decision of when to tell the nation that its prime minister was dead.

At 2.20 p.m. it was announced at the doors of the hospital that Indira Gandhi was dead. Ten minutes later, the news was broadcast over the BBC World Service in its 9.00 a.m. GMT news bulletin. Listeners to the BBC around the world, including its large regular audience in India, already knew of the shooting five hours earlier. But India's own radio and television services were not to announce the Prime Minister's death till much later, perhaps fearing the consequences when it became known that she was the victim of Sikh assassins.

Rajiv Gandhi was in the north-eastern state of West Bengal, not far from Calcutta, on a pre-election tour when he was told of the shooting. Those with him recall how calm he was on being given the news, perhaps out of a sense of fate. A helicopter brought Rajiv to Calcutta's Dum Dum airport, where he boarded an Indian Air Force plane sent from Delhi to collect him. On the way to Delhi the pilot tuned into the BBC and other stations. Though Rajiv was not told for certain that his mother had died until he reached Delhi, he was to say later that on the plane he 'sort of knew'.

Rajiv went directly from Palam airport to the All India Institute of Medical Sciences, where his wife, Sonia, had remained at her mother-in-law's side. By the time Rajiv reached the hospital, in the middle of the afternoon, India had lost its prime minister. There was no deputy prime minister, nor even any designated or pre-eminently qualified successor.

The person whose job it was to appoint and swear in a prime minister, President Zail Singh, was himself thousands of miles away in the Yemen Arab Republic. He was woken early by a telephone call from Delhi telling him of the shooting. The caller, the permanent head of the External Affairs Ministry, advised him to return immediately, saying 'your presence is needed'. Zail Singh was not told that Mrs Gandhi was dead – indeed, it was probably not known for sure at that stage. However, he followed the advice he was given and left San'a, the Yemeni capital, to return to Delhi aboard his Indian Air Force

Boeing. On the aircraft, he consulted the copy of the Indian constitution that he always carried with him and reassured himself that
the responsibility for choosing a new prime minister, if one should be
needed, was his and that he was not bound to consult anyone else. He
did, though, discuss the choice with his secretary and other officials
travelling with him over the course of the five-hour flight, before
reaching his decision. Zail Singh also listened to reports on the BBC
as he flew towards Delhi.

The first decision reached by the president was that there should
not be an interim prime minister. Twice before since Independence,
India's prime minister had died whilst in office: Indira Gandhi's father,
Jawaharlal Nehru, in 1964, and two years later his successor, Lal
Bahadur Shastri. On each occasion, it had been decided not to select
a new prime minister until after the customary thirteen-day period of
mourning was over. An interim prime minister had taken over in the
meantime. However, India's constitution makes no provision for an
interim prime minister, and Zail Singh made up his mind that he would
not appoint one. Secondly, recognising that Indira Gandhi's Congress
Party had an overwhelming majority in Parliament, he determined
that the new prime minister should be a Congress member. Without
majority support, a prime minister could not survive in office long.
Then he made his third and crucial decision; to ask Rajiv Gandhi to
form a government. Looking back on his reasons for selecting the least
experienced candidate from those whose names crossed his mind, Zail
Singh gives three reasons for his choice: 'He had always had a clean
image, his age was in his favour, and I thought at the time he was
intelligent.' Zail Singh, who was later to fall out with Rajiv, adds
rather sourly: 'I think differently now.' He had weighed up other
possible candidates: the finance minister Pranab Mukherjee would have
been his second choice, but he was not a popular figure in the party
and had the disadvantage of belonging to the *Rajya Sabha,* the upper
house of Parliament, rather than the *Lok Sabha,* or lower house, from
which all previous prime ministers had been chosen. His third choice
would have been the home minister Narasimha Rao. But Zail Singh
felt neither could carry a majority of the party with him, whereas Rajiv
could.

Zail Singh agrees that other factors influenced him in making his
crucial decision; factors unrelated to Rajiv's qualifications for the office
of prime minister. He thought that, in the tragic circumstances of his

mother's death, Rajiv deserved to be chosen, and he knew that is what Indira Gandhi would have wanted. 'I knew her mind and that was what she wanted, though we had not discussed it specifically; I just knew her mind,' he says. Zail Singh also admits to owing a debt to the Nehru family; to Jawaharlal Nehru, who brought him into politics, as well as to Indira Gandhi who chose him as Congress's candidate for president. But he denies suggestions that he would have done anything for Indira, or that his selection of Rajiv was his way of repaying the family a debt he owed, saying that, as president of India, his responsibility lay to the constitution and the people of India. Zail Singh's mind was made up long before he reached Delhi.

Zail Singh arrived at Palam airport some time after Rajiv. He was met by Vice President Venkataraman, and the Speaker of the lower house of Parliament, Balram Jakhar, amongst others. They confirmed to him that Indira Gandhi was dead. As a Sikh and a former chief minister of Punjab, Zail Singh weighed up the implications of the fact that India's prime minister had been shot dead by members of his own community. The president overruled advice that he return directly to the presidential palace, and drove instead to the All India Institute, arriving there at around 5 p.m. Accompanying him in the car were Mrs Gandhi's long-time special assistant, R. K. Dhawan, and one of the Congress Party general secretaries, Arun Nehru, a cousin of Indira Gandhi. Zail Singh told them he was thinking of appointing Rajiv prime minister. 'R. K. Dhawan looked happy, whilst Arun Nehru remained silent,' he said. After paying his respects to Mrs Gandhi and offering condolences to Rajiv, Zail Singh joined leaders of the Congress Party who had been meeting at the Institute.

Congress leaders had by this time made up their own minds on the succession. They too had decided that a permanent, rather than an interim prime minister be chosen immediately, though it was the circumstances of Indira's killing that seems to have influenced them most. Both Jawaharlal Nehru and Shastri had died natural deaths; Indira's death at the hands of Sikh gunmen gave rise to a very real fear that inter-community violence would erupt. A strong leader was needed if violence was to be averted and the nation held together in the face of such a threat. A constant theme of the Congress Party at elections has always been that it is the only party to provide the unity needed to keep in check the recurring separatist demands put forward by one community or another, like those now being called for by some Sikhs.

It is the job of Congress's Parliamentary Board, its policy-making cabal, to select a new party leader. Of its eight members, Mrs Gandhi was dead and several of the others were away from Delhi. Those absent included the finance minister Pranab Mukherjee, who had been in his home state of West Bengal with Rajiv Gandhi, and the home minister Narasimha Rao, who was in his home state of Andhra Pradesh in southern India. As long-standing members of the cabinet, both had some claim to succeed Mrs Gandhi. Amongst the many Congress figures who had assembled at the hospital were chief ministers and party leaders from some of India's most important states, such as Bihar, Madhya Pradesh, Maharashtra, Tamil Nadu and Rajasthan. In the atmosphere of crisis in which the party found itself, their opinions probably counted as much as those of members of the Parliamentary Board. The choice was not an easy one: there was no obvious successor. After feeling threatened from within the party during her earlier years as prime minister, Mrs Gandhi had made a point of removing potential rivals from positions of power. There was a widespread belief that, since her younger and more politically inclined son, Sanjay, had met an untimely death in a flying accident, Indira Gandhi had intended she would be succeeded by her elder son, Rajiv. Indeed, some people believe he had been drafted into politics with the express intention that the Nehru–Gandhi dynasty should be continued under his stewardship.

However, on that October day it was by no means a foregone conclusion that Rajiv would take over. It could have been argued that Rajiv's apprenticeship was not yet complete, and indeed, it has since been argued that he would have done better to have bided his time. He had, after all, entered political life just three years earlier, winning the by-election necessitated by his brother's death. He had never held cabinet office, nor even nursed any junior ministerial portfolio, though his mother, in a clear indication of her ambition for him, had made him one of the Congress Party's general secretaries. In this capacity he was already playing a key role in preparations for the forthcoming general election.

Yet, even before Zail Singh had reached Delhi, a consensus emerged amongst Congress leaders gathering at the hospital that Rajiv Gandhi should be selected as the new leader of the party and, therefore, of the country. According to the senior party general secretary, G. K. Moopanar, Rajiv was the only person who was acceptable to all those assembled at the hospital. He says the need to maintain stability was uppermost in their minds. There was no dissent from the choice of Rajiv, which was effectively achieved through consensus. Later, in the early evening, the full Parliamentary Board did meet at the prime minister's office, 1 Akbar Road, and endorsed the consensus decision.

Rajiv agrees that the decision that he should take over as prime minister had been reached by senior members of the party before Zail Singh arrived back in the country. The most senior Congressman, Kamlapati Tripathi, who claims credit for proposing that Rajiv take over, admits there was a sympathy element in the decision: 'I said, "We must not leave the throne vacant. That will be very dangerous. We all feel for Rajiv; let's put him up." '[1] According to Rajiv, there was even some talk of Vice President Venkataraman conducting the swearing in immediately, before Zail Singh's arrival, but that option was rejected. It was decided to await the president's return. Of the decision to choose him, Rajiv says: 'I hadn't really thought of being prime minister at all; the thought of being in government "yes", but not prime minister.' It did not occur to him that he might be asked until several people collared him at the hospital, saying he should accept the job. Rajiv says: 'I wasn't at all happy. I talked with Sonia and she was totally unhappy about the whole thing. We discussed it and we weighed up all the pros and cons, and finally we decided to accept.'

In the circumstances, Rajiv had little choice but to accept; he was not a free agent. The nation urgently needed a new leader, the more so because of the circumstances of Indira Gandhi's death, and the fear that it might lead to an explosion of communal violence. The Congress Party hierarchy had reached a unanimous decision that he should be that leader. The country's president had reached the same decision, for similar though not identical reasons. Even if Rajiv was unaware of what was widely assumed to be his mother's wish – that he succeed her as prime minister – or had been prepared to defy it, he could hardly refuse a request that was supported by the entire Congress Party leadership, and by the president.

Before he left the All India Institute, President Zail Singh had asked Rajiv Gandhi to come to Rashtrapati Bhawan, Delhi's grand presidential palace, to be sworn in as prime minister. The former president is adamant that he was acting on his own decision, and that he did not take any notice of the views of Congress leaders. Later,

[1] Speaking to *The Illustrated Weekly of India*, 25 January 1987.

when Congress Parliamentary Board members arrived to deliver their formal decision of Rajiv's selection as the party's new leader, Zail Singh says he ignored it. 'Moopanar wanted to give me a letter, but I did not take it, I did not see it,' he says. According to Zail Singh, there was no meeting of the Congress Parliamentary Board. 'Even if there had been, it would not have been binding on me; the choice of Rajiv Gandhi was mine and mine alone; nobody else contributed. I alone am responsible,' he says. When later Zail Singh and Rajiv Gandhi had their differences, the president never ceased reminding the young prime minister of the debt he owed him in having 'made' him prime minister.

With the power vacuum effectively filled, Zail Singh instructed Vice President Venkataraman to tell the nation of Indira Gandhi's death. It was announced at 6.00 p.m. through All India Radio and Doordarshan, the television network, that Indira Gandhi was dead – more than three and a half hours after her death had been confirmed and nearly nine hours after she had been shot. At around 6.40 p.m., in Rashtrapati Bhawan's Ashoka Hall, Rajiv took the oath of office to become the sixth prime minister of India, the third member of his family to hold that office. What should have been a happy ceremony was on this occasion a decidedly sombre affair. Thus, a young man who had hardly had opportunity to come to terms with the death of his mother, and its enormous implications for the nation, was unwittingly, and perhaps unwillingly, thrust into the most challenging role to which any Indian can aspire and one to which he had never aspired.

It was in many ways a cruel decision to ask one so inexperienced to take on a job that required so much experience, and at such a difficult time for the nation. It was an unashamed use of the Gandhi name, the Gandhi–Nehru legacy, to hold together both the party and the nation at a time of crisis. The Congress Party had been dominated by two members of the same family and was now to be led by a third. Even if Rajiv had contemplated one day succeeding his mother, he could hardly have imagined it would happen so soon, and in such tragic circumstances.

Shortly before midnight, Rajiv made his first address to the nation as prime minister over television and radio, recorded at the Akbar Road office, a few yards from where Indira Gandhi fell earlier that day. It was an address hastily cobbled together with the help of a number of key aides. They included Arun Nehru, R.K. Dhawan and

Mrs Gandhi's press adviser, Sharada Prasad. Sonia Gandhi, and two of Rajiv's close friends, Arun Singh and film star Amitabh Bachchan, were there too. One of the broadcasting team sent to record the address recalls helping Amitabh Bachchan to translate the text from English into Hindi so that it could be recorded in both languages. She was told to write in big bold letters so that the prime minister could easily read it; English is the first language of Rajiv Gandhi and most of those close to him, as indeed it continues to be the main language of government. Rajiv does not find it easy to choose the right words in India's official language of Hindi. The English version of his address was recorded without difficulty, but when the time came to record the Hindi version, Rajiv stuttered and fluffed. There were several retakes. 'He sounded very uncomfortable with the language,' recalls the producer. Now, as on subsequent occasions, he showed himself quite ready to have his Hindi corrected by the radio or television producer, or to agree to a retake where he had stumbled on an unfamiliar word.

Rajiv told his audience that the nation as well as he himself had lost a mother, a remark reminiscent of the announcement of the death of his grandfather, Jawaharlal Nehru, twenty years earlier, when it was said that the entire nation had been orphaned. He went on: 'You know how dear to her heart was the dream of a united, peaceful, prosperous India, an India in which all Indians, irrespective of their religion, language or political persuasion, live together as one big family in an atmosphere free from mutual rivalries and prejudices. By her untimely death, her work remains unfinished. It is for us to complete this task.' The broadcast also invoked comparison with the one Jawaharlal Nehru had made in 1948 to tell the nation of the assassination of its founding father, Mahatma Gandhi: 'The light has gone out of our lives and there is darkness everywhere. Our beloved leader, Bapu as we called him, the father of the nation, is no more.'

Nehru feared that Muslims would be blamed for Gandhi's death which could have exacerbated an already tense atmosphere between Hindus and Muslims. He was therefore quick to tell the nation that the assassin was a Hindu fanatic. Bearing similarly tragic news thirty-six years later, Rajiv Gandhi made no reference to his mother's assassins, or to their motives. He only alluded to the communal nature of the killing when he appealed for calm and national unity, saying nothing would hurt the soul of Indira Gandhi more than the outbreak of violence in any part of the country.

Violence had in fact broken out very soon after Mrs Gandhi's death was announced from the hospital. At first it was confined to the vicinity of the hospital, with turbaned Sikhs becoming conspicuous targets. Stones were thrown at the car bringing President Zail Singh from the airport. Other vehicles were set on fire, as was a Sikh *gurudwara* close to the hospital. It was what one eye-witness to the events which followed called a 'knee jerk' reaction to news of the assassination. If Rajiv Gandhi was hoping, as he made his first prime ministerial address to the nation, that further violence could be averted and peace restored, he was to be disappointed. It was three days before order was restored to the capital.

The following morning, Delhi was ablaze. Sikh homes and property all over the city became the targets of mobs intent on exacting revenge. It started in outlying districts, suburbs like Saket and Palam, where Sikh homes and *gurudwaras* were attacked, looted and set on fire. Before long, the mobs were attacking targets in the city's commercial centre of Connaught Circus, where Sikh-owned restaurants and hotels were set on fire. Sikh men can easily be identified by the turbans many of them wear to protect their long hair, which for religious reasons they keep uncut. Particular targets of the mobs were the many taxis driven by Sikhs. More than two thousand cars, taxis and trucks were burnt during the three-day orgy of vengeance and vio-lence. On the outskirts of the city, Sikh-owned factories, including the plant which makes Campa Cola, India's answer to Coca-Cola, were set alight.

It was not just property that was attacked; Sikhs themselves became victims of the frenzied violence during the course of 1 November. The initial 'knee jerk' response had given way to what appeared to be a more systematic and organised outbreak of blood-letting. Sikhs were stabbed, burned and butchered to death. Sikh taxi drivers were pulled from their vehicles and killed, their bodies left on the road. Some Sikhs arriving in the capital by train were slaughtered. In one notorious episode, a well-organised group spent several hours putting to death all identifiable Sikhs living in the suburb of Trilokpuri on the eastern bank of the river Jumna. Eventually, they were disturbed by journalists who found it difficult to comprehend what was going on, and even more difficult to fathom why police from nearby police stations had not attempted to prevent the massacre. At Trilokpuri, as well as other places, there was circumstantial evidence that the police may have encouraged – and most certainly turned a blind eye – to what was going on.

The anti-Sikh pogrom was undoubtedly further fuelled by various rumours that were circulating: one said that Sikhs had poisoned Delhi's water supply; another said that a train full of Hindus coming from Punjab had been slaughtered by Sikhs. There was no truth in either rumour, but people still believed them, and so the killings continued into a second, and then a third day. Later, Rajiv was to be much criticised for his seemingly insensitive remark suggesting the inevitability of the killings: 'When a mighty tree falls, the earth is bound to shake.'

While the bloodbath continued, Delhi's police and the civil administration were preoccupied with maintaining security in the more visible parts of the city in preparation for the scores of foreign VIPs who were arriving for Mrs Gandhi's funeral. Security was tight around Teen Murti House, the home of the late Jawaharlal Nehru, where Mrs Gandhi's body lay in state. Troops, who are not normally seen in the city, were put to work clearing away the debris of burnt-out vehicles. Delhi police gave a higher priority to keeping the streets clear for visiting dignitaries than to stopping the killings. Nobody, it seemed, had orders to seek out and try to prevent the holocaust that was taking place in areas like Trilokpuri, Sultanpuri and Mangolpuri.

It was later claimed that members and workers of the Congress Party were involved. Some gangs of killers were seen picking out the homes of Sikhs from the names on voters' lists. A report prepared by two civil rights organisations entitled 'Who Are The Guilty?' concluded that far from being a spontaneous expression of madness and popular grief at Mrs Gandhi's assassination, as the authorities claimed, the attacks on Sikhs in Delhi were 'the outcome of an organised plan marked by acts of both deliberate commissions and omissions by important politicians of the Congress Party at the top and by the authorities in the [city] administration'.[1] The report, which spoke of a 'determined group', named 227 people, identified by survivors, who had allegedly instigated violence or protected alleged criminals; they included Congress MPs and councillors and a number of policemen.

The death toll in Delhi during those three days of killings was officially

---

[1] 'Who Are The Guilty?' A report by the People's Union for Democratic Rights and People's Union for Civil Liberties, Delhi 1984

put at 2733, though a report by another human rights' organisation, the Citizens' Justice Committee, put the Delhi total at 3870. Several hundred more people died elsewhere in north India as a result of similar attacks. Outside the capital, the cities worst affected by the orgy of violence were Kanpur in Uttar Pradesh, where 140 people died, and the steel town of Bokaro in Bihar, with a death toll of 76. The worst attacks occurred in cities like Delhi where the Sikhs constitute a significant minority. The Sikhs' home state of Punjab remained quiet.

The way in which many Hindus turned on Sikhs, apparently seizing what they considered to be a long overdue opportunity to teach this troublesome minority a lesson, was an ominous reminder of the Hindu–Muslim killings which had accompanied the partition of the subcontinent into India and Pakistan thirty-seven years earlier. Hindus and Sikhs are usually considered to have more in common with each other than do members of India's other faiths, and it must be remembered that the anti-Sikh violence was by no means a community-wide response to the alleged misdeeds of the Sikhs. Many Hindus were only too ready to take Sikhs into their homes to give them protection from the rampaging and vengeance-seeking mobs. Just as very few Sikhs had espoused the cause of Khalistan, or followed the violent campaign of the late Jarnail Singh Bhindranwale, so relatively small numbers of Hindus were intent on teaching the Sikhs a lesson.

Even so, the killings inflicted a deep wound on all Sikhs, deepening the wound inflicted four months earlier with the army assault on the Golden Temple. One Sikh journalist wrote that the killings had 'left a volatile and proud community humbled and beleaguered ... [they] marked the end of normal life for Sikhs'.[1] What made the alienation worse was the refusal of the authorities at first to admit the extent of what happened, claiming repeatedly that the situation was under control. It was three full days after the assassination before the army, who had been called into the city on the day after the assassination, began to enforce the curfew and restore order. Until then, it was claimed they had no instructions to do so. The report 'Who Are The Guilty?' spoke of a lack of co-ordination between the police and army, and an absence of clear instructions to the army. President Zail Singh was one of those who urged Rajiv to take urgent action to halt the violence. Rajiv, still shell-shocked by the experience of taking power,

[1] Rahul Bedi writing in *The Assassination and After*, Shourie.

had difficulty in operating the levers of power. He was unaware of the procedure for calling in the army to assist the city police, and may well have been unaware at first of the seriousness of the situation.

The Sikh feeling that their community had been betrayed was deepened by the government's delay in initiating an enquiry into the massacre, despite many well-attested claims of police and Congress workers' connivance. Feelings were further aroused when, during the election campaign which was to follow the assassination, Sikhs were portrayed as an alien community, as if all of them were being blamed for Indira Gandhi's death. The low level of compensation offered to families who had lost breadwinners and other members, and often homes and property too, was an added grievance for a community which was entitled, like any other, to the protection of the authorities. Five years later, many Sikhs were still living in refugee camps around the capital and several thousand others had migrated across north India to Punjab in search of greater security.

Rajiv Gandhi seemed to be preoccupied with organising the funeral rites of his mother, and receiving the visiting dignitaries who had come to pay her their respects. As he lit his mother's pyre, his awesome new responsibilities had hardly struck home. Politically, he was very much the servant of his inherited advisers, none of whom seemed any wiser than he was as to how to stop the killings, beyond appealing for calm.

It was not till the morning of the day his mother was to be cremated, 3 November, that Rajiv visited some of the worst affected parts of the city. That visit, and the orders he then issued to the chief of the army staff, seem to have convinced lesser functionaries that their duty was not to stand by as innocent people were set upon and burnt, and India's capital city plundered. Later that day, the army opened fire on looters and began to take control of the city. It was three days since Indira Gandhi's death and thousands lay dead; an ominous start for India's new prime minister.

CHAPTER TWO

The Family

Although lacking direct experience of government, Rajiv Gandhi had plenty of indirect experience. As the son of Indira Gandhi and grandson of Jawaharlal Nehru, who between them had ruled India for thirty-three of Rajiv's forty years, he had been brought up 'in government'. Rajiv spent his childhood mainly in Teen Murti House in Delhi, Nehru's prime ministerial home. After returning from studies in England and marrying, he continued to live at what was by then his mother's prime ministerial home, 1 Safdarjung Road. In both homes, he was used to observing the comings and goings of politicians and foreign statespeople which would have given him a unique view of the day-to-day business of ruling India. It was, though, a superficial view and, since Rajiv never aspired to rule India himself, it probably never occurred to his mother to instruct him in the art of statesmanship, as she had been instructed by her father in letters written by him from jail. At that time, though, Nehru, was not so much preparing his daughter to rule India but for the freeing of India from colonial rule, the struggle for which formed the backcloth of Indira's childhood.

Rajiv was born in Bombay on 20 August 1944, at the home of his great-aunt, Nehru's younger sister. India still had three years to go to Independence, so Rajiv qualifies as one of what Salman Rushdie has dubbed 'Midnight's Children': he is the first Indian prime minister not to have experienced the freedom struggle in which other members of his family were so much involved, though he must have heard a great deal about it from them. Grandfather Jawaharlal Nehru was in a British prison at the time of his birth, his ninth and final incarceration. His mother, Indira, had been released fifteen months earlier and his father, Feroze, only a year earlier. Even his great-grandfather, Motilal, was twice imprisoned for his involvement in civil disobedience against British rule. By comparison, Rajiv's upbringing lacked the excitement and danger of the freedom struggle and the ever-present fear of being arrested. Nor did he have first-hand experience of what it meant to have to fight to win one's freedom.

Indira Gandhi told how Nehru had a first glimpse of his grandson. Rajiv's parents had heard that Nehru was moving prisons and might spend the night at Allahabad's Naini jail. Their information was correct and, as he entered the prison late at night, they held seven-month-old Rajiv up for his grandfather's inspection. 'Under a very dim roadside light, my father peered at him,'[1] Indira wrote. Prior to that, Nehru had been sent photographs of his grandson, which elicited the comment: 'The forehead seems to be rather like Feroze's'.[2] Indira also told how Nehru had selected his grandson's names from lists she and Feroze sent to him in jail. Rajiv was chosen because in Sanskrit it means 'lotus' – as does Kamala, the name of Nehru's wife who had died eight years earlier. Though he has always been called Rajiv, his full name is Rajivaratna. Ratna means 'jewel', which is one of the meanings of Jawahar; so he inherited names from both his maternal grandparents. Nehru was very fond of using Persian words in his writing, and wrote to his daughter that 'an additional Persian name would be desirable'. He proposed the name Birjees, a Persian name for Jupiter, the king of the gods, which also means 'the auspicious one'. Nehru's suggestion of a Persian name, which Feroze and Indira adopted, does not appear to have anything to do with the fact that Feroze was, by upbringing, a Parsi, a member of a small religious community which follows the teachings of the Persian prophet, Zoroaster. However, they rejected another suggestion that they also add Nehru as an additional name.

It is significant that even in such a straightforward matter as the selection of names, the influence of the Nehru side of Rajiv's family was paramount. Despite bringing the Gandhi name to the marriage (though he was no relation to Mahatma Gandhi), Feroze never got over a complex that he had married into the Nehru family, a family to which he felt very close, but to which he never felt he belonged. His marriage to Indira was a love match, not a marriage arranged by the family as is more usual in India. She had accepted his proposal on the

[1] This and subsequent Indira Gandhi quotations are taken from *My Truth* by Indira Gandhi, as told to Emmanuel Pouchpadass.
2 This and subsequent Nehru quotations are taken from *Selected Works of Jawaharlal Nehru* (first series), volume thirteen, Orient Longman, Delhi, 1972.

steps of Sacré Cœur in Paris after a prolonged courtship which began in Allahabad and continued when both studied in Britain, Feroze at the London School of Economics and Indira at Somerville College, Oxford.

On the eve of Independence on 15 August 1947, when Nehru became India's first prime minister, circumstances caused Indira and Feroze to be separated. Whilst Indira and baby Rajiv moved to Delhi to be with her father, Feroze stayed in Lucknow, where he was by then managing the Congress Party's daily newspaper, the *National Herald*. However, he regularly used to visit the family in Delhi, or they travelled to Lucknow. Rajiv's brother, Sanjay, was born shortly after the move to Delhi. In 1952, Feroze was elected to Parliament and followed his wife and children to the capital. MPs qualify for bungalows and, with strains in the marriage already showing, Feroze spent much of his time at his bungalow at Victoria – now Rajendra Prasad – Road, though he spent what hours he could with his sons. He resented being described as 'the nation's son-in-law' with its innuendo – probably not intended – that he was living off his father-in-law. He may also have resented the fact that Indira had chosen to become housekeeper and assistant to her father, although she was to claim later that 'it wasn't really a choice … there was nobody else to do it'. There was an unspoken tension between Feroze and his father-in-law, arising out of a family feeling that Indira had married beneath herself; Feroze came from a lower social and poorer background – facts that seem to have mattered more to the Nehru family than his not being a Hindu, like them.

Feroze was a popular MP, winning a reputation for exposing corruption. His uncovering of one particular instance of questionable practice on the part of India's largest insurance company led to the resignation of the finance minister and other senior officials, causing some embarrassment to Nehru, but enhancing his own reputation for probity. Speaking of the influence his father had on his upbringing, Rajiv talks with obvious approval of 'the way he acted in Parliament, independent and a little outspoken, without caring too much for the consequences'. Feroze had been a bit of a revolutionary in his student days, and was once briefly arrested for taking part in a leftist demonstration in Paris. Rajiv likes to think he has inherited something of his father's leftist streak, though he has never really demonstrated it.

The strains in Rajiv's parents' marriage increased as Indira took a more prominent role within the Congress Party. Their political differences brought into the open their personal ones as well. One issue on which they publicly clashed was about the Communist government that had been elected to power in the state of Kerala in 1957, the first time a Communist administration had come to power by democratic means anywhere in the world. Indira, who was by then Congress Party general secretary, was wary of the state government's intentions, especially when they introduced state laws to give protection to tenant farmers and to regulate privately-run schools and colleges. She encouraged her father to dismiss the government. Feroze was adamantly opposed to the principle of dismissing a properly elected government, and he made his views known. Not surprisingly, it was Indira's views that prevailed and, giving a foretaste of a technique she was to use often after she became prime minister, she persuaded her father to dismiss the Kerala government by the constitutional device of declaring President's Rule, which means that central government takes over. The Kerala crisis marked the low point in relations between Rajiv's parents.

When Rajiv was sixteen, his father suffered the second of two heart attacks, and died. Rajiv recalls that it happened shortly after an attempt at reconciliation between his parents. The family had taken a long and enjoyable holiday in Kashmir; 'some of the old strains had disappeared', he told Simi Garewal in the video, *India's Rajiv*. Feroze was a few days short of his forty-eighth birthday when he died. Indira had confided to an American friend that she was deeply unhappy in her domestic life, saying she and Feroze 'quarrelled over every conceivable subject'. She told of her sorrow at having missed 'the most wonderful thing in life, having a complete and perfect relationship with another human being'.[1] Rajiv remembers the good times and, being away at boarding school from the age of nine, may not have been conscious of the extent to which strains were growing in his parents' relationship. In any case, he had an extra father figure in Nehru, to whom he was devoted – more so than was his brother, Sanjay. Nehru enjoyed spoiling both his grandchildren.

Rajiv inherited from his father a love of working with his hands.

---

[1] From *Indira Gandhi: Letters to a Friend, 1950–1984* by Dorothy Norman, Weidenfeld and Nicolson, London, 1985.

Feroze had a talent for making toys and used to get his sons to help him in the small workshops they had at both the homes in Delhi. It was largely due to Feroze's influence, teaching them to take things apart and put them together again, that both Rajiv and Sanjay went on from school to study engineering. Rajiv says his father taught him the 'dignity of labour, not hesitating to work with your hands, being straight and truthful, not hesitating to speak out'.[1] Rajiv also inherited from his father a taste for Western classical music since, according to his mother, 'the Nehrus were very unmusical people'.[2] Two traits Rajiv did not inherit were Feroze's heavy smoking and drinking; Rajiv has never smoked and has never acquired a taste for alcohol, being a virtual teetotaller his entire life.

The Nehrus were a high-caste family belonging to the Kashmiri community known as the Pandits, who hail from the Vale of Kashmir. The family had migrated in the eighteenth century to the Mughal capital of Delhi in response to a summons to serve the Emperor Farrukhsiyar. It was in Delhi that they acquired their name, having previously been known by the caste name of Kaul. Rajiv's ancestor, Raj Kaul, had built his house on the banks of a canal. The Urdu word for 'canal' is *nehar* so he became known as Kaul-Nehru. Towards the end of the nineteenth century, Rajiv's great-grandfather, Motilal, migrated again, this time to the city of Allahabad in Uttar Pradesh. Motilal was a lawyer and his move was prompted by the shifting of the High Court for the then northern provinces to Allahabad.

Motilal, who deserve to be regarded as the founder of the political dynasty – he was the first member of the family to become Congress president – had developed a taste for British language, literature and education. He had himself enjoyed an English-style education in India, and was determined that his son, Jawaharlal, complete his education in England, though he warned him sternly against marrying a foreigner. When the young Nehru returned from Britain, where he had been educated and called to the Bar, his father described him as 'more an Englishman than an Indian'.[3] Jawaharlal Nehru, in turn, sent his only child, Indira, for education in Switzerland and Britain, maintaining the cosmopolitan upbringing of a Hindu family which had served at

[1] Quotations of Rajiv here and throughout the book are taken either from *India's Rajiv*, a video by Simi Garewal, or from conversation with the author.
[2] Quoted in *Indira Gandhi; a Personal & Political Biography*, Inder Malhotras or from published speeches.
[3] Quoted in *Indira Gandhi: a Biography*, Zareer Masani.

the Mughal Muslim court before espousing British ways and tastes.

Indira described the newly born Rajiv as 'quite ugly', but his birth as 'one of the most joyful moments of my life'. He was a happy, laughing baby until, at the age of two, his brother Sanjay was born. From then onwards, Rajiv frequently threw tantrums. His mother tried reasoning with him, but he replied: 'What can I do? I don't want to cry, it just comes!' She told him: 'There is a nice fountain in our garden. When you want to cry or shout, go to the fountain and do it there.'

There is no doubt that the two boys enjoyed privileged upbringings even though they also suffered the frequent absences of their mother. Being both her father's housekeeper and hostess, with the onerous responsibility of entertaining important visitors from India and abroad, as well as a senior official of the Congress Party in her own right, it was inevitable that the time Indira had left to attend to her sons was limited. Sometimes, however, whilst they were still small, she took them with her. The two-year-old Rajiv went with his mother on 29 January 1947 to visit Mahatma Gandhi, who was being blamed by Hindu refugees from Pakistan for allowing the partitioning of India and the creation of Muslim Pakistan which had accompanied Independence four months earlier, and had sparked widespread killings between members of the two communities. Rajiv played with the Mahatma's robe whilst the adults talked. The following day Gandhi was shot dead by a Hindu fanatic.

Indira had been lonely as a child, with her parents in prison for so much of the time. She wanted her own children to have a more normal upbringing, and tried to arrange her political activities when her boys were at school. Sometimes there were conflicting demands on her. At the age of twelve, Rajiv needed a small operation at a time when his mother, who had recently become president of the Congress Party, was required at an important meeting to choose the party's election candidates. The meeting was shifted to the verandah of the hospital as his mother refused to leave him.

Both Rajiv and Sanjay were fond of animals, and kept a succession of them in the grounds at Teen Murti House. They included dogs, parrots, pigeons, squirrels and a Himalayan Red Panda called Bhimsa, which had been given to Nehru during a visit to Assam. They also had three tiger cubs, one of which was later presented as a gift to Marshal Tito of Yugoslavia, one of many foreign heads of state to visit the Nehru household.

34

As well as the constant foreign visitors, there were also other early foreign influences on Rajiv's upbringing. For a time, he had a Danish governess, a strict disciplinarian and ardent believer in cold showers and exercise. Later he was sent to an exclusive kindergarten run by a German lady, Elizabeth Gauba, who had married an Indian. At that tender stage, Rajiv showed a special talent for drawing aeroplanes, and also enjoyed taking the lead in play-acting. When Nehru and Indira went to London for the Coronation in 1953, Rajiv and Sanjay were put into school in Switzerland for a short time.

After early schooling in Delhi, Indira and Feroze had sent their children to boarding school at Dehra Dun, several hours' drive north of the capital in the Himalayan foothills. They went first to Welham Boys' Preparatory School, presided over by a formidable English disciplinarian, Miss Oliphant. Dehra Dun has many claims to fame, but is probably best known as the home of Doon School, one of a number of English-style public schools in India and where Rajiv and Sanjay went after Welham.

Doon was founded in 1935, and had been dubbed 'the Harrow of India'. Nehru, who had studied at Harrow, was a great admirer of the English public school system. Rajiv's headmaster, John Martyn, had taught at Harrow before accepting a job on the staff at Doon, to become its headmaster in due course. Rajiv was eleven years old when he joined the school.

Despite being a post-Independence child, Rajiv's formative school years were spent at schools whose head teachers and many of whose staff were British. The schools themselves were run on the pattern of English boarding schools, albeit with their own Indian characteristics. English was, and still is, the teaching medium. Boys slept in dormitories distributed between four houses, which were the boys' homes during term time. Rajiv was in Kashmir house, and was assigned his school number: 203K. Rajiv's name was short enough for him to avoid acquiring a nickname, which many boys and all members of staff had. Some nicknames remained with boys well into adulthood. Houses were presided over by the housemaster and a formidable lady called a dame who was responsible for housekeeping and feeding up to a hundred boys in her care. Another feature borrowed from the English public school and Oxbridge system is the practice that each boy has a tutor to oversee his welfare and to take him on occasional outings. Good school work is rewarded with a 'good chit', whilst misdemeanours are punished with a 'bad chit' and detention, or a run around the playing fields.

A contemporary of Rajiv lists what he regards as the special merits of a Doon School education: 'Some very good old-fashioned values like a basic honesty, telling the truth, admitting to mistakes, a sense of camaraderie, the value of friendship; things of this kind which mixed tempered achievement with an absence of over-riding ambition.' Another old boy says one of the outstanding things Doon taught its boys was a great sense of equality: 'When we came to Doon School, everybody was brought down to the same level by the simple fact that nobody was allowed to possess any money. We had a very elaborate system of cheque books by which boys could spend their pocket money. This pocket money was allocated to you equally depending on the time you were at school. It increased by a few rupees each term. At Doon, you had this little world of your own in which you evaluated each other totally on your merits as human beings, a very good system in which to develop a sound value system.' This equality, however, is only relative, since only wealthy parents could afford to send their sons for a Doon School education. The vast majority of Indian children have scant education and certainly no pocket money. To go to any school is a privilege, whilst to go to boarding school is the prerogative of a lucky few. Whilst Doon School undoubtedly provides a good education, and prepares its pupils to go on to university, there is also a snob value attached to it which marks its old boys out as a class apart. This was seen to be true when Rajiv later brought several of his Doon School contemporaries into government or advisory posts, and there was much comment about the Doon School clique, or mafia.

Rajiv and Sanjay received no special favours by virtue of being the prime minister's grandsons, or 'the nation's grandchildren', as the press had dubbed them. At any time, the school had a number of sons of Indian nobility, which reinforces its image as an academy for the élite. The sons of erstwhile rajahs and maharajahs mingle with those of senior members of the armed forces and captains of Indian industry. What they have in common at a school which draws its intake from all corners of India is, almost invariably, English as a mother tongue, a wealthy family background and parents committed to the British style of public boarding school education. In India's caste-ridden society, those of noble birth or privileged upbringing, like those who are fluent in English, are more likely to be the objects of envy than of resentment.

Like most boys there, Rajiv enjoyed his time at Doon, after the initial homesickness. He spent his spare time in the wood and metal workshops making things, or at the photographic club. His grandfather had given him a Russian-made camera. The school encouraged outdoor activities, especially mountaineering, but Rajiv does not seem to have starred in this respect, or at the school sports of cricket and hockey. He is remembered at Doon School as a quiet, unassuming boy of average intellect, who nonetheless entered into the spirit of the place. He did not stand out as a scholar, and was considered to be 'very average' academically. His favourite subjects were geography and maths, in which in his final year he was in the upper half of the class according to his teacher. He is remembered for his shyness, his wish to be ordinary and not be marked out as the prime minister's grandson. He recalls: 'I was embarrassed at being the prime minister's grandson.' When Nehru came to call at the school, said Rajiv, 'I stayed somewhere at the back; they couldn't find me'. Were it not for his membership of India's ruling family, he probably would not have been much remembered at school. A prefect remembers Rajiv as 'a very ordinary boy, but not naughty enough, and not interested enough in anything in particular'.

Rajiv made a number of close friends at Doon School, some of whom have remained close friends even after embarking on very different careers. In the closed atmosphere of Delhi's élite, the Doon School bond is evident. Rajiv retains a special affection for the school and his time there, as was clear when, as prime minister of one year's standing, he arrived as 'chief guest' at the school's golden jubilee celebrations in November 1985 wearing his old boys' blazer and tie. Addressing old boys and their families, he told a story of the old Doon School boy, or 'Dosco' as they like to be called, who arrived as an undergraduate at Cambridge. His tutor asked him about the significance of the lamp emblem on the school's old boy blazer. On being told it represented the lamp of learning, his tutor is said to have replied: 'What a pity they didn't light it while you were still there!' The apocryphal story emanated from Rajiv's speech writer, Mani Shankar Aiyar who had, like Rajiv, gone on to Cambridge from Doon School.

Prime Minister Nehru was meticulous in not seeking special privileges for his grandsons. He used to observe the rule, for example, that whilst boys could be taken out for lunch or tea at the weekend, they had to be back at school by nightfall. Boys were not allowed to spend the night away from school during term time, even those like Rajiv and Sanjay whose family had a house at nearby Mussoorie. So, members of the school's staff were surprised when, many years later after Rajiv had become prime minister, he sought special leave to take his son, Rahul, out of school to accompany him on an overseas tour. Sonia, it has been suggested, may not have been quite so committed to the boarding school education that kept both their children away from the family home for more than nine months of each year.

During school holidays at Teen Murti House, Nehru took pleasure in spoiling his grandsons. Sharing their passion for speed, he gave them their own racing car, which they used to drive around the grounds, and later around Delhi. It is said that Indira rang up the police, asking them to treat her boys like anyone else if they broke the law, which, of course, they were hardly likely to do. A visitor to Teen Murti when Rajiv was sixteen and Sanjay fourteen recalls how Nehru used to indulge his grandchildren – much to the distress of their mother. The boys were usually late for the formal English-style meals which were the habitual practice at Teen Murti. Later, when they arrived hungry and only mildly repentant, it was Nehru who took them into the kitchen or summoned the servants to find them something to eat, rather than reprimanding them for keeping the household and guests waiting.

After Doon School, Rajiv was sent to London. He stayed at the home of India's High Commissioner in Kensington Palace Gardens while attending tutors to study for 'A' levels. He used a bicycle to get around London. At this stage in his life, there was no special security for the grandson of the Indian prime minister. On one occasion, Rajiv was knocked off his bicycle in Bayswater Road by a London cab which did not stop. He suffered mild concussion. His Indian companion picked him up off the street, and after a few minutes they continued their ride. After narrowly passing his 'A' levels, he was offered a place at Trinity College, Cambridge to read mechanical engineering – largely, it is said, because of the influence of Nehru, who was himself a Trinity man and had very much wanted one of his grandsons to follow him to Cambridge.

Rajiv led a quiet existence in Cambridge where, for the first time in his life, he was not marked out as a prime minister's son. He is said once to have explained to an enquirer that he was no relation of Mahatma Gandhi, without admitting that he was a relation of Nehru. Like most undergraduates, he was constrained by a shortage of funds, making do on a relatively meagre allowance. His parents may not have appreciated the cost of living, though even the family's wealth by Indian standards may have been strained by the cost of supporting two sons studying in England. Sanjay had meanwhile become apprenticed to Rolls Royce Motors in Crewe. Following the tradition amongst British students, Rajiv made his allowance go further by working during his vacation, variously picking fruit, selling ice cream, loading trucks and doing the night-shift in a bakery. One friend from Cambridge days remembers him as 'not very academic but always keen on cars, and flicking through car magazines'. He could not afford his own car, but one evening he turned over a Volkswagen Beetle that he and three friends had borrowed to go for a meal outside Cambridge. Nobody was seriously hurt, but the car was a write-off; they forked up twenty-five pounds each to pay for it. At Cambridge, Rajiv also developed a taste for listening to music, especially jazz – Gerry Mulligan, Stan Getz, Zoot Sims and Jimmy Smith were his favourites, though his tastes also took in the Beatles and Beethoven. Rajiv says of his Cambridge days: 'We had a great time, enjoyed ourselves and didn't do enough study.' He says his time in Cambridge gave him 'a view of the world you didn't get in India, especially if you're related to a prime minister.' It was probably truer of Rajiv than it had been of Nehru that his time in Britain left him 'more an Englishman than an Indian'.

At the end of his second year, news came of the death of his grandfather. Within four years, he had lost first his father and then his grandfather, to whom he was equally devoted. Rajiv hurried back to Delhi for the funeral, but returned the following term for his final year, which he did not complete. Though there were many undergraduates from India in Cambridge at that time, some of whom – like writer Gita Mehta and her publisher husband Sony Mehta – have found fame in their own fields, Rajiv was not a great socialite and had eyes only for a quiet language student from Turin, Sonia Maino. He first set eyes on her in a Greek restaurant and, according to Rajiv, 'organised through a friend for them to meet'. It seems to have been love virtually at first sight as far as he was concerned: 'The first time I saw her, I knew she was the girl for me. Then we fell in love.' Sonia was his first and only girlfriend. He introduced her to his mother as she passed through London on a trip.

Rajiv left Cambridge without a degree, just as his mother had failed to gain a degree from Oxford. Using his own word, he 'flunked', not even sitting for his degree examinations. He had enjoyed Cambridge life, but found the course hard going. Possibly he lacked the incentive that most undergraduates have of the knowledge that a degree enhances the prospects of finding a good job. However, he did have a fiancée, Sonia, and had decided by this time to train as a pilot, having inherited a love of flying from Nehru. He had been hooked after his grandfather took him for his first ride in a glider: 'It gives you a certain freedom ... takes you away from it all,' he says. During holidays from Cambridge he joined the Delhi Gliding Club, which whetted his appetite to go on to powered flight. In England, he saw an advert for flying lessons at Wiltshire Flying Club at Thruxton. He enrolled for a course during a vacation from Cambridge, training on a four-seater variant of the Tiger Moth. By the end of the course he had gone solo.

On returning to India, Rajiv continued his training with the Delhi Flying Club, first to private pilot's level and then going on to gain his commercial pilot's licence. His initial training there was on the Indian-built Pushpak. Colleagues recall what a diligent student he was – of the theory as much as the practical side. He had what one friend describes as 'a peculiar kind of inquisitive nature – always wanting to know how things worked, not being content just to fly'. Unlike other pilots, he used to come into the maintenance hangar if there was a fault, to have the problem explained to him. In that way he got to know the aircraft inside out and later, as a pilot with Indian Airlines, he helped prepare the evidence in defence of the Hawker Siddeley Avro 748 when its safety was called into question. One colleague described him as the 'ace' Avro pilot; before long, he was instructing other pilots on the Avro.

Rajiv is an intensely practical man who enjoys the challenge of trying to understand how something works, and fixing it if it doesn't. He used to travel between the Flying Club at Safdarjung airfield and his mother's home at 1 Safdarjung Road on a motorbike, which he maintained himself. Changing a car wheel is second nature to him in a country where car owners do not normally need to get their hands dirty: there's always someone around willing to do the job for a reward. A technocrat through and through, Rajiv used to enjoy fiddling with electrical equipment, and even helped a friend set up in business making amplifiers. The enjoyment of listening to his large collection of classical records, meant he was naturally interested in the quality of their reproduction. Later, after he had become prime minister, he was one of the first people in India to have a Sony Walkman compact disc player, and even had a compact disc player installed in his bullet-proof Range Rover. Another 'toy' he enjoys is a short wave radio which can be tuned by pushing buttons. A friend continued to send her push-button radio to Rajiv to re-tune long after he became prime minister. Flying led to another hobby when Rajiv took up amateur radio. Using a Japanese-made Yaesu transmitter, he became an enthusiastic 'Ham' conversing with others around the world. Amateur radio and listening to music were two of the pastimes he most missed as prime minister.

Rajiv and Sonia were married in February 1968. Though Indira's own marriage showed she was not averse to inter-community marriages, she had encouraged Rajiv to wait until he was quite sure of himself. She did not oppose the marriage when they both made clear they were sure, and had herself developed a close bond with Sonia from the start. The Nehru-Gandhi family had followed a liberal, Westernised tradition, which included a tendency to select their own marriage partners. Even so, Rajiv was the first member of the immediate family to have chosen to marry a foreigner. Before the wedding, Sonia had stayed in Delhi at the home of Bachchans, close family friends of the Gandhis. There she had learnt to speak Hindi and other Indian skills like how to tie a sari, and a little Indian cooking. The wedding was a simple non-denominational ceremony in the garden of 1 Safdarjung Road with just a few close friends present. Sonia wore a pink sari made from cotton which Nehru had spun whilst in prison – the so-called *khadi*, or homespun cotton, which was symbolic of the independence movement. It was the same sari that Indira had worn for her wedding. By wearing it, Sonia seemed to be accepting that she was marrying into a noble Indian family, and that she would abide by their customs and traditions. She was clearly enjoying the process of becoming an Indian through marriage, and there was no suggestion at this stage that they would ever live in Italy, or away from India. The wedding was followed by a large reception at Delhi's Hyderabad House before the couple and Sonia's family, who were visiting India for the first time, went off to a wildlife reserve. On the way back to Delhi, they encountered a traditional village-style Hindu wedding, which can last for several days. Rajiv and Sonia's wedding had lacked the style and flamboyance of a traditional Indian marriage ceremony. They had opted for a low-key ceremony rather like a registry office marriage in the West.

It is a marriage that, as Rajiv says, 'has worked very well'. Explaining his initial attraction, he says: 'I found her very understanding and warm as a person.' Indira, who had become prime minister two years earlier after the sudden death of her father's successor, Shastri, drew the line at Rajiv's suggestion that they move to a flat of their own after marrying. Marriage outside the community was one thing, but living apart was strictly contrary to the joint family tradition of India. Indira may have found it more difficult to enforce Nehru's tradition of speaking only Hindi at meals until Sonia became familiar with the language which was, in any case, only their second language, after English. Within the confines of 1 Safdarjung Road, Sonia was to develop a very close personal relationship with her mother-in-law, whom she used to call 'Mummy'. It may have had something to do with the strains which developed between Indira and her other, Indian, daughter-in-law, Sanjay's wife, Maneka, that she came to trust in Sonia, who took on many of the responsibilities of running the household in the same way that Indira had looked after her father's household affairs. Indira used to consult Sonia over matters of dress in particular; what sari she should wear on what particular occasion. Though Sanjay, the political son, was Indira's favourite, Sonia soon became her favourite daughter-in-law. Sonia and Rajiv's first child, a son whom they called Rahul, was born in 1970. Their daughter, Priyanka, followed eighteen months later. Indira loved to be with her grandchildren, and tried to spend as much time as possible at home.

Throughout Indira's first period as prime minister, up to 1977, Rajiv kept out of the limelight. It was different with Sanjay. He had embarked on an ambitious project to build an Indian 'people's car', the Maruti, a successor to the aged British-designed models then on the roads in India, which was meant to be within the financial reach of even middle level government servants. There were charges of favouritism and nepotism when Sanjay's application was favoured over many others and he was granted a licence to develop the vehicle. Indira could never see, or at least would not admit, that Sanjay had been favoured because she had such complete faith in his abilities, though this faith turned out to be misguided. The project was highly controversial from the start, and slow to produce its first car, which it did only after the Japanese firm, Suzuki, was brought in to bail out the project.

At the same time as developing his pioneer car, Sanjay was establishing himself as his mother's right-hand man in the political arena. He played an especially prominent role after his mother declared the Emergency in 1975, allegedly on Sanjay's advice, after the High Court in Allahabad had set aside her election victory at Rae Bareilly in Uttar Pradesh in the 1971 general election. Her defeated opponent had complained that she violated electoral law to win the election. It had taken four years for the case to come before the High Court, allowing Indira to dismiss it as a politically-motivated vendetta against her. Though the verdict was subject to appeal to the Supreme Court, that would have taken some time, and she may have had to step down from office, or at least to lose her right to vote in Parliament, while the appeal was pending. If upheld, the Allahabad court ruling would have barred her from holding any elective office for six years. Instead of bowing to any curtailment of her power, she followed advice and asked the president to impose an Emergency. It was an unashamed attempt to hang onto power which, in the short term at least, succeeded. Opposition leaders were arrested and restrictions imposed on the country's free press, as Indira exercised near-dictatorial powers.

This was a bad time for the family. Rajiv and Sonia wanted to move to Italy to avoid the additional attention and resentment the Emergency brought to Indira and Sanjay, who were daily being accused in the press of destroying Indian democracy. It was Indira who dissuaded them, saying the family should stick together at this difficult time. Things were no easier when the Emergency led to the defeat of Congress at the 1977 elections and its replacement by a Janata government. This was the first time Congress had lost power since Independence thirty years earlier, and only the second time that a member of the Nehru-Gandhi dynasty – as it was beginning to be described – had not been at the helm. The humiliation went deeper. Indira was defeated by a large margin in her own bid for re-election at Rae Bareilly. Her defeat was followed by her brief arrest: she was held for one night as the Janata government sought its revenge for many of their number having been detained during the Emergency. Later, after being returned to Parliament in a by-election, she was imprisoned again, for a week, for contempt of Parliament after refusing to answer questions about Sanjay's Maruti car project, into which the Janata government had launched an investigation. Whilst in jail Indira was brought food cooked by Sonia. Sanjay was also imprisoned for a short time.

The naked display of vengeance against Indira Gandhi was one of the factors that precipitated the collapse of the Janata government after two and a half years. Another was the personal ambition and rivalry of its leaders which was never far from the surface. Fresh elections were held in January 1980 and, in a result that was more a rejection of Janata than a strong show of support for Congress, Indira returned to power for her second stint as prime minister. Remaining at her side in the political arena was Sanjay who had, for the first time, taken the conventional road to a political career by contesting and winning election as the new MP for Amethi near Lucknow in Uttar Pradesh. It was very much a family constituency, having been re-presented in Parliament at different times by both his grandfather and his great-aunt. Later, Rajiv was to inherit the Amethi seat. Indira's second term as prime minister, was to end four years and ten months later with her death.

Rajiv was impatient with the security which by now surrounded him as the son of a prime minister who had an increasing number of enemies. He often tried to escape from the security men, who made it their business to escort him at all times. One thing that made him lose his temper was being suffocated by the over-diligent attentions of those entrusted with his security. This feeling of claustrophobia was one reason he had preferred to keep out of public life. Even after he became prime minister, Rajiv still preferred to drive himself when possible, especially when visiting the farm he bought at Mehrauli to the south of Delhi. He used to indulge his passion for speed in the Mercedes-Benz and Range Rover given him by the King of Jordan, by outpacing his security escort.

Around the time of the Emergency, Rajiv had graduated from the Avro aircraft to the Boeing 737, which was to become the mainstay of the Indian Airlines fleet. One day, when Rajiv had flown to Bombay and was going to the hotel for an overnight stop, the car in which he was travelling was diverted by police off the main road into a lane to allow a VIP car to pass by. The VIP turned out to be his brother, Sanjay. Though still without formal authority in the Congress Party, Sanjay was considered to be the second most powerful person in the land. Rajiv's companion in the car commented: 'Younger brother is going, elder brother is diverted into the lane! How do you like it?'

Rajiv replied: 'That's politics!' It was as if Rajiv was saying: 'Sanjay is welcome to his high profile, political life; for my part, I prefer the relatively inconspicuous life of an Indian Airlines pilot.' It also shows up an important difference between the two: Sanjay had first acquired power simply because he was the prime minister's son; election had come later, after he was already well-established politically. Rajiv, who had consciously hidden from his prime ministerial connections at school and at Cambridge, had achieved his position as a senior and respected Indian Airlines pilot entirely on his own, without making use of any family advantage.

However, Sanjay's political career was to be cut short. Like Rajiv, he had inherited his grandfather's love of flying, but for him it was merely a pastime. He used to fly at the Delhi Flying Club whenever he had the chance. On 23 June 1980 he took off on his last flight. Seemingly attempting aerobatic manoeuvres without enough height, he failed to recover and crashed into the ground close to the house his mother had occupied whilst out of office. Aged just thirty-three, he left his widow, Maneka, and their baby son, Varun, as well as an inconsolable mother, who never entirely recovered from the tragically premature death of her younger son and chosen heir. He had been an MP for only six months. Ten days before his death, she had installed him in his first formal party office as one of the Congress Party's general secretaries.

CHAPTER THREE

The Party

Sanjay's death created a cruel dilemma for Rajiv. He had not the slightest inclination to enter political life, yet it was clear that Indira had been grooming Sanjay to succeed her, and equally clear that she would now turn to Rajiv to replace him. Rajiv, the elder son who had been at his mother's side when she lost her husband, her father and now her younger son, had never gone against his mother's wishes in anything that really mattered. But he was not to be hurried into making a decision and, as with all his more important decisions, it was taken in conjunction with Sonia. Though neither could foresee the circumstances in which he would later become prime minister, they knew that the decision they were now faced with – whether Rajiv should enter politics – carried a strong possibility that it would lead to the prime ministership.

The decision was made all the more difficult because Rajiv loved flying, which he said was 'more like a hobby than a job'. It was, he said, 'man and machine working very closely together' and something that 'makes you feel very good when you do it well'. He considered himself fortunate to have 'a well-paid job with a lot of leisure time'.

Sonia and Rajiv were staying with her parents in Italy when Sanjay's death occurred. The cremation was delayed while they hurried back to Delhi. In an early act of wisdom on assuming the *de facto* role as his mother's chief political aide, Rajiv dissuaded her from cremating Sanjay too close to the spot where Nehru had been cremated. Rajiv saw that it would do the family no good for the unpopular Sanjay to be so honoured. This was not the first time he had distanced himself from the unpopular politics of his brother. Even as a pilot, Rajiv is reported once to have taken a judge aside and apologised to him for his brother's action in transferring him to an undesirable posting, an act of vindictiveness because Sanjay had not appreciated one of his judgements.

Indira Gandhi had lost not only a son, but her closest political adviser, which made the shock doubly wounding. In his biography of Indira Gandhi, Inder Malhotra suggests that after what she regarded as her betrayal by those around her in the Congress Party after its 1977 defeat, she was virtually incapable of trusting anyone except her son and a very small coterie of aides. It was certainly true that she had no really trusted ministers around her, and the frequency with which she reshuffled her cabinet bears this out. Sanjay had also been her line of communication with Congress leaders, leaving her feeling isolated from them after his death. He even had his own block of Congress MPs in Parliament who owed greater loyalty to him than to the prime minister. For these reasons she needed her other son to replace Sanjay. The immediate need was probably more important than the dynastic aspiration, though that was certainly present too. There have been suggestions of another reason for wanting Rajiv to join politics: that Sanjay's death made her hate aircraft to the extent that she was determined to persuade her surviving son to give up flying. This seems unlikely as neither she nor Rajiv showed any reluctance to travel by air, and Rajiv continued to pilot himself whenever he had the chance.

Whatever the motivation, Indira did turn immediately to Rajiv to fill the void left by Sanjay's death. Formally, the approach came from Congress MPs who started a 'draft Rajiv' movement, but they were clearly acting in accordance with that they knew to be their leader's wishes. The reluctant son accepted his filial duty even though he was on the point of getting his command as a Boeing captain, which made his dilemma more acute. Nonetheless, he took leave from Indian Airlines to be at his mother's side and provide her with support.

Following Sanjay's death, it was probably inevitable that Rajiv would enter politics, but there remained the task of reconciling his mother's wishes with Sonia's opposition. According to Indira Gandhi, Sonia had threatened to divorce Rajiv if he ever entered politics.[1] Rajiv said later that Sonia 'felt she would be losing me'. However, when he did eventually resign from Indian Airlines, eleven months after Sanjay's

[1] Said to Khushwant Singh, and quoted in From Raj to Rajiv, Tully and Masani.

death, he said 'it was a joint decision' arrived at after 'long talks' between the two of them. Sonia had perhaps bowed to the wishes of her mother-in-law, or else had reconciled herself to the thought that being a politician's wife was not such a bad life. Rajiv's explanation for his decision is strongly reminiscent of his mother explaining why she had to become housekeeper to her father: 'It wasn't really a choice ... there was nobody else to do it.' Rajiv explained: 'I felt that there was a void and I couldn't see anybody else filling it; there was in a sense an inevitability about it.'

The drafting of Rajiv into politics can be seen as the action of a selfish politician who was thinking of her own need to control the party and to prevent any alternative centre of power from emerging. Indira did not need Rajiv for his political acumen, which was undemonstrated, as yet, and if she had put his own happiness first, she would certainly not have encouraged or persuaded him to give up flying and enter politics. What she needed him for was to help her retain the loyalty of the party, and by drafting him into the political arena as a Sanjay-substitute, she was cruelly using him, taking advantage of the family bond, and his sense of family duty.

The day after resigning from the airline, Rajiv filed his nomination papers for the by-election at Amethi, which had been Sanjay's seat. He was elected the following month, June 1981, and duly took his seat in the *Lok Sabha,* the lower house of Parliament around the time of his thirty-seventh birthday. There had been another factor in Indira's urgency to draft in Rajiv: Sanjay's widow, Maneka, was making it apparent that she considered herself to be Sanjay's political heir. She would have challenged Rajiv for Sanjay's parliamentary seat of Amethi – as she did later at the 1984 elections – had she not been too young at the time to become a parliamentary candidate.

Rajiv was not like Sanjay. He spoke of having ambitions, not for himself but for India and he was critical of the calibre of many politicians who had joined politics solely for power and money. He rejected Sanjay's followers in favour of his own school, university and airline friends one of whom, Arun Singh, said of his group of foreign university-educated friends: 'We're all Indians first; we are all secular Indians by any definition. Irrespective of what anyone might say, we operate on a very high level of integrity – personal integrity. I'm not talking only about money, for after all, money is only one aspect of personal integrity. Let's say we have a fairly high moral standard, and I think these are assets.'[1]

Rajiv's own political beliefs were not very clear cut, but one thing which did mark him out, and was to characterise many of his speeches, was his technological orientation. Like his grandfather, he believed that science and technology, properly applied, held the solutions to many of India's problems.

At his own wish, Rajiv had a gradual apprenticeship into politics, though behind the scenes he was fulfilling the role of key adviser to his mother from an early stage. His first major test began towards the end of 1980 when he was given the task of organising the Asian Games, which were due to be held in Delhi two years later. More than just the Games themselves were at stake, since the government had decided to put on a grand show which involved building new hotels, flyovers and rail links, as well as several stadiums and a village for the athletes. Rajiv found himself liaising with architects, builders and accountants and spending large sums of money. The country was also introducing colour television in time for the Games, and rapidly extending television's reach. The whole event was, in large part, designed to boost the image of Rajiv Gandhi and to launch him onto the political stage.

Rajiv passed the test with flying colours when the Games took place in November 1982. According to Mark Tully and Satish Jacob in their book *Amritsar*: 'He had bulldozed his way through the Indian bureaucracy and achieved what by the standards of any country was a miracle: starting from nothing he had built all the facilities for the largest ever Asian Games in two years.' But it was at some cost to his reputation and that of the government. The many lucrative building contracts had encouraged serious exploitation of workers. The matter was taken to the courts as an issue of workers' rights. The Supreme Court eventually found against the government, ordering that bonded labourers be transported back to their villages in the nearby state of Haryana, and that conditions be improved for stone-miners in the quarries of Faridabad, whose labour was providing the materials for the building boom.

A second bout of criticism came from the Sikhs, whose demands for greater autonomy in their home state of Punjab were occupying the government more and more. Shortly before the Games, talks between

[1] Quoted in *The Nehrus and the Gandhis*, Ali.

the government and the leaders of the Sikh party, the Akali Dal, had broken down, leading to a threat from the Akalis that they would demonstrate in Delhi while the Asian Games were on. However, nothing was to be allowed to spoil the triumph of Rajiv. So, after a further attempt at compromise with the Akalis had failed, orders were given to the police to throw a cordon around Delhi to prevent any disruption. Sikhs passing through Haryana on their way to the capital, including prominent judges and senior army officers, were searched by an over zealous police force. Fifteen hundred Sikhs suspected of planning to demonstrate were arrested. The Games were not disrupted, but the searches and arrest heightened the Sikhs' sense of alienation, and played into the extremists' hands when it was claimed that Sikhs had been prevented from attending the Asian Games. The alienation of Sikhs was the gravest problem that Rajiv was to inherit on becoming prime minister.

In February the following year, 1983, Mrs Gandhi had responded to party setbacks at the polls by appointing Rajiv as one of seven new Congress general secretaries. Since the party had little doubt by this time that he was the intended heir, he was considered to be the senior general secretary. The brief his mother gave him was to reorganise and revitalise the party, which had been in a state of decay for many years. Congress, the mass movement through which Indians had fought for and won their independence from Britain, had derived its strength from its deep roots in the villages of India. But, under Mrs Gandhi, the party had been centralised to such an extent that it had become virtually her party. With the party controlled from the centre, its grass roots structure diminished in importance.

Nineteen seventy-one, the year of Indira Gandhi's biggest electoral triumph, had marked the turning point: collective leadership and internal democracy within Congress were replaced by the cult of an undisputed leader. The following year was the last year in which internal elections were held for party office bearers. From then on, Congress presidents were selected according to their loyalty to the prime minister. They no longer needed to have an independent power base of their own. In due course, this came to apply to the chief ministers of individual states as well, who were appointed or fired at Indira Gandhi's will or whim. The party had twice split under Mrs Gandhi – in 1969 and 1978 – resulting the second time in the suffix 'Indira', or (I), being used to denote the faction led by Indira Gandhi.

Long before Rajiv came into politics, the Congress Party had become, for all practical purposes, his mother's party, to be used for ensuring her political survival, although the idea that she should bequeath it to one or other of her sons had probably only gradually come to her.

Shortly before Indira's death, there was a graphic demonstration of the arrogant manner in which Congress had come to behave. During the course of 1984, state governors appointed by the Congress government had dismissed the elected non-Congress governments in Jammu and Kashmir and Andhra Pradesh. (Governors are appointed to their posts by the central government.) The technique used in each case was the same – members of the state legislative assembly were encouraged to defect from the ruling party, enabling the respective governors to claim the chief ministers had lost their majority support in the assembly. A different technique, that of declaring President's Rule, was used to oust the government in the Himalayan state of Sikkim. In Andhra Pradesh, whose deposed chief minister was the colourful film star N. T. Rama Rao, the ousting of the government became a *cause célèbre* and led to claims that democracy had been butchered by Congress. Mrs Gandhi denied that she had any prior knowledge of the governor's action in dismissing NTR, as he is widely known, and it was the governor who was forced to resign over the issue. There was suspicion that Rajiv had ordered the chief minister's removal, perhaps on his mother's instructions, or else thinking he would be doing his mother a favour. However, he maintains that he and his mother had taken a firm decision against dismissing the state government, and that the governor was acting on his own, or at least following orders from someone else, whom Rajiv will not name.

The dismissals in all three states left a bad impression of Congress's respect for democratic institutions, provoking suggestions that, after destroying democracy within the Congress Party, Mrs Gandhi was now intent on destroying it in the states. The respected news magazine *India Today* said: 'The ruling party appeared to have perfected a technique of snuffing out opposition-led ministries,' adding: 'Democracy could not have been betrayed in a more sordid manner.' In the case of Andhra Pradesh, the technique had not been fully refined. After a month of public outcry, capitalised on by all non-Congress parties, N. T. Rama Rao was restored to office after demonstrating to the new governor's satisfaction that he continued to command the support of a majority of members of the state assembly.

Indira's death came at a crucial moment for the party. Within two months, it was due to face the first general election since Indira's triumphant return to power in 1980. It was going to be a struggle for Congress to hold onto power. At a time when the party should have been united in preparation for that contest, there was a great deal of bickering and criticism of the leadership style, especially from those who still considered themselves to be loyal to Sanjay's style of leadership. They were not happy with the way Rajiv, as party general secretary, was carrying out that role, perhaps because they feared he would not give them party 'tickets' to contest the election. Last time, it had been Sanjay who handed out the tickets.

In taking over this key source of patronage, Rajiv consciously rejected so-called Sanjay loyalists. He also readmitted to the party many former members who had left or been expelled during the Emergency. This angered the party's 'old hands' who resented the readmission and, in some cases, the giving of party offices to those who had not remained loyal throughout. However, at this stage Rajiv was anxious to attract back to the party anyone who might be an electoral asset; he was totally guided by the need to win the election. To this end, he had been involved with a complicated computerisation of constituency data to help the party determine who would have the best chance of winning any particular seat.

The swearing in of Rajiv as prime minister within hours of his mother's death was technically a response to his selection by the Parliamentary Board as the party's new leader. As we have seen, though, the party's decision was largely immaterial: Zail Singh intended Rajiv to become prime minister even without the party's approval. The following day, the Congress parliamentary party overwhelmingly endorsed the Parliamentary Board's choice. Two weeks later, the process of succession was completed, albeit in the reverse of the natural order, when Rajiv Gandhi was formally selected by the Congress working committee as party president, the post Indira Gandhi had combined with that of prime minister since returning to power in 1980. As nobody within the party had any doubt that Indira Gandhi had been preparing Rajiv to succeed her, there was virtually no dissent at the fact that he had now done so, even if the succession had taken place rather sooner than anyone could have predicted. This indicates the extent to which the party had become, in effect, the property of the Nehru–Gandhi family. The selection process was described later by an opposition MP as 'a conspiracy of circumstances'.

Within days of becoming prime minister, Rajiv announced that the general election would take place from 24 to 27 December. It was not immediately apparent that the assassination had provided a new factor in Congress's favour: a wave of sympathy towards the party and its new leader. Rajiv believed he still had a hard fight on his hands and was determined that candidates would be chosen according to their ability to win. He has been criticised for giving party tickets to known criminals where he thought they had the best chance of winning as a result of local factors, and for failing to take the opportunity at this stage to cleanse the party of such people. However, unlike others, he was not sufficiently confident of victory to attempt this now.

The elections gave Rajiv and the party he had led for less than two months the largest mandate it had received in any of India's eight general elections. With the subsequent polls in Assam and Punjab, Congress took 415 of the 543 seats in the *Lok Sabha*, better than anything Rajiv's grandfather or mother had ever achieved. It was rightly regarded as a personal triumph for Rajiv who had campaigned exhaustively, travelling more than 30000 miles by plane, helicopter and car in twenty-five days. It seemed that the people of India wanted to give this newcomer to politics, this 'Mr Clean', as he was being portrayed, the chance to show his worth. According to *India Today*, the election result 'demolished the myth of the political novice, of a soft pilot-turned-politician being manipulated by weightier personalities'. At the same time, there was no doubting the importance of the sympathy factor, with people choosing to demonstrate their sympathy by showing solidarity with the assassinated prime minister's son. In the circumstances of the assassination, as well as the separatist violence in Punjab, there was also a greater tendency to believe Congress's claim that it was the only party which could prevent India from being dismembered.

Opinion polls suggested the unity of the country was the factor that weighed most on the minds of the electorate. In its campaign, Congress had combined the twin claims that Mrs Gandhi had given her life in the cause of national unity – promoted with gruesome posters of her blood spilled over a map of India – and that now only Rajiv could hold the country together in these difficult times. It promoted this unity call with a much criticised publicity campaign which showed Pakistan encroaching through Punjab to the outskirts of Delhi above the appeal:

'Will the country's border finally be moved to your doorstep? India could be your vote away from unity or separatism.' With memories of Indira Gandhi's assassination still fresh in people's minds, there was a clear anti-Sikh undercurrent to Congress's campaign. Rajiv had made much play in his campaign meetings of Sikh demands for a separate state. Indeed, in what has been described as the dirtiest election campaign in Indian history, Rajiv came within a whisker of blaming the opposition for his mother's death, by accusing them of supporting Sikh separatism.

Congress's argument that only Rajiv could keep India united was strengthened by the limited degree to which the Opposition had united to contest the poll. Attempts by the Opposition to argue that Rajiv was not a man of the people – 'Neither he nor his mother could distinguish between a paddy field and a wheat field', claimed opposition leader Charan Singh – apparently went unheard or unheeded. Rajiv himself, in an interview with *Time* magazine, described the vote as a 'mandate for change, for cleaning up, for efficiency.' To *Newsweek* he said: 'A new generation has taken over the country.' When asked if the change would herald the end of ideologies which dated from the independence period and which were not as relevant now as then, he replied that there was nothing wrong with the ideologies, but the application of the ideologies to the changed circumstances on the ground had to change: 'It requires new thinking,' he told *Newsweek*. Amidst the euphoria that surrounded his triumph, he was likened to John F. Kennedy, and a similarly high expectation was put upon him. Rajiv described this high expectation as 'scary'.

Rajiv himself won a handsome personal victory at Amethi for the second time in four years. The victory was more significant on this occasion as one of his defeated opponents was his sister-in-law, Maneka Gandhi, standing for the Rashtriya Sanjay Manch, the party she had formed in memory of her late husband, Sanjay. The result settled once and for all the family row as to who was Sanjay's political heir, his wife or his brother. Rajiv, who had never hidden his criticism of Sanjay's political style, preferred not to see it that way. He could rightfully regard it as his own victory.

Rajiv was not the only member of the family in the new Parliament. His cousin, Arun Nehru, who had played a key role in making him prime minister, had contested and been elected for Indira's former constituency of Rae Bareilly, recalling perhaps Indira's comment that 'the people of Rae Bareilly are not happy without a Nehru'.[1] When Indira made that remark, she was forgetting that she had inherited the seat from her late husband, Feroze Gandhi, or else she regarded him as a Nehru by adoption. Perpetuating the Nehru–Gandhi's reputation as India's ruling family, Rajiv made Arun Nehru minister of internal security in his first post-election government.

With Congress holding four-fifths of the seats in the Lok Sabha, Rajiv had the power to amend India's constitution, though he could not always be sure of a similar majority in the upper house, the Rajya Sabha, whose members are elected by an altogether different system. In keeping with his pledge to introduce electoral reform, one of his first parliamentary bills amended the constitution by providing for the expulsion from either parliamentary house or any state assembly of any elected member who changed parties. If an elected member were to defect from his party, he would lose the right to sit in that chamber, unless more than a third of elected members of that party were involved in the defection, in which case it was regarded as a party split. Defections between parties had been a debasing feature of Indian democracy for two decades, and it had become routine that a process of 'horse trading' would follow a close election result. By offering financial incentives or promises of ministerial portfolios, Opposition parties had brought about the downfall of numerous state governments. Congress had itself encouraged defections the previous year to bring about the downfall of state governments in Jammu and Kashmir and Andhra Pradesh. Under the new law, that would not have been possible.

Rajiv's mother had introduced similar legislation twelve years earlier, but it never reached the statute book. The Janata government made another abortive attempt. The defection of members from the Janata government in 1979 was the crucial factor in the collapse of that government and the subsequent return to power of Mrs Gandhi. Rajiv told the Lok Sabha that his bill was 'the first step towards cleaning our public life'. He promised other electoral reforms in due course. Even from the Opposition parties, the new prime minister won wide praise for putting an end to an abuse that had more often benefited Congress than any other party.

Rajiv's 'bombshell' to the Congress Party came at its centenary

[1] Quoted in The Nehrus and the Gandhis, Ali.

gathering at the Brabourne stadium in Bombay, in December 1985. It launched one of the boldest initiatives of his political career. After deferring to his limited political experience, saying he was a mere 'apprentice in the great school of politics', he took his fellow members of Congress to task for allowing the party to lose touch with the masses of India. He told delegates: 'We are a party of social transformation, but in our preoccupation with governance we are drifting away from the people.' He complained of 'the brokers of power and influence' who ride on the backs of millions of ordinary Congress workers, 'dispensing patronage to convert a mass movement into a feudal oligarchy. These self-perpetuating cliques', he went on, 'are reducing the Congress organisation to a shell from which the former spirit of service and sacrifice has been emptied ... We talk of the high principles and lofty ideals needed to build a strong and prosperous India, but we obey no discipline, no rule, follow no principle of public morality, display no sense of social awareness, show no concern for the public weal. Corruption is not only tolerated but even regarded as the hall-mark of leadership. Flagrant contradiction between what we say and what we do has become our way of life. At every step, our aims and actions conflict. At every stage, our private self crushes our social commitment.'

The speech recalled to mind a description of Congress a decade earlier as 'a party of self-seekers and spineless opportunists'. Those words came from the veteran nationalist, Jayaprakash Narayan, in a letter to the person he blamed for the party's downfall and who had put him in prison – Indira Gandhi. Rajiv's speech can be seen as his own criticism of what his mother had done to Congress, another attempt to distance himself from the politics of both his mother and his brother. By promising to 'break the nexus' between political parties and vested interests, to change the electoral laws to ensure cleaner elections, to make political parties accountable for the funds they receive and to wage an ideological war against those who exploit the poor in the name of caste and religion, he was demonstrating a desire to purge Congress of the decay which had accumulated over the previous decade. He promised that Congress would be reorganised and revitalised, repeating the pledge he had made eight months earlier that party elections would soon be held to 'cleanse the party and the nation'.

These were powerful words coming from someone whose membership of the party was so recent and whose presidency was little more than a year old. Given the subsequent failure to transform them into actions, it is important to identify whose advice he was following in making such pledges. The speech had been written by a committee under his close friend, political adviser, and fellow technocrat Arun Singh. There had also been contributions from Narasimha Rao, who had become human resources development minister, and Gopi Arora, another key member of Rajiv's staff. It was an early example of Rajiv following the advice of those he had brought into positions around him, but clearly the advice to clean up the party was in accord with his own instincts. Rajiv followed up the speech by appointing Arjun Singh, the former chief minister of Madhya Pradesh and latterly governor of Punjab, to the new post of party vice president, much to the chagrin of the existing number two in the party hierarchy, Working President Kamlapati Tripathi.

Like other senior party apparatchiks, the octogenarian Tripathi felt threatened by the promise of elections and reform. In a subsequent letter to Rajiv which was leaked to the press, he blamed the party's electoral setbacks in state assembly polls on Rajiv for allowing the party to be run by inexperienced newcomers who, in his opinion, were not running it well. In fact he blamed Rajiv for many things – for what he called 'the rapid disintegration of the party at all levels', for pursuing economic policies which 'favoured the rich' and for rushing in to sign accords over Punjab and Assam without weighing up all their implications. He criticised Rajiv's speech at the centenary session, asking whom he had meant when he spoke of 'power brokers'. He complained of a lack of respect for himself, pointing out that he had been one of the co-founders of the Congress (I) after the 1978 split, and had been appointed to his party position by Indira Gandhi.

Previously Rajiv had taken steps to oust the Sanjay loyalists, now he was being confronted by those who regarded themselves as Indira loyalists. There was no doubt that Rajiv was the focus of their attacks. When Kamlapati Tripathi resigned from his post at the end of 1986, it was seen as a victory for Rajiv over the 'old guard' in his attempt to reform the party. Other 'dissidents', including old-timer Pranab Mukherjee, had been expelled for opposing party legislation. Yet Rajiv had already moved his reformist vice president, Arjun Singh, back to the cabinet as communications minister after only ten months in the party post. Arjun Singh's sudden and unexplained departure, having made no obvious progress in bringing about the promised reform, brought into question Rajiv's commitment to the path he had outlined at the centenary meeting. There was no urgent need for Arjun Singh to rejoin the cabinet, so it seemed that the true significance of the move was his departure from the controversial post. It was an early indication of Rajiv's tendency to vacillate on important initiatives.

The promised party elections did not take place in 1986, or in 1987. Self-imposed deadlines kept on being put back. In early 1987, Rajiv appointed a ten-member committee to work out how the elections should be held, but its conclusion – that the elections could be held by June 1988 – was never adopted, and the elections still had not taken place by the time Rajiv was voted out of office. The main obstacle was the party's membership list: it was claimed that many of the 10 million listed members were bogus – they did not exist and thus could not vote. Also, there were clear vested interests with some Congress stalwarts fearing they would lose their power if elections were held. There is no reason to believe that Rajiv's pledge to reform the party was not genuine, but, in making it, he committed himself to a task that was too ambitious, and which defeated him.

Rajiv admits that it is one of the greatest failures of his five years in office not to have reformed the party and inculcated his own modernist values into this centenarian organisation. 'I should have stuck to my guns and gone through with them, but it got very complicated and we backed down,' he reflects. He saw his 1989 proposal to extend village level democracy through *panchayati raj,* a system of elected village committees, as a way round the failure to hold party elections. 'If we could hold elections in the local bodies, then we would automatically clean out not only the Congress but all the politics at that level, and take out the vested interests and have the answerability there,' said Rajiv. It seems very doubtful that this would have worked, since the party organisation has a momentum of its own which would hardly be upset by extending the system of elected village councils. The problem of the lack of democracy with the party could only be tackled within the party itself. Rajiv might well ask himself what the value was in putting constituency details onto a computer database if the party office bearers are still appointed rather than elected? Rajiv left office still promising that the party elections would take place soon, saying: 'I don't think we can do without them.'

Generally, Rajiv resisted the temptation to dismiss non-Congress state governments, which had come so easily to his mother from the 1959 Kerala dismissal onwards. But dealing with Congress governments was quite another matter. In an effort to maintain the strong central control of the party, he was wont to dismiss Congress chief ministers until, in 1989, a revolt by Congress assembly members in Bihar against the chief minister that he had installed a year earlier forced him to recant and change chief ministers again. Similar revolts followed in Gujarat and Rajasthan. Rajiv started reappointing members of the party 'old guard' against whom his barbed comments about the state of the party had been directed. Confronted by Congress rebellions in the states, Rajiv also reappointed his mother's special assistant, R.K. Dhawan, who was acknowledged to have a unique understanding of the party organisation in the states. By the time of the 1989 elections, Rajiv was again depending on the party bosses he had so roundly condemned and had, to a considerable extent, surrendered party power to them. It was they who handed out Congress tickets for the 1989 election, the most powerful form of patronage the party has.

It was the Congress Party meeting at Maraimalainagar near Madras in April 1988 that marked the end of Rajiv's commitment to reform, though he would continue to pay lip service to the commitment until after he left office. The 'young man in a hurry' with hardly a good word to say about the party had been replaced by the more seasoned Rajiv, veteran of several state electoral defeats, who had nothing ill to say of the party. At Maraimalainagar, he reserved his criticism for the opposition, proclaiming: 'The Congress Party is the only party with the poor and the oppressed ... is the only party which can protect India's independence, unity and integrity ... and is the only party of principle.' The party dissidents who had troubled him the previous year were no longer in evidence, or else were no longer dissidents. With the party's focus on the forthcoming general elections and its energies devoted to devising winning slogans, Rajiv felt no need to explain why internal party elections had not taken place. It seemed as if the Congress Party was back to normal after the aberration of Rajiv's Bombay speech two years earlier. The wheel had turned full circle, and Rajiv finally became his mother's son at Maraimalainagar, leading a party that for all intents and purposes was his own electoral vehicle.

Rajiv did not reform the party because he could not – vested interests ran too deep. Possibly he could have done so if he had acted immediately, but his repeated failure to win state assembly elections and his poor campaigning performance weakened his power base within the party. What is difficult to believe is that he did not hold party elections simply because he feared the humiliation of not being re-selected as party president, as some have argued. It is inconceivable that a party which had shown such loyalty over so many years to its ruling family would vote against that family simply because its current representative had decided to restore some democracy to the party.

Rajiv once likened the Congress Party to the river Ganga, or Ganges: 'The Congress is to politics what the Ganga is to our culture – the mainstream.' He went on: 'The political unity of modern India is itself a reflection of the united political will which the Congress built up.' Whether or not Congress's days as the natural party of government are past, Rajiv at least recognised that if it was to survive – if not to retain what it had come to regard as its virtually divine right to rule India – it needed to reform itself and smarten up its own democratic credentials. He saw that only in that way could it hope to resist the challenge from others, and in particular from the new regional parties emerging on the Indian political stage. But it was not enough to recognise this, he needed to carry through those reforms, and that is where he manifestly failed.

CHAPTER FOUR

Towards the Twenty-First Century

On the thirteenth day after her death, Indira Gandhi's ashes were scattered over the Himalayas from an aircraft by her son, according to her wishes. Hindus believe the Himalayas to be the abode of the gods. The following day, Rajiv addressed the nation over television and radio. It was his first policy speech and was rich in science, technology and national self-reliance. Rajiv credited his grandfather, a science graduate, with laying the foundations of a technologically modern India, and his mother with having made the nation self-reliant in agriculture, industry and some branches of technology. The speech ended with the pledge which came to be regarded as the hallmark of Rajiv's rule: 'Together we will build for an India of the twenty-first century.'

The speech was revealing of Rajiv's outlook in other respects, too. For example, he emphasised his continuing commitment to India's public sector which he credited with laying the foundation of a modern economy. However, he said it now needed to shoulder greater responsibilities and to become more efficient and 'generate surpluses for investment'. Was this a sign that Rajiv was about to reduce the size of the large state sector, and perhaps allow unprofitable public enterprises to go to the wall? 'Private industry should acquire the strength competition provides by reducing costs and absorbing new technology. Both public and private sectors should venture into new fields and develop indigenous technology.' Was this an indication that he would lift protectionist barriers and expose Indian industry to competition from imports? The fact that he also reaffirmed his adherence to socialism and central planning seemed less important than the overall stress he placed throughout his speech on modernisation and the 'all-round induction of new technology'.

Rajiv read mechanical sciences at Cambridge, so it is hardly surprising he placed so much importance on science and technology. It is a constant theme of his that Indian science must be equal to the best. Nehru had shown the way by establishing a number of scientific research institutes. As a result, Indian scientists have carried out research into a wide range of specialist fields, including space and nuclear technology. Rajiv's mother, though no scientist herself, had continued to support scientific research by pouring funds into research institutes. During Indira's rule, India had become a nuclear power-generating nation, had launched its own satellites into space and – most important of all – achieved self-sufficiency in food-grain production, very largely as a result of investment in the development of high-yield and disease-resistant varieties of grain, thus giving birth to India's 'green revolution'.

Rajiv's philosophy is that science and technology must be relevant to the needs of the country. He does not believe in research for its own sake. With a typically scientific metaphor, he once told an audience of scientists that 'the litmus test for any scientific activity in India is how far it helps to remove poverty'. He defends himself from criticism of the costs of ongoing research by arguing that the farmers of the Punjab would not have succeeded with their green revolution had they not had access to tissue culture and genetic engineering. At an award ceremony honouring scientists for technological achievements, Rajiv told his audience: 'Indian scientists have ... transformed the image of India from a land of rope-tricks, snake charmers and elephants, to a land that today is the repository of a wide spectrum of science and technological ability.' He is convinced that most scientific advance has a relevance even for the Indian villager, and that the introduction of technology is itself a means for eliminating poverty. 'Development through science' and 'technology for the benefit of the people' could very well be his campaign slogans.

But Rajiv had already won the election, and was now attempting to implement his modernist philosophy. Signifying his intention of keeping a close eye on technological development, he retained for himself the ministerial portfolios of Science and Technology, Electronics, Atomic Energy, Space and Civil Aviation, as well as Environment and Forests, and Ocean Development. He subsequently demonstrated the importance he attached to science by identifying six areas of underdevelopment where he thought a scientific approach would help in achieving targets. He called these target-orientated projects 'technology missions' and, in most cases, the deadlines he set for achieving the targets were, significantly, the arrival of the twenty-first century.

The aim of the most basic technology mission is to provide drinking water to every Indian village, only about one in five of which currently has its own potable water supplies. The drinking water mission involves finding, extracting and cleansing water supplies, and combines the disciplines of geology, civil engineering and biochemistry, with help from India's space scientists who already had satellites for identifying hidden water resources in orbit and were planning to launch more sophisticated ones. A literacy mission was given the task of reducing illiteracy, from which over sixty per cent of the population suffer, by using video and audio cassettes. This mission was also expected to look to the space scientists for help by extending India's existing satellite communications systems as a means of bringing learning to the villages. The theory was that bringing television to India's villages would advance literacy, or provide a means for teaching reading and writing skills, and would at the same time promote other social needs such as birth control and sanitation. The immunisation of all children and pregnant women against a range of diseases was to be tackled by another mission. A mission to develop dairy productivity by im-proving the milk yield of cows and buffaloes and combating cattle disease was added later.

A less obvious priority, to expand edible oil production, was entrusted to another technology mission. This was Rajiv's response to the high level of imports of edible oils, which was costing the nation dear in foreign exchange. As part of a programme to reduce imports in general, he entrusted this mission with the task of matching the various oil-bearing crops which India grows, to the climate and soil of each region, with a view to achieving self-sufficiency. Lastly, Rajiv was persuaded that India's unreliable and insubstantial tele-communications network was itself a major constraint on develop-ment. India's 800 million population was served by fewer than 5 million telephones, which is a hindrance to business as much as to communication with the villages. The mission has a target to bring the telephone to every Indian village by the turn of the century.

The man who helped inspire the technology mission approach was a brash young American-trained Indian, Sam Pitroda. A graduate of Baroda University and the Illinois Institute, who had made a fortune in the United States from telephone switching systems before selling out to Rockwell International, Sam Pitroda epitomises everything Rajiv believes in. He has plenty of drive and initiative and refuses to allow bureaucracy, or prejudices of caste or upbringing, to stand in the way. Above all, he is firmly committed to self-reliance, and believes India should develop its own telephone technology suited to the conditions and needs of the country. From the moment Sam Pitroda and Rajiv first met in November 1981, they got on well: 'We clicked, and I felt encouraged,' Sam Pitroda recalls. He had come to India from Chicago to demonstrate his theories for developing telecommunications in India to Indira Gandhi's cabinet. Rajiv sat in on the slide show presentation, and it was probably partly as a result of his influence that Indira was persuaded to set up an experimental Centre for the Development of Telematics (the science of combining telecommunications with computer-based informatics) with the objective of designing and building an indigenous Indian telephone exchange. It was a controversial project because it was based on Pitroda's no-nonsense style and American methodology. This did not go down well with India's enormous telecommunications bureaucracy which had its own way of doing things. Resentment against him and his methods increased when he was appointed chairman of the newly constituted Telecom Commission in May 1989.

At the same time as developing three different sizes of telephone exchange, the Centre for the Development of Telematics, or CDoT, claims to be masterminding a management revolution by replacing a bureaucratic, hierarchical approach with an informal and, according to Pitroda, 'irreverent' approach. The project has a much lower budget than equivalent research establishments in other countries, but Sam Pitroda is confident it can produce results because of the pool of scientifically trained manpower in India, and the relatively low salaries that they command when compared with the United States. Although set up at his instigation, Sam Pitroda turned down an invitation from Rajiv to head the new centre, which is based in Delhi and the southern city of Bangalore, preferring to act as adviser whilst still commuting regularly to India from his base in the United States.

Sam Pitroda found Rajiv very committed to technological advance and to overcoming the prevailing atmosphere of low self-esteem and high resistance to change. Two years after Rajiv became prime minister, Pitroda decided to bring his family back to India. He gave up a lucrative

1 Rajiv with his father, Feroze, mother, Indira, and grandfather, Jawaharlal Nehru.

2 Rajiv with his mother and grandfather on a visit to Palam airport, Delhi, to inspect a Canberra jet bomber. Rajiv inherited his interest in flying from Nehru.

3 Rajiv with his younger brother, Sanjay (**right**), their mother, Indira, and grandfather, Jawaharlal Nehru, and the family dog. There were always animals around the Nehru household, and a small zoo in the garden.

4 Doon school-days; Rajiv (**centre back row**) pictured with fellow members of Kashmir house in his last year at school.

5 Twenty-five years later, Rajiv returns as prime minister to Doon School, wearing his old boy's blazer and tie, and is shown the chemistry laboratories by the headmaster, Gulab Ramchandani.

6 During his student days in England, Rajiv rode a bicycle, but here he indulges his passion for fast cars by pretending he owns this Jaguar.

7 At Cambridge, Rajiv met Italian language student, Sonia Maino. They are pictured shopping together in Harrods' book department.

8 Rajiv (**left**) with his younger brother, Sanjay, at the factory in Delhi where Sanjay's controversial Maruti car project was based.

9 Rajiv, the family man and pilot, standing in front of the aircraft he flew, with Sonia and their children, Priyanka (**left**) and Rahul.

10 Rajiv consoling his mother at Sanjay's funeral. Indira turned to Rajiv for political and personal support at this hour of need.

11 The Sikh Golden Temple at Amritsar, Punjab. By sending the army in to clear the temple complex of Sikh gunmen, Indira Gandhi effectively signed her own death warrant.

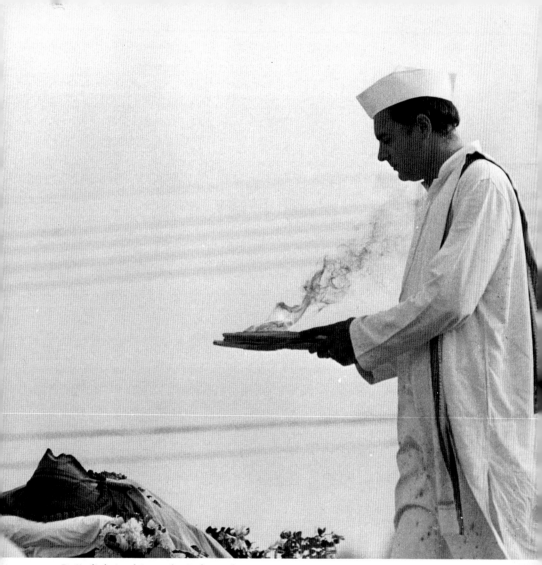

12 Rajiv lighting his mother's funeral pyre.

13 Rashtrapati Bhawan, the Indian presidential palace in Delhi, where Rajiv Gandhi was sworn in as the sixth prime minister of India, shortly after his mother's assassination, on 31st October 1984.

14 President Zail Singh administers the oath of office as prime minister to Rajiv Gandhi.

and luxurious life in Chicago, readopted Indian citizenship, and put his children into Delhi's American school. The following year, he agreed to become Rajiv's adviser on technology missions, having persuaded him to include telecommunications amongst them. He was dubbed 'Rajiv's new missionary'.

Sam Pitroda's brash, enthusiastic style and modern management approach have earned him enemies, curiously from the academic community as much as from those who feel directly threatened by his innovations. There is a feeling that he is 'not Indian' but is playing out an American dream in India; that he has breached some unspoken understanding by combining scientific talents with entrepreneurship. Perhaps there is also resentment at his unwillingness to do things 'the Indian way', or at least adjust his methods to allow for Indian sensitivities. Brashness is not a quality that appeals to Indian employees or managers. The prevailing distrust of Pitroda was summed up by the *Statesman* newspaper when it warned: 'The nation must be wary of persons waving magic wands to wish away complex problems.'

As Telecom Commission chairman, Pitroda's five-year target is to double the five million telephone connections whilst, at the same time, replacing and improving existing lines with the help of his indigenously developed exchanges, which he admits are running a little behind target. He insists that India's telecommunication system needs to be reformed but agrees, when pushed, that what he really wants is 'massive administrative reform' of what he calls 'India's antiquated system of doing things'. He believes the role of information is critical to the development of new work habits. He talks of 'the poverty of mind' which he sees as part of a refusal to 'think big'. He believes these are the weaknesses that have prevented India from becoming a modern nation. At the same time, he says the nation 'must address the needs of the 250 million below the poverty line'. Like Rajiv, he sees no conflict between the introduction of advanced technology and the need to improve the situation of India's rural masses, arguing that using technology is the only way India can afford to tackle the problem on a large enough scale.

Sam Pitroda is very much in the style of his master, Rajiv, a young man in a hurry, with the commercial achievement to back up his commitment to modern methods. Two years Rajiv's senior, he shares Rajiv's vision of an India in which the application of technology has pulled the nation up from the poverty trap to take its place amongst the best in the world. He says that, to have meaning, this vision needs to be broken down into 'manageable packages of work' and given to people to implement. As a result of his close professional friendship with Rajiv, Pitroda even offered him his thoughts on how the Congress Party might be reformed, as well as a computer-based 'SWOT' analysis, to use his jargon, of Rajiv's performance as prime minister under the headings 'Strengths, Weaknesses, Opportunities and Threats'. In early 1989, he came up with a strategy for re-election, based once more on the approach of identifying problems and then trying to tackle them. There is no evidence that any of Pitroda's strategies in this area were adopted. Analysing Rajiv's electoral defeat later, Sam Pitroda says there were not enough 'modern men' around him. Sam Pitroda's foray into the political arena nearly led to his own undoing. The new government were naturally suspicious of someone who had advised Congress on a re-election strategy, and appointed a committee to investigate Pitroda's approach to telecommunications. However, when the committee reported, it was the telecommunications minister who was transferred; Sam Pitroda was given the benefit of the doubt and allowed to continue to develop indigenous telecommunications systems.

Indian scientific research, to which Rajiv was so committed, has not been one long success story. During Rajiv's premiership, the space programme suffered setbacks when its new augmented satellite launch vehicle twice failed on take-off. Also, the programme for putting more sophisticated satellites into orbit suffered a setback because of the American Challenger disaster, which delayed all satellite launching by the United States, and the subsequent damaging of an INSAT satellite as it was being prepared for launch at the Kennedy Space Centre. However, India still has ambitious plans to improve its own capacity to put satellites into low earth orbits, and ultimately into high orbit for remote sensing and weather forecasting, as well as for defence applications. India's first indigenously produced, remote-sensing satellite went into orbit in 1988, and has already led to successes in locating water resources in Gujarat and Rajasthan, as well as helping the mulberry farmers of Karnataka, the tea planters of the north-east, and would-be diamond miners in Andhra Pradesh find the right kind of terrain for their respective products.

The road to nuclear energy has been a difficult one, from the days in the 1960s when India was the first nation in Asia, outside the Soviet

Union, to have a nuclear research reactor. Its first nuclear power station was eight years late in generating electricity and the newest one, at Narora on the Ganges, was also years behind schedule when it 'went critical' in March 1989. All the five power stations in service by the time Rajiv left office had experienced difficulties operating at full capacity, and the electricity they provided was less than three per cent of India's total. In 1988, Rajiv's government signed a deal with the Soviet Union to build two giant, enriched-uranium power stations. The deal was fiercely opposed by those who champion self-reliance in the nuclear field as it signified the abandonment of the policy of self-sufficiency in designing, building and commissioning nuclear power plants in order to reach the target of providing ten per cent of the country's electricity needs from nuclear power by the dawn of the next century. Importing enriched uranium for these Soviet-built power stations will mean they will have to be open to inspection by the International Atomic Energy Authority, something India had previously been reluctant to allow for fear of foreclosing its nuclear weapons option. Under Rajiv, India inaugurated a pilot plant for enriching its own uranium, one of a number of fields of nuclear research which suggest that at least the Atomic Energy Commission in India has its sights firmly focused on the twenty-first century.

Rajiv has a reputation as a man of computers, to the extent that he is sometimes accused of overrating their usefulness. It's the old argument that the computer is only as good as its programme, or as the data fed into it. Rajiv is certainly an enthusiast, as he is with all electronic equipment; the more sophisticated, the better. Rajiv has two Toshiba lap-top computers on which he enjoys organising databases, keeping his appointments in order, revising speeches and making notes. He chose the software and taught his staff how to use it, and usually takes one with him when he travels at home or abroad, allowing for last minute adjustments to speeches, or enabling him and his staff to work ahead on future speeches.

Within a month of becoming prime minister he ushered in a new computer policy that was being prepared under his mother. This gave a considerable boost to the indigenous manufacture of computers by reducing the import duties on component parts, generally relaxing controls on the industry and encouraging the use of computers in offices, banks and schools. Competition was introduced by allowing foreign manufacturers to enter the home market, the first example of controlled foreign imports being used as a means of encouraging domestic producers to lower prices and raise or maintain standards. The new policy also prescribed that jobs were not to be lost as a result of computerisation, something which would seem to defeat one of the developed world's major justifications for computerisation – that it cuts down on manpower. Because manpower remains cheap in India, other reasons have to be found for introducing computers. The effect of the new policy was to bring down prices, thus making computers more widely available; there were well over 100 000 in use around the country by the time Rajiv left office. Newspapers and magazines are full of advertisements for personal computers, at prices not out of line with those prevailing in the West, and the computer in the office or at home has become something of a status symbol.

The effects of computerisation are plain to see by anyone who makes an airline or railway booking at one of the main booking centres, or uses a bank in a big city, though it will clearly be years before the same facilities are available outside the major cities. Behind the scenes, movements of railway freight and passenger wagons are planned and co-ordinated on computers. A large network provides all government offices in Delhi with a fund of data, and schools are increasingly being provided with computers as part of their teaching programme. Computers have also been introduced into the immigration service and the army.

Rajiv is guided by the thought that India missed out on the industrial revolution which gave Europe its pre-eminent position and he believes it is vital not to miss out on another revolution, the electronic or computer revolution. India has the mathematical skills needed for research in electronics, and is well advanced in applying those skills to the manufacture of electronic goods, from television sets and video recorders to desk top computers. The regret – and it is his regret as much as anyone's – is that India is not yet exporting hardware or software in appreciable quantities, only the manpower that has developed those skills, with computer scientists of Indian origin to be found in American computer laboratories and centres of manufacture. Rajiv calls these overseas Indians a 'brain bank' rather than a brain drain, and cites Sam Pitroda as an example of how resources – or personnel – can be attracted back to India to utilise their skills there. India's own 'Silicon Valley', its so-called Electronics City, is taking shape on the outskirts of Bangalore, where the telematics centre and many of India's foremost scientific research institutes are based. The arrival of the US computer giant, Texas Instruments, to produce goods for export, has fostered hopes that the city may take off in the computer world as it has already done in the manufacture of watches and aircraft. Rajiv's long term hope is that India can make a name for itself as a producer of software, capitalising on its relatively cheap skilled labour.

A key objective of Rajiv's fiscal policy was to boost India's exports. Much emphasis has been placed on self-sufficiency over the years; but not enough energy has been applied to exporting the products of Indian industry. The heart of the problem, it is recognised, is that self-sufficiency has been achieved in the past by erecting barriers on imports in order to nurture India's fledgling industry. The cost of that policy is that Indian goods are not often up to the standards of foreign goods, which has generated a belief that goods from abroad are, *ipso facto,* better than Indian-made goods. This is often true, but Indians do not have the chance to judge for themselves, or to know how their goods compare with foreign manufactured ones, because the Indian market is virtually closed to foreign consumer goods, and is, in any case, large enough to absorb all domestic output.

Under Rajiv, the drive to encourage exports was linked to a relaxation of the blanket ban on foreign goods; with a view to improving competitiveness amongst Indian manufacturers as much as anything. By virtue of its size, India is an attractive market for foreign firms. But the strict government controls – which have meant, for example, that companies such as Texas Instruments were only allowed into India to manufacture goods for export – have had the effect of reducing India's appeal as a place of investment. Foreign companies' rights to repatriate profits are limited too.

Rajiv and his able finance minister, V. P. Singh, set about reducing controls over industry. 'We have to get rid of the controls without getting rid of the control,' said Rajiv. His aim was to ease the disincentives on enterprise and investment, indigenous and foreign, but to do so in such a way as not to stifle weak or sick industry. It was not an easy task, particularly as another aspect of fiscal policy had been to crack down on the so-called 'black money' that notoriously forms a large part of business in India. Black money can take many forms. The term includes money hidden abroad in violation of India's strict foreign exchange laws, money which should have been paid as tax or customs duty but which has been avoided, bribes paid to officials to gain licences without which the private entrepreneur can do very little, and other undeclared and often illegal payments.

It is not only a problem of big business, since even in India's villages it is acknowledged that government and bank officials take their cut from any aid or project funds, or else demand payment in return for granting approval for virtually any enterprise. Black money has to be paid even by the tobacco seller who wants to erect a stall at the side of the road, or by the merchant who wants to borrow money from a bank to stock his shop. Indian politicians too are not above accepting bribes, and it is common knowledge that international companies will pay handsome commissions, to an individual or as a contribution to a political party, in return for winning a lucrative contract, or even for gaining an audience with a minister in the hope of winning the contract. Just as greedy Indian workers, returning from the Gulf, want to smuggle back more video recorders and television sets than they are allowed, so big companies that try to avoid paying import duty on electronic typewriters, by falsely describing them as sub-assemblies, are motivated by commercial greed as well. In both cases domestic shortages may have been a contributory factor. Announcing his determination to tackle what he called 'the menace of black money', which he said permeates 'every part of our lives', Rajiv appointed a committee to advise on ways of doing this. Unfortunately, one of its conclusions was that eliminating black money would generate its own problems, since black money is a lubricant for all economic activity.

Meanwhile, as the finance minister, V. P. Singh set about cracking down on black money with a series of raids on firms where his department believed there was evidence of fraud or financial wrongdoing. Five weeks into Rajiv's premiership, excise officials raided offices of the large Pune-based Kirloskar industrial group and arrested its eighty-four-year-old chairman, S.L. Kirloskar. The firm was charged with not paying customs duty on the import of air compressors, and with violating foreign exchange regulations by investing money in a West German company. The authorities lost the case in the courts, but it had served as a warning that even the largest and most respected privately owned firms in the land were not to be exempt from what had come to be known as 'raid raj' – rule by raids.

The cleansing drive of the Finance Ministry knew no bounds. By the time V. P. Singh was transferred from the Finance Ministry in early

1987, when Rajiv took over control of Finance himself, officials had raided over 5000 firms, and claimed to have detected evasion of taxes and duties of the magnitude of Rs 5000 million (around £200 million). Revenue collection increased as firms put their affairs in order out of fear of being raided. When raided, many firms found that the easiest way out was to admit the offences, to pay unpaid duty or tax, and promise not to repeat the offence, which allowed them immunity from prosecution, thus avoiding the risk of a heavy fine.

A notable raid, in late 1986, was against the fifth largest privately owned industrial company, the Thapar group, controlled by Lalit Thapar who, besides being an acquaintance of Rajiv, is an old boy of Doon School and chairman of the school's board of governors. The raid stunned industrialists everywhere, particularly as Lalit Thapar himself was arrested and charged with failing to repatriate earnings from companies abroad owned by his group, which is against India's foreign exchange controls. It seemed to them that nobody, not even a friend of the prime minister, was exempt from the attention of the new cleansing regime. India's ambassador in Washington reported that Lalit Thapar's arrest had affected business confidence amongst potential investors in the United States.

Quizzed about the Thapar raid on returning from a trip abroad, Rajiv indicated that perhaps the authorities had gone too far. This was taken as a sign that even Rajiv was unhappy about the zeal being exercised by the Finance Ministry. Yet Lalit Thapar, within days of denying the charges against him, admitted his guilt, apologised for the offence and gave an assurance that it would not happen again. The admission seemed to justify the raid, and undermined Rajiv's suggestion that the ministry had gone too far. The Thapar raid had an important effect on the relationship between industry and government, and may, at the same time, have begun the process which was to lead to the departure of V. P. Singh from the Finance Ministry. Certainly his drive – or, as some saw it, 'witch hunt' – against black money was widely resented by industrialists. At the same time, it was immensely effective. Even India's foremost industrialist, J. R. D. Tata, who boasted never knowingly to have paid a bribe to an official, was forced to admit hiding abroad the profits from the Tata group's worldwide hotel chain when the Tata group in turn fell victim to the ubiquitous raids.

The raids generated discussion about the system itself, the so-called 'licence raj', which puts a price on everything – from permission to open a factory to permission to import a needed piece of machinery, and even permission to export. What V. P. Singh's department was doing, it was claimed, was trying to enforce an outmoded system by making sure that unnecessary regulations were adhered to. If the government was serious about liberalising the business environment, it would do better to lift the restrictions altogether, ran the argument of the industrialists. The system itself gave rise to black money, they contended, and warned Rajiv that he could not expect a smooth ride into the twenty-first century, or the country's high rate of economic growth to continue, if he went around alienating the captains of industry.

But sweeping away the 'licence raj' system was not as easy as that, as Rajiv was to find out. Many of the restrictions on business activity or imports are designed for the protection of Indian business against foreign imports and to protect state monopolies. Rajiv had, after all, reaffirmed his commitment to socialism, something he was bound to do since India's constitution, in its preamble, enshrines socialism as one of the pillars of nationhood, together with democracy and secularism.

The relationship between state enterprise and the private sector was laid down in a five-year plan drawn up by the planning commission, of which the prime minister was chairman. As a result, any change to the economic status quo takes time, and is within defined parameters. The 220 or so public sector corporations play a key role in the economy, especially in the defence, oil and gas, steel, mines and metals sectors, which they dominate. Only about half of them make any profit. Rajiv's target was to make state corporations more profitable and to stop the state from taking over so-called 'sick' industry, which had often been the practice in the past – usually with the justification that jobs would otherwise be lost. That target in itself risked undermining Rajiv's commitment to provide opportunities for work.

Rajiv promised to provide employment to at least one member of each family. He went further in his 1989 election campaign by pledging to eliminate unemployment altogether – not a realistic objective even by the dawn of the twenty-first century. These employment promises were a major restraint on doing what many economists considered to be necessary – allowing lame duck state corporations to go to the wall. Nor did Rajiv consider privatisation to be the solution; the privatisation of a state-owned scooter concern had earned him brick-bats from workers who feared their jobs were threatened. Employment is an emotive issue in India, and for that reason it was never going to be easy for Rajiv to take harsh measures against unprofitable state enterprises unless he had new industries to put in their place. One consequence of Rajiv's industrial liberalisation policy is that private industry has been afforded a leading role in the eighth five-year plan, which also promises a liberal trade regime. However, the plan did not begin until April 1990, four months after Rajiv left office.

Rajiv's commitment to technology did not mean he was blind to environmental concerns. Indeed, there had been a powerful reminder of the need to balance economic activity and the environment five weeks into his premiership. The giant Union Carbide insecticide plant at Bhopal, in central India, leaked deadly methyl isocyanate into the night air. At least 2500 workers and inhabitants of the nearby shanty town died within hours or days of inhaling the gas. Many thousands more suffered permanent injury, including blindness, as a result of the world's worst ever industrial accident. Accusations of blame were traded as the government faced the powerful United States-based Union Carbide parent company in the courts in pursuit of compensation for the victims.

It was to be the end of Rajiv's premiership, five years on from the disaster, before any compensation was paid after a settlement of $470 million was agreed. The Indian government had originally asked for $3.3 billion. Lawyers for Union Carbide had taken the attitude that there was contributory negligence from the Indian side – by allowing a dangerous chemical process to be established within the Bhopal city limits, for example, or not preventing shanty dwellings from being erected close by. There were also suggestions in India that, in granting permission for the plant to be built, officials may have been influenced by the willingness of Union Carbide to allow them the use of their rest house, and by the payment of bribes.

Nobody blamed Rajiv or his government for the disaster, but it did increase pressure on his government to enforce safety regulations and not allow the power of big business to lead to the neglect of necessary controls. Addressing a news conference during a visit to Washington, Rajiv accused American companies of being less responsible abroad than they were at home. Yet the Indian government was a minority shareholder in Union Carbide's Indian subsidiary, which increased its share of moral culpability. The Madhya Pradesh state government had also inspected the plant thirty days before the disaster and found nothing wrong. Rajiv's government did tighten up the system of granting licences for 'polluting industries', but there was concern expressed that, even five years after Bhopal, neither Congress nor any other major political party had made protecting the environment a top priority.

Rajiv's government did take an interest in certain types of environmental protection; the need to replace non-renewable energy resources, for example. Research has been done into alternative energy sources, which has led to the production of a cooker which uses solar energy. The development of nuclear power has been balanced by research into manufacturing bio-gas from cow dung, in pursuit of what has been dubbed a 'brown revolution', and into the harnessing of wind power. National water and forest policies treat both commodities as scarce resources, the importance of which was brought home to the prime minister by the severe drought of 1987. As he travelled to drought stricken areas, he said he could clearly see that where there had been drought there were no trees so that when it rained the water was not conserved in the top soil, causing floods in the lower reaches. He encouraged the reforesting of upper catchment areas of rivers.

In 1987, Rajiv told the United Nations General Assembly about the efforts of India's Chipko Movement to prevent the cutting down of trees in the Himalayas and, more generally, to end the commercial exploitation of Himalayan forests. 'Chipko' means 'hug', with women volunteers saving trees destined to be felled by literally hugging them. They won the support of Rajiv's government which committed itself to conserving and replanting forests. This is an area where successive Indian governments can claim only very limited achievement in their ambitious target of, under Rajiv, 'trying to achieve thirty-three per cent forest cover when the [currently] available cover is only thirteen per cent, maybe even less'. It would have taken a great deal longer than Rajiv's five years in office to achieve such an ambitious target.

One of Rajiv's favourite environmental projects achieved a much greater degree of success. This was his programme to clean up the river Ganga – or Ganges – which nourishes the people, cattle and crops of much of north India, as well as being their main sewage outlet and a conduit for industrial effluent. The river is considered by Hindus to be a goddess, and is thus a place of pilgrimage. Hindu rites dictate that the remains of cremated bodies be cast into the river, making the challenge of cleaning up the waters that much greater. One of the more imaginative schemes under Rajiv's cleansing programme was to release into the river flesh-eating turtles, which do not actually attack people but do digest their remains. In his post-election broadcast, Rajiv pledged to 'restore the pristine purity of the Ganga'. Eighteen months later he launched the project from the holy city of Varanasi with the inauguration of the Central Ganga Authority. Rs 2930 million (£110 million) were allocated for the first stage of the task and by the time Rajiv left office, the Ganga was already a cleaner river.

Rajiv considered reforms in education to be an essential propellant towards his vision of the twenty-first century, and introduced a new education policy. It was based on his belief that development is as much as anything about investing in people. He aimed to create an education structure that would allow India to catch up with the most advanced countries in every field, but, like many of his schemes, it was extraordinarily ambitious, stressing as it did both the excellence of education at the top, and the reach and quality of basic education. The three planks of the policy were Operation Blackboard: to provide the infrastructure for schools, such as furniture, teaching aids and teachers; the achievement of universal education, together with the related target of 100 per cent literacy; and the promotion of vocational training, since the high number of educated unemployed was itself a major social problem, as well as a waste of resources. Education, like science, technology and the environment, was a subject about which Rajiv was always very ready to speak, because he holds firm views about its importance. All these subjects have a place in Rajiv's vision of twenty-first century India.

There are those who regard Rajiv's India as a Golden Age; indeed, Rajiv is one of them. Asked by journalists to sum up his five years as prime minister, moments after he had surrendered the post to V. P. Singh, he said: 'I think India has never had the sort of development and progress and international standing that it has gained in these five years.' Indeed, he had some justification for that boast: economic growth averaged over six per cent, with every prospect that it would sustain that level; tax revenue was at record levels allowing ambitious programmes of government expenditure; exports were up, though imports were also up, leaving a substantial trade deficit; employment levels, a particular target of Rajiv's, were also higher than they had ever been as a percentage of population, but, of course, the population level was up too, at well over 800 million. Perhaps the greatest cause of satisfaction for Rajiv's government was the fact that, despite severe drought, nobody had died from starvation thanks to judicious use of food buffer stocks. Not only that, but grain output once more reached record levels during 1989.

Thanks, in large measure, to his relaxation of controls on business, Rajiv's rule had been a period of expansion. There had been a price to pay, though, in an exceptionally high foreign debt, depleted foreign currency reserves and a deterioration in the exchange value of the rupee, and there were fears that the country would have to seek a loan on international markets before long. Under Rajiv, there had been something of a consumer boom, triggered by reductions in taxes, the greater availability of personal loans and a dilution of the austere regime of self-sufficiency. The dilution was deliberate – designed to make industry competitive and its products more attractive and hardy by exposing them to foreign competition.

The boom was, of course, only experienced by the middle classes, those whose incomes allowed them to benefit from a greater availability of consumer goods, often at lower prices. This Indian élite has been estimated at as many as 150 million people, which is a considerable amount of buying power. People who previously could not afford a vehicle suddenly found they could now afford one of the 100 000 Maruti cars that are coming off the production line each year. The state-owned Maruti corporation is a good example of an industry that has gained from the boom; there was an increased demand at home and, for the first time, Maruti exported cars beyond India's immediate neighbours to Hungary and France.

The Maruti is also a good model of how India has changed over fifteen years, and especially since Rajiv came to power. What was conceived by Sanjay Gandhi as an indigenous 'people's car' had become, with Japanese help, a relatively costly status symbol which has spawned an accessories industry. The idea is that, since the limited range of vehicles available means you cannot flaunt your wealth by upgrading cars, instead you pamper your car with all sorts of accessories. As *Sunday* magazine said in a report entitled 'Have Money Will Spend', you can get anything you require to make your Maruti feel like a Ferrari; more surprisingly, people are willing to pay exorbitant prices for anything that makes their Maruti different from the next one.

The same competitive consumerism exists in relation to homes, where bathrooms have been receiving particular attention. Imported Italian marble, 'designer' tiles, saunas, jacuzzis and gold-plated taps are much sought after by the new conspicuous consumers of Delhi and Bombay; as always, there is a premium on imported goods, whether or not they are better. Foreign food at foreign restaurants is also much in demand, whilst the wearing of expensive jewellery and designer fashions are other ways in which the new Indian beneficiary of Rajiv's 'Golden Age' can flaunt his or her wealth. Rajiv is often portrayed as a 'Gucci' prime minister whose exotic tastes are evident from his choice of an Italian wife. If he can buy his Lacoste tee-shirts and Christian Dior sunglasses at the best stores in London, Paris and New York, runs the argument, then we shall do our best to follow suit.

The Rajiv years were good for the consumer; they were good for business too, especially for the 6000 or so companies quoted on one or other of India's stock exchanges. Antagonism to the Finance Ministry raids on industry distracted attention from the fact that business activity had never been greater, or more profitable. As one businessman put it: 'For the first time since Independence the creation of wealth is no longer considered to be a crime, and "profit" is no longer a dirty word.' Many fortunes were made as a consequence of Rajiv's liberalisation, which was praised in business circles at least as much as V. P. Singh's 'raid raj' was condemned. It seemed that self-reliance as a national target had given way to the encouragement of commercial self-interest.

The other side of the coin is that most Indians do not have the buying power to benefit from the essentially urban boom. For those close to the poverty line, rises in prices, especially during Rajiv's fifth year in power, have knocked out whatever gain had come from increased subsidies. The rapid rise in the cost of sugar in particular, allegedly because of bureaucratic delays in meeting shortages with imported supplies, was undoubtedly a factor in Rajiv's electoral defeat. While some people have climbed out of the poverty trap and become consumers with purchasing power, the vast majority – at least 600 million – remain at subsistence level with little to show by way of any improvement in their circumstances after five years of Rajiv's liberalised socialism. Increased expenditure on health, education and anti-poverty programmes takes longer than five years to bring significant advances. Despite the slogans – eliminate poverty, eliminate unemployment, education for all – there had been no sustained attack on poverty and few examples of technology benefiting the ordinary people. 'You've never had it so good' was true only as far as the consuming minority were concerned. The argument of economists that there are in reality two Indias, that of the 'haves' and that of the 'have nots', had never been truer.

Rajiv found it frustrating that his policies made little impact on poverty. Any number of good ideas and endless quantities of money did not seem to him to be having much effect. It is a frustration which reveals itself when he is asked how piloting a nation compares with piloting a plane, a question he has been asked dozens of times. By way of reply, Rajiv invariably complains of the slow response time or inertia in 'piloting the nation'. 'There is so much free play in the controls that you can almost shake them at one end and nothing happens at the other end,' is how he once put it in a BBC interview. Even for an experienced airline pilot with the right instincts and ideas, the challenge of piloting a nation like India into the twenty-first century is a daunting one.

CHAPTER FIVE

International Statesman

As befitted a pilot, Rajiv loved to travel and visit other countries during his time as prime minister. This may have been as much because he wanted to project India on the international stage, as because he enjoyed being his country's chief diplomat, a role for which he felt his upbringing equipped him well. When he told those attending a banquet given in his honour by the British prime minister, Mrs Thatcher, during his first visit to London after taking office that 'it is good to be among friends', he meant it. It was not just memories of his 'carefree days' in London as a student, but the fact that he has been meeting international statespeople in his grandfather's and mother's homes for as long as he can remember. He feels at ease with such people, which is not true of all Indian politicians, and that may explain why he decided to retain the external affairs portfolio for himself in his first government after the elections. It certainly provided a pretext, if one were needed, for the foreign tours he undertook to fifteen different countries during his first year after being elected to office.

There is a tradition in the subcontinent of watching to see whether a new leader goes first to Moscow or Washington, as an indicator of ideological leanings. When Rajiv came to office, it was suggested he would lean more towards the West because of his fondness for computers and other electronic gadgetry that is more widely available there. He was not thought to be as committed to socialism as Nehru or Indira Gandhi were. As it happened, the decision about his first visit abroad was decided not by Rajiv or the External Affairs Ministry, but in Moscow with the sudden death of the Soviet leader, Konstantin Chernenko, in March 1985. The funeral necessitated a quick dash to Moscow, where Rajiv was warmly received by the new Soviet leader, Mikhail Gorbachev. Any remaining doubts about Rajiv's foreign policy priorities were finally dispelled two months later when he made a fully fledged six-day visit to the Soviet Union. This visit established a special relationship between the reform-minded leaders of both countries, with Rajiv particularly impressed by Mikhail Gorbachev's apparently genuine commitment to nuclear arms reduction. They were to visit each other regularly after this, and had a total of eight meetings over five years.

Rajiv's strangest visit to Moscow came later the same year when he ordered the jet bringing him back from a six-nation tour, which had included visits to the Commonwealth Conference in the Bahamas and the United Nations General Assembly in New York, to divert to Moscow after his last scheduled stop in the Netherlands. Brief talks were followed by a visit to the ballet by Rajiv and Sonia before they headed home. This unscheduled stop provoked some consternation in the United States, coming so soon after Rajiv and President Reagan had met at the United Nations in New York, and just a month before the first Reagan-Gorbachev summit in Geneva. Apart from creating an impression that Rajiv could not meet the American president without straight away reporting back to Moscow, the Moscow stop-over gave rise to worries that he might be giving Mikhail Gorbachev advance information of an American posture at Geneva. In India, the rushed visit was considered rather unseemly: one journalist suggested to the prime minister on his return that 'normally a prime minister of a country of India's size doesn't go to another country all of a sudden, and that just after your meeting such a big ...'. The questioner was cut off by Rajiv defending his visit saying the Moscow visit was not entirely unscheduled, just unannounced, but had only become feasible after his stay in New York was cut short. The mystery remained, but the impression of undue deference to Moscow had been created. The following year, there was to be another brief unscheduled stop in Moscow on the way back from Mexico, but this time the cause was a technical failure on Rajiv's aircraft.

Despite the warmth of his relationship with Mikhail Gorbachev, Rajiv would not agree that he or his government were closer to Soviet thinking than to Western. Whenever it was put to him that India tilted towards the Soviet Union in the great ideological divide, he would quote his mother: 'We are upright, we don't have a tilt.' When interviewers persisted and pointed out that India had invariably voted the same way as the Soviet Union at the United Nations and often voted against the United States, he replied by saying that India never voted with or against anyone but for the principles it believed in which, he said, was the meaning of non-alignment. Non-alignment had been the guiding foreign policy principle of Jawaharlal Nehru who, together with Gamel Abdel Nasser of Egypt and Josip Broz Tito of Yugoslavia, had been instrumental in the early 1960s in forming the Non-Aligned Movement, which brings together countries which share this ideal of neutrality. The main tenets of non-alignment are that a country is not party to any defence alliance and does not have foreign troops stationed on its soil. In 1983, Indira Gandhi became the Non-Aligned Movement's chairman, and Rajiv Gandhi succeeded her in the post when he became prime minister.

Under successive prime ministers, India had enjoyed a close relationship with the Soviet Union for more than thirty years. The relationship had been formalised when the two countries signed a Treaty of Peace, Friendship and Co-operation on the eve of India's third war with Pakistan in 1971. The relationship was strengthened during the war when a United States aircraft carrier sailed into the Bay of Bengal in threatening posture, an incident that has been cited ever since as justification for India's determination to keep superpower navies out of the region, and for building up its own naval force. The Soviet Union is regarded in Delhi as a dependable friend, unlike the United States, which Rajiv has accused of cutting off supplies of military spares and equipment at times of war when they are most needed. The Delhi–Moscow axis is further strengthened by non-military co-operation. Since the early fifties, the Soviet Union has helped India develop its indigenous industrial base and the two nations have become signficant trading partners in the process.

However, India's major trading partner is the United States and, whether to correct the impression of a tilt towards Moscow or not, it was just three weeks after his first substantive visit to Moscow that Rajiv was warmly welcomed in Washington. He had come to inaugurate one of a series of international cultural festivals of India, but was also afforded the honour of addressing both Houses of Congress. He reminded members of Congress that India and the United States are the world's two largest democracies, and raised a cheer when he told them that it was the throwing of Indian tea into Boston harbour during the Boston Tea Party of 1773 that had helped stimulate the American revolution! (History had not been a strong point of Rajiv's at school, otherwise he would have been able to point out to his speech-writer that tea was not introduced into India from China until the middle of the nineteenth century.) Rajiv perhaps best captured the imagination of members of Congress when he told them: 'India is an old country but a young nation: and like the young everywhere we are impatient. I am young and I too have a dream. I dream of an India – strong, independent, self-reliant, and in the front rank of the nations of the world in the service of mankind.'

Rajiv also had a chance to talk with President Reagan after which he told the National Press Club: 'I think we will get on very well together.' Whilst still in America, a flying visit to Texas in the Company of Vice President George Bush gave him the opportunity to develop a relationship with the next president. Rajiv's talks with both men covered a range of subjects, including scientific and technological co-operation. Rajiv told President Reagan that India wanted to buy an American super-computer to help predict the onset of Indian monsoons with a high degree of accuracy. The United States had been refusing to supply India with high technology equipment out of a fear that India might use it for military applications. Worse still, they feared that once in India's hands the technology would leak out to the Soviet Union. However, at this meeting the American president agreed that India should have the computer. Whether this was an indication that India was henceforth to be taken off the 'suspicion' list or simply a sweetener in the hope that the United States would be well placed when India made up its mind on its defence shopping list, is a matter for speculation. Even so, anyone looking for signs of a 'tilt' will have noticed that it was to the Soviet Union that India turned three years later for help in building nuclear power stations.

Rajiv clearly felt as much at ease in Washington as in Moscow, or indeed in London, Paris, Cairo or most of the other capitals that he was to visit during his five years in office. International hob-nobbing comes easily to him, and not only in the major centres of power. Other countries of which he seems especially fond include less prominent ones like Vietnam and tiny Bhutan (he made return visits to both), Yugoslavia, which he also visited twice, and Indonesia. He recalled visiting both Yugoslavia and Indonesia as a boy with his grandfather and mother, the latter when he was only six years old. He had not previously visited Bhutan, a tiny Himalayan kingdom which depends on India for a large part of its development budget, but had obviously heard a lot about it from Nehru. 'After my grandfather and my mother returned from Bhutan twenty-seven years ago, they told me about their adventurous journey on horse-back and yak-back, and of the picturesqueness of Bhutan's landscape and its shimmering air,' he recalled at a banquet given by King Jigme Singye Wangchuck on his first visit to the kingdom.

When visiting a new country. Rajiv often begins his banquet speech by recalling a visit made to that country by Nehru many years ago, and quotes something his grandfather had said or written about that visit. Rajiv likes to speak about common or shared heritages or early links between the country he is visiting and India – of the Buddhism that links India with China and Vietnam, for example, or even when he told a British audience: 'We in India have long ago forgiven you for ruling over us.' Rajiv may not have been schooled in world history by Nehru, as his mother was, but Nehru was his favourite source of quotations for illustrating his speeches abroad. His second favourite was 'our great national poet', Rabindranath Tagore. Rajiv's speech writers were well read or briefed and included, for example, a Turkish proverb when he spoke at a banquet in Ankara, a quotation from Ho Chi Minh at a reception in Hanoi, and one from Dag Hammarskjold in Stockholm.

Rajiv's style on all these foreign trips was not to deal with the specifics of Indian foreign policy, which he left to the professional diplomats; instead he was much more interested in the broad principles and with campaigning to put right what he considered to be wrong and evil. If he had an overriding international philosophy it could be described as 'one-worldism', the breaking down of barriers between nations. It is a philosophy he attributes to his mother who, he says, saw herself as an 'earth citizen'. 'She rejected the fashionable division of our common earth into the First, Second and Third Worlds,' he said, 'affirming her belief in One World'. That is not a view of his mother's foreign policy imperatives that would be widely accepted, as Indira Gandhi went out of her way to turn foreign difficulties to her political advantage, the most notable example being her intervention to help Bangladesh break away from Pakistan, an act which won her a great deal of support at home and abroad.

Rajiv may have learnt a lesson from this episode and tried to follow her example when he signed a treaty with Sri Lanka that, as we shall see, was very much to India's advantage. Less successfully, he searched for a role for India in resolving the Afghan conflict after the Soviet troop withdrawal, without finding one. He certainly emulated both his mother and his grandfather in his commitment to non-alignment. However, he was just as inclined as his mother to see a foreign hand at work – in stirring up unrest in Punjab or Kashmir, behind spy scandals, in association with Opposition parties during the election campaign or in other areas of public life. There was nothing very original in Rajiv's foreign policy, though his style of personalised diplomacy was his own.

In travelling so widely, Rajiv was committed to projecting India's voice more forcefully on the world stage and, indeed, to making its voice count in international affairs. At the same time, he was an ardent supporter of the United Nations, which he considered offered the best hope for peaceful co-existence. His speeches were riddled with talk of the need to free the oppressed peoples in their struggle to win freedom and shape their own destiny; to create a more equitable world order in which the developing countries could have a larger voice; to stand up for co-existence in the family of nations and solve differences by peaceful means, with reaffirmation of the principles of non-alignment, and with determination to combat racism. He believed India had much to contribute in all these respects, having won its own freedom from oppression by the Gandhian path of non-violence, and because Nehru had been a co-founder of the Non-Aligned Movement. However, as with so much that he attempted, Rajiv's was a diplomacy of dreams and ideals rather than one based on the harsh realities of co-existence with friends and enemies. The relatively low priority he gave to developing relations with India's immediate neighbours is an indication of this, as well as being another way in which he followed his mother's example.

Rajiv particularly enjoyed addressing big set piece occasions, demonstrating the importance he attached to membership of the various international bodies. He attended three Commonwealth conferences – at Nassau in 1985, a 'mini-summit' on South Africa in London in 1986 and Vancouver in 1987 – and would have attended another in Kuala Lumpur in 1989 had he not decided to call elections instead. He went to two meetings of the Non-Aligned Movement – at Harare in 1986, which ended his tenure as the movement's chairman, and Belgrade in 1989. He represented India at summits of the newly-formed South Asian Association for Regional Co-operation in Dhaka (1986), Bangalore, South India (1987) and Islamabad (1988). This group of seven

South Asian nations had been formed as a counter-balance to India's overwhelming dominance of the region. Rajiv also addressed three sessions of the United Nations General Assembly, including its fortieth anniversary session in October 1985 and the special session on disarmament three years later. One writer described 'this youthful man from India' as the main attraction at the United Nations' fortieth birthday party. 'Whenever he came to the UN complex . . . heads would turn and hearts would flutter. He looked handsome in his buttoned-to-the-neck Nehru jacket, he smiled a great deal, he was appropriately deferential to more seasoned world leaders who had come to the UN that autumn, and he made a couple of well-received speeches. Needless to say, media coverage of his trip was extensive and laudatory.'[1]

One of Rajiv's favourite causes was nuclear disarmament, and he inherited from his mother the ideal forum in which to promote it: the Six Nation Five Continent Initiative, which brought together the heads of government of Argentina, Mexico, Tanzania, Greece, Sweden and India. The group had been formed by Indira Gandhi a few months before her death as an international pressure group to encourage the superpowers to move towards the elimination of nuclear weapons and to reduce other forms of weapon stockpiling as well. Four weeks after winning the December 1984 election, Rajiv hosted in Delhi the first summit meeting of this group of like-minded would-be disarmers, who included Prime Ministers Olof Palme of Sweden and Andreas Papandreou of Greece. This was at the time when the superpowers were still engaged in talks about arms reduction talks, with very little to show for them. President Gorbachev had yet to come to power, and President Reagan had yet to visit Moscow.

Rajiv believed the cause of disarmament to be a logical extension of the Gandhian ethic of non-violence and adopted it as his own, introducing the theme of disarmament, and particularly the Six Nation Initiative, into most of his international speeches. He pointed out to one audience that he had been just one year old when the first nuclear bomb was used, and has credited Mahatma Gandhi with identifying the fallacy of the theory of deterrence when he said that 'the supreme tragedy of the [atom] bomb is that it will not be destroyed by counter bombs'. India's principled stand against nuclear weaponry is often considered by others to be flawed. For one thing, India has not signed

---

[1] *India: The Challenge of Change*, Pranay Gupte.

the Nuclear Non-Proliferation Treaty, which it considers to be a pact by the nuclear weapons-possessing club of nations to prevent other nations from acquiring them. Secondly, India has itself progressed a long way down the road towards nuclear weapons' manufacture, having tested a device in 1974, and, although it says it neither has 'the bomb' nor has any intention of acquiring it, Rajiv Gandhi often threatened to re-examine its decision not to develop nuclear weapons if Pakistan continued to do so.

A few months after the Six Nation summit, at talks in Moscow with the newly installed Soviet party leader, Rajiv found that Mikhail Gorbachev shared his own strong views on disarmament. Rajiv believed he had won his first superpower convert. Long before the White House woke up to the seriousness with which the new Soviet leader was talking peace and arms reduction, Rajiv was calling the Soviet leader a peace-maker and nuclear disarmer. Together they developed a programme for disarmament – dubbed the Delhi Declaration – during the Soviet leader's first visit to the Indian capital in November 1986. At two further meetings in Sweden and Mexico, the six summiteers developed their own initiative into what they call an Action Plan for nuclear disarmament.

By the time Rajiv Gandhi presented the Action Plan to the United Nations General Assembly's third special session on disarmament in June 1988, the group was able to point to the success of the superpower arms reduction talks, which had by then brought the ratification of the INF treaty with its ban on one class of nuclear weapon. Rajiv told the special session that this had come about 'partly in response to the hopes and aspirations of ordinary people across the globe to which the Six Nation initiative had sought to give voice'. However, in reality it was Soviet and American realpolitik that was responsible for the success of disarmament initiatives; the pleadings of Rajiv and the other members of the Six Nation Initiative had not been given much attention in Moscow or Washington. It is doubtful, too, whether President Gorbachev remembered much of the Delhi Declaration, which is significant as a stage in the development of Indo-Soviet relations rather than as a milestone on the road towards nuclear disarmament.

At the special session, Rajiv also pushed for the adoption of his group's Action Plan with its target of a binding commitment by all nuclear powers to eliminate all nuclear weapons by the year 2010. Unfortunately for him, or at least for India's standing in the matter, relations between President Reagan's United States and President Gorbachev's Soviet Union had by then developed in all fields, and international optimism on disarmament was running so high, as to drown completely the views of six non-nuclear nations on how nuclear disarmament should be brought about. The Initiative in which Rajiv played a key role – even composing the Action Plan himself on his lap-top computer – was well-intentioned but futile. It was overtaken by a convincing demonstration that only the nuclear powers can determine when and how to give up their weapons.

Another favourite cause of Rajiv's was the fight against apartheid in South Africa, where there is a substantial community of Indians, as well as the related target of ending South African rule in Namibia. Indian leaders have closely identified with the plight of the non-white in South Africa since Mahatma Gandhi worked there as a young lawyer. It was there that Gandhi discovered that he 'had no rights as a man because I was an Indian'. Nehru had been the first world leader to raise the issue of racial discrimination in South Africa at the United Nations, and in 1954 India was the first country to take sanctions against Pretoria by breaking off diplomatic and trade links.

Rajiv fought a strong battle within the Commonwealth to introduce and enforce mandatory trade sanctions against South Africa. It was a losing battle, with Mrs Thatcher determined to stick to the path of gentle persuasion to eliminate apartheid, a path that no other Commonwealth leader believed would bear fruit. Commonwealth Secretary General, Sir Shridath Ramphal, paid tribute to Rajiv's campaigning role on South Africa saying: 'His voice is among the clearest insisting that the Commonwealth has a special responsibility to hasten apartheid's demise.'

It was the Indian prime minister's proposal that a group of eminent Commonwealth statesmen visit South Africa and advise on a course of action. Despite the recommendation of its report that mandatory sanctions be applied, Britain would still not endorse the majority feeling. A subsequent initiative of the Indian prime minister was the setting up of the Africa Fund at the 1986 Non-Aligned summit in Harare. The Fund, an acronym for Action for Resisting Invasion, Colonialism and Apartheid, set out to collect funds to help compensate front-line African states for the inevitable economic losses arising from sanctions against South Africa. Three years later, at the Belgrade Non-Aligned summit meeting, Rajiv was able to report that the fund had collected nearly half a billion dollars from developing and developed nations, especially those of Scandinavia and Eastern Europe, and that most of the money had already been committed to bodies such as UNICEF and UNHCR, as well as to African liberation movements like the African National Congress (ANC) and the South West African Peoples' Organisation (SWAPO). Rajiv had left office by the time two of his southern African dreams were realised. He nonetheless greeted Nelson Mandela by telephone, and later took up an invitation extended by Sam Nujoma to attend the Namibian independence celebrations, during which he had an opportunity to meet Nelson Mandela.

Except on very short trips, Sonia invariably accompanied her husband, though she shied away from addressing functions on her own as she was asked to do. Rajiv calls Sonia 'a very private person who likes to keep out of the spotlight'. They traveled in style on an Air India Boeing fitted with a bed, a conference room and a small lounge. Rajiv revises the speeches he will make at his various stops on the travelling computer. He wears casual clothes on board, and is sometimes to be seen indulging his sweet tooth with a cake that Air India have learnt to provide for him. Apart from his personal staff, the aircraft carries a squad from the Special Protection Group, the force set up shortly after Rajiv took over to provide twenty-four-hour protection for the prime minister. Journalists are sometimes invited along too. One, who accompanied Rajiv on his 1985 tour of Europe, the Caribbean and the United States – a two-week round trip of nearly 20 000 miles – described the prime minister's sense of calm throughout: 'He's always in control of himself.' Addressing the Commonwealth Conference, he was 'one of the stillest leaders on stage, moving only to take his speech out of his pocket and give it a few quick glances'.[1]

Rajiv's frequent forays abroad earned him criticism at home, and the attention of India's sharp political cartoonists. One Opposition politician greeted the prime minister in Parliament on what he suggested was 'one of his occasional visits to India'. The cost of his trips also came in for criticism, as well as the disruption his visits caused to the schedules of Air India, which had to take two Boeings out of service for each prime ministerial tour (one as reserve) and allow time to equip the aircraft with its VIP accommodation. The provision of aircraft for one four-nation tour of Europe and the Middle East in mid-1988 caused

[1] Ashok Mahadevan writing in *Reader's Digest,* Indian edition, January 1985.

the cancellation of twenty-three scheduled flights, it has been claimed. A question asked in the upper house of Parliament about the revenue loss to Air India resulting from the prime minister's travels elicited a figure for his first three years in office of 28 million rupees (about £1 million). The junior minister who made the reply reassured members that there was in fact no loss to Air India since a calculation for the loss of revenue was included in the charter price charged to the government. These charter costs have not been revealed although the total cost of Rajiv's foreign travel has been estimated at more than 300 million rupees (at least £12 million) by the time he left office.

In December 1988, Rajiv and Sonia made an historic visit to China. It had been thirty-four years since Rajiv's grandfather went there on the only previous visit by an Indian prime minister. Nehru's sense of common cause with this Asian neighbour had been shattered in 1962 when the two fought a border war. Two vast tracts of land in the Himalayas, each of them larger than Switzerland, remain disputed, with India claiming China has in both cases intruded deep into Indian territory, in violation of treaties drawn up in British times. During 1986 there was a serious increase in tension on the disputed eastern sector. It was reported that China was constructing a helipad in an area to which India lays claim, known as Sumdorang Chu, and it seemed for a while as if border conflict might break out again. The failure to solve these border problems has held up normalisation of relations between Beijing and Delhi, even though it was agreed during Rajiv's premiership to resume cross-border trade and extend consular contacts.

The fact that Rajiv felt able to go ahead with his visit to China, despite the impasse over disputed territory, was the clearest indication of a desire in both capitals to put border disputes to one side and end nearly thirty years' estrangement between Asia's two giants. The meeting between Deng Xiaoping and Rajiv Gandhi, with the former addressing the latter as 'my young friend', was of deep significance, but in itself did little to resolve 'the problems left over from history', as the Chinese are wont to describe their border disputes. Some observers believe Rajiv failed to exploit an opportunity for concluding a lasting peace with China when troop levels in Tibet along the frontier with India were reduced following his Beijing visit, though he had started a process of strengthening relations that continued under V. P. Singh. Six months after visiting China, Rajiv failed to condemn the massacre of pro-democracy demonstrators in Beijing's Tiananmen square, drawing comparisons with Nehru's failure to condemn the Soviet suppression of the Hungarian uprising in 1956, and his mother's lack of protest in 1968 when Soviet forces invaded Czechoslovakia. Perhaps Rajiv believed that to have done so would have imperilled the gradual improvement in relations which was one of the few undoubted foreign policy achievements of his period in power.

By visiting Beijing, Rajiv had been to the capitals of all five permanent members of the United Nations Security Council, most of them several times. In fact, there were few capitals of any significance that he had not visited in just over five years in office – more than sixty visits in total, an average of one foreign visit a month. He had been to all neighbouring countries, including the Maldives, Burma and Mauritius. He had been to Australia, New Zealand, Thailand, Indonesia, and four times to Japan, as well as to a dozen or more European nations, several Middle Eastern ones and four in sub-Saharan Africa. He had also made forays into the Caribbean, and to Latin America for the Six Nation disarmament conference in Mexico. No Indian, and few world, leaders have covered so much ground in such a short time.

CHAPTER SIX

Rule by Accord

After winning his massive election mandate, Rajiv declared, in a broadcast to the nation: 'My government will give top priority to the problem of Punjab. The Sikhs are as much a part of India as any other community.' Promising to solve another of the main problems he had inherited, he also ensured that 'earnest efforts' would be made to settle the foreigners issue in Assam. Punjab and Assam were the only two states where elections had not taken place in December 1984, because of fears that they would have been marked by violence. In due course, Rajiv made clear the terms on which he would negotiate to settle problems like those in Punjab and Assam: 'Discussions can only be with those willing to operate within the framework of our constitution. There cannot be any concession to separatist ideologies or to the cult of violence.' Within ten months of coming to power, Rajiv appeared to have made breakthroughs towards solving the disputes in both states, and went on to reach accords with other agitating – and potentially secessionist – communities. However, making the accords work proved to be the greater challenge and one which, in the case of Punjab, defied him.

The Punjab problem had been occupying Rajiv for some time before he became prime minister. As his mother's key aide and Congress general secretary, he was closely involved with negotiations over three years with the Sikh party, the Akali Dal, which was articulating Sikh demands for greater autonomy. In this, he had been assisted by the two Aruns, Nehru and Singh, the former his cousin and the latter a schoolfriend. Both had given up business positions to become his associates within the Congress Party apparatus. Since it was the Punjab problem that was responsible for Rajiv becoming prime minister, it was only natural that finding a solution to it should become his government's 'top priority'.

Many people consider the origins of the Punjab problem lie in Indira Gandhi's decision in 1966 to accede to demands for the creation of a Punjabi-speaking state. This involved carving off Hindi-speaking areas into the two new states of Haryana and Himachal Pradesh. The bulk of the original Punjab, including its capital city of Lahore, had gone to Pakistan at partition. Nehru had resisted demands to split the state again, saying the Punjabi language was not sufficiently distinctive from Hindi, but his daughter reversed this decision. Sikhs were only narrowly in a majority over Hindus in the resulting state, which fell short of being the Sikh state that the Akali Dal really wanted – a state based on religion rather than language. The first call for a Sikh state had come before Independence, prompted by the demands of the much larger Muslim community for their own state of Pakistan, articulated in the Lahore resolution of 1940. Four years later, at a meeting in the Sikh holy city of Amritsar, the claim was first made that the Sikhs were a 'separate nation'. Significantly, it was 20 August 1944, the very day that Rajiv Gandhi was born.

However, Sikh militancy in pursuit of a separate state is more recent, and stems from a resolution adopted at the sacred Sikh city of Anandpur Sahib, in 1973, and from the presentation of the demands of that resolution to the prime minister Indira Gandhi nine years later. In calling for a separate Sikh state – using a Punjabi word which did not necessarily imply separate nationhood – the Anandpur Sahib resolution demanded that the central government limit its 'interference' to matters of defence, foreign relations, currency and communications. This resolution was to form the basis for negotiations between the Akali Dal and Mrs Gandhi's government. It also gave rise to the demand by some Sikhs for a Sikh homeland separate from India, to be called Khalistan, 'land of the pure'. This demand was never adopted by the mainstream Akali Dal, and the government was to claim, with some justification, that it was mainly espoused by Sikhs living abroad, in Britain and Canada for example.

The Anandpur Sahib resolution's demands for greater recognition of the separateness of the Sikh faith were closely interwoven with two more down-to-earth demands. These had nothing to do with Sikhdom as such, but concerned the sharing out of resources when the two new states were separated from Punjab in 1966. Punjabis believed they had got a poor deal in the division of river waters, one of two resources (energy was the other) whose shortage was hindering the expansion of agricultural output. Punjab is the home state of India's green revolution and the granary of north India, so its farmers thought their state deserved more water. Punjabis also wanted Indira Gandhi to fulfil the promise she made after Punjab was divided in 1966 – that the state capital of Chandigarh, built by Nehru after Lahore went to Pakistan, become exclusively Punjab's capital instead of being shared with neighbouring Haryana.

One of the main difficulties in responding to the Akali Dal demands was that, long before Rajiv came to power, the religious and temporal demands had become mixed up with political rivalry between the Akali Dal and the Congress Party. Not only that, but the Akali Dal had split along religious lines, particularly with the emergence of the fundamentalist Sikh preacher, Jarnail Singh Bhindranwale. In one of the less savoury chapters of recent Indian political history, Congress, in the persons of Rajiv's late brother, Sanjay, and Punjab's chief minister, Zail Singh, had encouraged Bhindranwale in a successful attempt to split the Akali Dal, to Congress's advantage.

Nor did they distance themselves from him when he started shooting dead anyone with whom, for political or religious reasons, he did not agree. On one occasion, Bhindranwale was arrested in connection with a murder, only to be released on the orders of Zail Singh, who had by then moved to Delhi to become India's home minister, who said there was no evidence against him. It was a clear attempt to protect his political protégé. Mark Tully and Satish Jacob suggest in their book, *Amritsar*, that Bhindranwale's release 'was the turning point in his career. He was now seen as a hero who had challenged and defeated the Indian government.'[1] Bhindranwale was a homicidal monster created by Mrs Gandhi's own Congress Party. He had emerged at a time of disenchantment amongst Sikhs, thus finding the ground ripe for his brand of fundamentalist preaching. By 1980, he had become the leading force behind a militant campaign in pursuit of Sikh autonomy, eclipsing the less extreme leadership of the Akali Dal.

This presented Mrs Gandhi's government with a dilemma: how to cut Bhindranwale down to size without alienating his followers. The dilemma was more acute because Bhindranwale was out of reach. Early in 1984, hearing rumours that he might be arrested for ordering the killing of a senior Sikh police officer who was shot as he went to

---

[1] *Amritsar*, Tully and Jacob.

pray at the Golden Temple, Bhindranwale took refuge inside the Akal Takht, a sacred building within the temple complex. In terms of its sanctity for Sikhs, the Akal Takht compares with the Kaaba at Mecca for Muslims and the Vatican in Rome for Roman Catholics. From there, Bhindranwale controlled his campaign of murder, directed initially at members of a minority Sikh sect, the Nirankaris, whom he said were not part of the faith. Later his gunmen turned to other targets.

After much dithering, Mrs Gandhi eventually sent in the army to flush Bhindranwale and his supporters out of the Golden Temple in June 1984. It was that action which effectively signed her own death warrant. Operation Blue Star resulted in heavy loss of life, not only of Bhindranwale and his armed followers, but of innocent pilgrims and soldiers as well. Officially, the death toll from Operation Blue Star was around 500, though the Akali Dal believe that the true figure was as high as 3000. The army action had been a messy affair; it took much longer than anticipated, and suffered from poor intelligence as to the whereabouts of the gunmen. The Golden Temple complex is spacious and has many small rooms in its outer perimeter, which is surrounded by narrow streets and dwellings making it very difficult to seal from the outside. Operation Blue Star appalled Sikhs, not least because the gunfire caused substantial damage to the Akal Takht.

One of the most worrying consequences for Mrs Gandhi, apart from the heightened risk to her own security, was the number of Sikhs who mutinied in the armed forces as a result of the operation. Because of their traditional role as warriors, Sikhs are disproportionately represented in the army; though Sikhs constitute only two per cent of India's population, they make up as much as ten per cent of the army. Attempts in recent years to reduce this proportion may have further fuelled Sikh alienation by restricting a traditional avenue of employment. The mutinies were an indication of the depth of the wound to the Sikh psyche created by the army's desecration of the Golden Temple, even amongst Sikhs living outside Punjab.

Many non-Sikhs believed the Punjab problem had become much bigger than it need have done because of Mrs Gandhi's long delay in sending in the army to dispose of Bhindranwale. This delay can only have been on the advice of Zail Singh, whom she had made India's president, and who continued to support Bhindranwale, or at least his ability to divide the Akalis. Rajiv, who was also advising his mother on the Punjab situation from an early stage but was not a member of her government, said in a BBC interview at the time that he did not agree with the government's policies on Punjab, and that he favoured sending the police in much earlier.

The challenge Rajiv faced on taking office five months after Blue Star was to end the extremist violence in Punjab and to placate wounded Sikh feelings in such a way as to end the pressure from India's richest state to secede. However, whatever concessions he made could not be seen to be encouraging other distinctive communities to copy the Sikhs in demanding greater autonomy. Rajiv's task was made even harder by the killings of large numbers of Sikhs in Delhi and elsewhere following his mother's assassination. Many Sikhs who would not consider themselves fundamentalists were deeply hurt both by Operation Blue Star and the failure to punish those responsible for the killings after Indira Gandhi's death. These events heightened the feeling that Sikhs had become second-class citizens in their own country, and fuelled a belief that the nation was forgetting its secular traditions and becoming more closely identified with the Hindu majority. In his post-election broadcast, Rajiv had given an assurance that 'Sikhs are as much a part of India as any other community'. This was welcomed by Sikhs, but they also wanted action: the arrest and punishment of the mobs which for four days had been allowed to get away with the killing of innocent Sikhs, for example.

Immediately after his election victory, Rajiv formed a cabinet committee to tackle the Punjab problem. It was March 1985 before he made significant moves, but when he did so he moved on several fronts: he ordered the release from prison of eight key Akali Dal leaders who had been detained since Operation Blue Star, and lifted a ban on one of the main militant Sikh organisations, the All India Sikh Students' Federation; he made a visit to the Punjabi town of Hussainiwala, close to the Pakistan border, to honour memorials to three Sikh martyrs; he announced the building of a dam, to alleviate the electricity shortage in the state, and a package of economic measures which he hoped would, by creating jobs for the educated unemployed, go some way towards tackling one of the underlying causes of Sikh agitation; and he announced the setting up of a north Indian cultural centre in the state. He also appointed a new state governor, Arjun Singh. The role of Punjab governor was especially important since Mrs Gandhi had, in October 1983, brought the state under central government rule, which means the governor, who normally has only a figurehead role, is in charge.

In Delhi, the home minister reinforced the government's conciliatory tone on Punjab by clarifying to Parliament that some parts of the Anandpur Sahib resolution were negotiable, and he announced the belated setting up of an enquiry into the anti-Sikh riots in Delhi which had followed Mrs Gandhi's assassination. The cabinet committee on Punjab toured the state seeking the views of its people. The Akalis, after all, did not represent all Sikhs, let alone all inhabitants of Punjab, and had never won more than fifty per cent of votes cast by Sikhs in a state election. Support for the Akalis came mostly from the Jat farming caste, the state's landowners, who had been largely responsible for the green revolution. At this stage, there was much talk by Rajiv of applying 'the healing touch' in Punjab.

Four months later, in July 1985, Rajiv announced a Punjab settlement, and proceeded to sign a peace accord with the leader of one wing of the Akali Dal, Sant Harchand Singh Longowal. Rajiv had been careful to keep President Zail Singh out of the negotiations, seemingly blaming him, in part, for creating the problem in the first place during his time as Punjab's chief minister. At the signing ceremony, the two signatories, Rajiv and Sant Longowal, were perhaps tempting providence with their declaration that 'this settlement brings to an end a period of confrontation and ushers in an era of amity, goodwill and co-operation, which will promote and strengthen the unity of India'.

The accord promised Punjab exclusive use of the state capital, Chandigarh, in return for some compensatory territory which was to be given to Haryana. It also provided for the setting up of a commission to adjudicate on the sharing of river waters between Punjab, Haryana and another state, Rajasthan, and referred the Anandpur Sahib autonomy demands to the Sarkaria commission, which was already looking into the relationship between central and state governments. The accord also appeared to remove an unacknowledged quota restricting the recruitment of Sikhs into the army, and to offer some rehabilitation – though not reinstatement – for post-Blue Star mutineers.

In signing the accord, Rajiv seemed to have solved the problem that had defied his mother and led to her death, a problem that was as old as he was. Rajiv's technique had been to use a different team in Delhi and a new Akali negotiating partner to reach this accord, whose terms were similar to previous draft settlements drawn up under his mother but never agreed. Rajiv's achievement strengthened a reputation he was fast acquiring for undermining those who opposed him by conceding many of their demands. It was an approach that had already won the respect of Opposition politicians. As his first major achievement since coming to power, and the fulfilment of his government's 'top priority', the Punjab accord brought the prime minister a great deal of kudos and the respect of friend and foe alike, even though the Opposition claimed he had compromised his principles by referring the Anandpur Sahib resolution to the Sarkaria commission. Not many months earlier, a key part of Rajiv's election campaign had been the charge that the resolution was anti-national, a theme to which he was to return during the 1989 election campaign.

In the build up to the signing of the accord, there had been two further instances of mass killing outside Punjab, which were assumed to be linked with Sikh demands and provided further evidence of the capacity of extremists to bomb and maim. In Delhi and neighbouring states, bombs concealed in transistor radios exploded on buses and trains, killing more than eighty people. Rajiv came under pressure to rearrest some of those Sikhs he had recently released, but wisely he resisted these demands, knowing that such action would risk undermining the delicate negotiations on which he had already embarked. He asked Parliament for its support saying 'we must adjust and accommodate' on political aspects of the problem whilst at the same time 'we must be very firm where there is any question of using violence towards those ends'.

On the other side of the world, an Air India Boeing 747, on a flight from Toronto and Montreal to Delhi via London, crashed into the Atlantic Ocean off Ireland, killing all 329 people on board in one of the worst air disasters ever. It was believed that a bomb was smuggled aboard, in circumstances very similar to those in the Pan Am crash over Lockerbie three years later. Though nobody has ever been arrested or charged, and no definite proof found that a bomb had been planted, the Indian judicial enquiry concluded that a bomb explosion was 'the most likely explanation'. Two militant Sikh organisations – one of them the recently legalised All India Sikh Students' Federation – and one Kashmiri group, claimed responsibility. Two circumstantial facts pointed to a Sikh connection: there is a large community of Sikhs in Canada, many of whom support the extremist demand for Khalistan; and, on the day of the disaster, a bomb exploded in baggage at Tokyo's

Narita airport as it was being transferred from a Canadian Pacific airliner, which had arrived from Toronto, to a Bombay-bound Air India flight, killing two baggage handlers. Coming shortly after Rajiv's first prime ministerial visit to the United States, the Air India disaster was a reminder to the world of the extent of the terrorist problem he was trying to tackle, particularly when it later emerged that police had thwarted an attempt on his own life during his visit to the United States.

At home and abroad, Rajiv moved around behind a high barrier of security involving a large number of bodyguards. After Operation Blue Star, even before Rajiv had become prime minister, his children had been removed from their boarding schools in Dehra Dun in great haste after the Intelligence Bureau became aware of a threat against them. They have since led a lonely existence behind Rajiv's security cordon. Late in 1986, there was an attempt on Rajiv's life when a Sikh concealed up a tree fired shots as Rajiv paid his respects at the cremation site in Delhi of Mahatma Gandhi. The gunman seemed to have acted on his own initiative rather than as part of a wider conspiracy.

Amidst this increasing violence, Sant Longowal was undoubtedly exposing himself to the wrath of orthodox Sikhs by signing an accord with the son of the woman who had committed sacrilege against Sikhdom's holiest shrine. He was to pay with his own life for, less than a month after signing the accord, he was shot dead whilst addressing an Akali Dal meeting in Punjab. News of the killing came as Rajiv was celebrating his forty-first birthday. He was later to regret that Sant Longowal had not been provided with better security, conceding that the Punjab accord, which was originally described as the Rajiv Gandhi–Sant Longowal accord, had a weak point in that 'it hinged entirely on one man [whose] death made it very difficult to complete it'.

This was a belated recognition by Rajiv that any successful Punjab settlement would need to involve other key Akali Dal figures. Sant Longowal may have seemed like someone with whom Rajiv could do business, and was a clear favourite of Punjab governor, Arjun Singh, but his killing showed that he did not enjoy universal support amongst Sikhs. He was no substitute for the strong men of Akali politics, who accused Longowal of having 'sold out' to the government in an accord which, they said, did not even secure the release from prison of all those Sikhs who had been detained without trial since Operation Blue Star, or the reinstatement of Sikhs who had deserted from the army at that time. With the hindsight of later events, Rajiv might have acknowledged too that the accord would have been stronger still, even cast-iron, had it been signed by representatives of Haryana and Rajasthan as well, since these states were crucially affected by the water-sharing and territorial provisions. The tragedy of Longowal's killing was that it came just as he seemed to be winning the agreement of his rivals in the Akali Dal to take part in the state elections, which were to follow the accord.

To his credit, Rajiv did not allow the killing of Sant Longowal to delay the holding of the state election, which went ahead amidst tight security on 25 September. The people of Punjab responded with a massive sixty-six per cent turnout, rejecting the boycott call of one Akali faction. The Congress Party, which had previously dominated the state assembly, was heavily defeated by the Longowal-wing of the Akali Dal which captured nearly two-thirds of assembly seats. With a vote of that scale, it was clear that the Akalis had won the support of many Hindus as well as Sikhs. Like Sikhs, they were voting for peace and for the accord, giving victory over extremism to the moderate line of Sant Longowal, a victory he had not lived to taste. The election had been largely free and fair, despite some intimidation by extremist gunmen who, more than a year after Bhindranwale's death, were still active in the state. An Akali Dal state government was formed under Surjit Singh Barnala, who had succeeded Sant Longowal at the head of the moderate wing of the party. This brought to an end two years of central government rule in Punjab. Though Congress had been soundly defeated, Rajiv praised the result as a victory for democracy over terrorism, saying it was more important to restore democratic government to the state than for any particular party to win.

Although the accord did restore a democratic state government, it was less successful in its other aims. While the elections were proceeding, two judicial commissions had been set up: the Mathew Commission was to determine which parts of Punjab were to be transferred to Haryana in compensation for Chandigarh, and the Eradi Commission was to investigate the sharing of river waters. The Mathew Commission was asked to report in time for the formal transfer of Chandigarh to take place on India's Republic Day, 26 January 1986, but it found it had been given an impossible task. Under the accord, the villages to go to Haryana had to be contiguous with Haryana, but no Hindi-speaking villages in the prescribed districts of Abohar and Fazilka had a border with Haryana. Despite three extensions, the commission still failed to make any recommendations, nor did a subsequent commission. Since the two transfers were linked and, according to Rajiv, he had been specifically asked by Punjab's chief minister Barnala not to transfer Chandigarh without first resolving what Haryana was to get in lieu, the transfer of Chandigarh did not take place on Republic Day 1986, or subsequently. Nor was the Sutlej-Jumna link canal – one of the key water-sharing provisions – completed as promised by 15 August 1986, or subsequently.

The failure to implement the accord in two such crucial respects left little hope that it would survive. The worst consequence of the failure was that it undermined the standing of Chief Minister Barnala, who was already on unstable ground in the face of continuing Akali opposition to the accord. The failure of the Chandigarh transfer provided the chance the extremists had been waiting for; they re-entered the Golden Temple and tore down the Akal Takht, which had been painstakingly rebuilt under government supervision by outcast Sikhs. The extremists considered the holy building had thus been defiled. Once more, they brought arms into the temple complex, with Surjit Singh Barnala's government seemingly unable to prevent this resurgence of militancy. Barnala was himself humiliated when several hundred extremist youths charged at a platform from which he was addressing an audience in the town of Anandpur Sahib, and the Akali Dal office in the Golden Temple was ransacked. By March, the extremists were fully in control of the Golden Temple complex once more; it was a return to the pre-Operation Blue Star scenario. The campaign of violence around the state flared up again, with Hindus as particular targets. The aim of the extremists was to make Punjab uninhabitable for Hindus, and to make the rest of India uninhabitable for Sikhs, by provoking an anti-Sikh backlash. Ten times as many people were killed in the state during 1986 as had died in 1985. The extremists also demonstrated that their reach went far outside Punjab when they claimed another VIP victim in August 1986 with the assassination in Pune of General Arun Kumar Vaidya, who had been chief of army staff at the time of Operation Blue Star.

Longowal's killing had undermined the foundations of the accord, but the failure to implement the territorial and water provisions, coupled with the extremists' reassertion of control over the Golden

Temple complex, and seemingly of the entire state, threatened the whole peace-building process. Rajiv's Punjab accord was in ruins, and to some considerable extent he had himself to blame. The failure to implement the territorial provisions of the accord was a result of pressure from within the Congress party; party members were worried that Congress would lose control of the adjoining state of Haryana in elections the following year if the accord were to be implemented. The accord was extremely unpopular in Haryana because it would have deprived the state of its capital and reduced its share of water.

Congress party fears over Haryana had been heightened by the fact that the electoral loss of Punjab to the Akali Dal had been followed by the loss of another state, Assam, after another Rajiv-negotiated accord to end years of unrest there. The non-implementation of the Punjab accord badly damaged the reputation of the prime minister who, only a short while before, had been hailed as a peace-maker. What use, his critics were now to ask, is an unimplemented – or perhaps unimplementable – peace accord? Rajiv denied the charge that the Mathew commission's terms of reference were designed to frustrate its implementation. Indeed, he made light of this fatal flaw, telling a news conference: 'There was, unfortunately, a slight drafting problem and they put in one of the standard clauses which they put into all their commissions of enquiry and it has slipped in . . . this has been extremely unfortunate.' However, he was unwilling to remedy the situation by revising the terms of reference.

It was later suggested that a Hindu lobby within the government had rebelled against Rajiv's conciliatory line towards the Akalis, thus preventing him from implementing the accord. Whether or not that was true, there can be little doubt that it was a political decision a year later that led to the dismissal of the Barnala government and the reimposition of President's (central government) Rule in the state. This occurred in April 1987, just five weeks before the people of Haryana went to the polls. Officially the Punjab government was dismissed because of its failure to check the increasing lawlessness in the state, but it was widely seen as a cynical attempt by the Congress leadership to win the Hindu vote in Haryana, where any concession to Sikh demands was viewed with disfavour. If so, it failed badly with Congress being humiliatingly defeated by the Lok Dal, a farmers' party, paying the price, perhaps, for signing the accord in the first place. The dismissal of the Barnala government and the Punjab assembly did nothing to restore confidence in Rajiv's ability to solve the Punjab problem. He was now seen to be vacillating on the matter, a victim of his advisers, rather as his mother had been, with no new initiative to offer. As an Akali Dal MP put it: 'Now people have lost faith in the prime minister and the situation has become so dangerous that no Akali leader is willing to show the sort of courage and initiative that Sant Longowal showed. No Akali leader is willing to meet the fate of Longowal and Surjit Singh Barnala.'[1]

It was 1988 before Rajiv offered any new ideas, which was almost certainly too late. The death tolls from random killings had once again soared, and even the appointment of the country's most experienced police officers to posts in the state had failed to quell the growing urban insurgency. Killings were routinely carried out by gunmen who escaped on motorcycles. At different times, their targets were those they claimed to be apostate Sikhs, Hindus, politicians, journalists, tobacco, liquor or meat sellers, and barbers, all of whom, for different reasons, earned the displeasure of the fundamentalists who were once more in virtual control of the state.

The action plan Rajiv introduced in 1988 was an attempt to revert to political moves to tackle the problem, but offered rather more stick than carrot, and was designed to attack the effect rather than the cause of the terrorist campaign. It included a programme to explain to the people the policies of the government in an attempt to woo them away from supporting the extremists. In fact, the extremists did not enjoy widespread support, but they did wield power by virtue of their arms and their terrorism, something that a propaganda campaign would hardly change. More of the Sikhs detained without trial since Operation Blue Star were released. Security measures along the border with Pakistan were improved out of the government's belief that gunmen were being armed and trained inside Pakistan, and the policing operation throughout the state, including the intelligence machinery and the quality of weapons carried, were improved. Village protection forces were set up in the worst affected villages, and the area surrounding the Golden Temple complex was to be improved in a programme which would also make it easier to control access to the temple.

Not long after the action plan was outlined in April, Rajiv's govern-

---

[1] Akali Dal MP, Balwant Singh Ramoowalia, quoted in *Sunday*, 30 July 1989.

ment had some good fortune. The shooting of a senior police officer in the jaw near the Golden Temple led to a ten-day siege, as a result of which nearly two hundred people, many of them gunmen, were eventually starved into surrendering to the security forces surrounding the complex. It was a triumph for a patient operation, which Rajiv had personally directed from Delhi, and which had avoided desecrating the temple by allowing the police or army to enter its precincts. The gunmen themselves were seen to have desecrated the temple when pictures were shown on national television of the mess they had left inside, and of the bodies found buried within the complex, demonstrating that the militants had at some stage turned their guns on each other.

Operation Black Thunder, the second clearing of arms and gunmen from the Golden Temple, this time executed with minimal loss of life or bloodshed, was a major propaganda coup for the government. It could have provided an ideal foundation for a new attempt to talk peace had the government known to whom to talk. However, despite maintaining secret contacts with various Sikh leaders since the collapse of the accord two years earlier, including several still held in jail, and especially trying to win the support of the five Sikh high priests, who were moulders of opinion within the community, the government faced almost insoluble difficulties. As soon as it became known that a person or group was in touch with the government, their standing was undermined in the eyes of the Sikh community, who by now had been alienated as never before by the increased security measures involved in the tight policing of the state, where the searching and arrest of ordinary people had become routine.

The only new initiative the government took after Operation Black Thunder came much later in the year when Rajiv twice visited the state – his first visits since 1985. He offered *panchayat*, or village level, elections, perhaps as compensation for the absence of democratic rule at the state level. Rajiv's offer was seen as an attempt to win popularity for Congress in advance of the forthcoming parliamentary elections rather than as a serious attempt to recover the confidence and trust of the Sikh community. (This view was strengthened when he made the holding of *panchayat* elections throughout the country a plank of his national election campaign.) Though the *panchayat* elections were promised by mid-1989, they had not taken place by the time Rajiv stepped down at the end of that year. In public, at any rate, there were no new talks with a community whose need for a demonstration of trust had never been greater. Such was the difficulty of knowing which religious or temporal figures had the support of the Sikh people that Rajiv was to leave office at the end of 1989 still complaining that since Sant Longowal's death 'we have been able to find no leader of his stature together with whom we can work'.

The 1989 general election provided the leader Rajiv had been looking for. Nine of Punjab's fourteen *Lok Sabha* seats were won by members or sympathisers of a faction of the Akali Dal led by Simranjit Singh Mann. A former police officer who had resigned after Operation Blue Star (or been dismissed according to the authorities), Mann had gone underground and subsequently been arrested in Bihar whilst attempting to cross into Nepal. He was held in solitary confinement and severely tortured in a Bihar jail by police who wanted him to admit to being involved in Mrs Gandhi's assassination. His detention had given him folk hero status amongst his followers. In May 1989, he and four others were charged with, amongst other things, involvement in the murder of Indira Gandhi, attempting to kidnap the children of VIPs, including those of Rajiv Gandhi, inciting disaffection amongst the police in Punjab and 'doing sensational things' like hijacking planes, breaching canals and poisoning water supplies to create chaos, confusion and anarchy. He was also accused of waging war against the government of India by attempting to establish a separate Sikh state of Khalistan.

Rajiv's government had sent envoys to Mann in jail and are said to have offered to make him Punjab's chief minister, a curious offer if they seriously believed the charge of his complicity in murder. But once more the carrot side of the policy on Punjab – in the form of yet another Punjab package announced in March 1989 – had been accompanied by the stick; in the same month that Rajiv was offering further releases and the partial lifting of unpopular special policing provisions in Punjab, his government hurried a constitutional amendment through Parliament that, according to Simranjit Singh Mann, 'spells genocide for the Sikhs'.

The 59th constitutional amendment allowed for 'internal disturbance' to be grounds for the declaration of a state of emergency. As Sikhs were quick to point out, it also provided that article 21 of the constitution, which guarantees the right to life, be suspended where a state of emergency is declared. International human rights conventions have categorised the right to life as one that should not, under any circumstances, be suspended, and indeed, it had previously been a non-suspendible right in India. Consequently, lawyers and human rights lobbyists considered the 59th amendment to be a danger-ously retrograde step and, since the scope of the amendment was restricted to Punjab, it was an understandable interpretation to see it as a direct attack on Sikhs.

The lawyer who later became attorney general in the government of V. P. Singh described the 59th amendment as 'the gravest folly' committed by the Rajiv regime, and evidence of his government's 'desperation over Punjab'. Less than a month after V. P. Singh took office, and before even seeking a vote of confidence, his government repealed the 59th amendment. Ironically, despite V. P. Singh's con-demnation of the 59th amendment, his government was later to seek Congress's help in amending the constitution in another respect to allow a further term of President's Rule in the state. Rajiv had left office with the Punjab problem unresolved. However, the initial euphoria that V. P. Singh's government would succeed where Rajiv's had failed, dissipated when President's Rule was extended once more.

Simranjit Singh Mann contested the 1989 parliamentary election from jail in Bihar, winning with a majority of close on half a million votes, the second largest of any victor in the election. He and his supporters trounced other factions of the Akali Dal, demonstrating he had the mandate to lead the party. Rajiv ordered Mann's release from jail so that he could take his seat in Parliament. It was a magnanimous gesture by the prime minister who, later that same day, offered his resignation to the president following his party's electoral defeat. In ordering Mann's release, Rajiv never made clear whether he was admitting the weakness of the charges against him, or just recognising the strength of his electoral support. The ease with which the charges against Mann were dropped inevitably raised questions as to why he had been detained in the first place, and whether the charges of complicity in Mrs Gandhi's assassination were not contrived. However, the new government had someone to negotiate with who appeared to have the people's mandate. Simranjit Singh Mann arrived back in Amritsar, a free man after five years, the day that V. P. Singh was sworn in as India's new prime minister.

*

A month after concluding the Punjab accord, Rajiv announced in his Independence day speech from Delhi's Red Fort that another key problem he inherited had been solved with the signing that morning of the Assam accord. For six years, students in Assam had been agitating over the influx into the state of 'foreigners' – immigrants from Bangladesh and the former East Pakistan, who had crossed the border into Assam and adjoining states in search of employment opportunities. The immigrants were mainly Muslims, and agitators claimed that Hindu Assamese were fast becoming a minority in their own land.

The Assam accord, in which Rajiv again played a key role, provided for the disenfranchisement of immigrants who had settled in the state between 1 January 1966 and 25 March 1971 (the day the state of Bangladesh was proclaimed) and the expulsion from the state of those who had arrived after that date. It also provided for the erection of a wall or barbed wire fence to prevent any further immigration. More people had been killed in the violence in this important oil-producing state than in Punjab, especially in a series of massacres that had accompanied the February 1983 state assembly elections. The conclusion of the Assam accord within a year of his taking office seemed like yet another triumph for Rajiv. He was strengthening his credentials as a problem-solving prime minister.

It would be wrong to say the Assam accord has not worked. It brought an end to the student-led agitation and cleared the way for elections to be held in December 1985. These were won by the newly formed Assam Gana Parishad (AGP), the former student agitators, who were an unusually young and well-educated government: the sixty-four assembly members of the ruling party had an average age of around thirty, with only twelve of them married, and all but four college graduates. More significantly for Rajiv, the AGP's victory made Assam the fifth Indian state to be ruled by a regional rather than a national party, and the eighth to be lost to Congress, a worrying trend for the party which was less inclined to see the result magnanimously as a 'victory for democracy' than it had been after its defeat in Punjab.

However, the expulsions for which the Assam accord provided never took place. Perhaps Rajiv never intended that they would. In any case, it had never been clear to where those affected would be expelled – whether to Bangladesh or to another Indian state; no other state had been asked to accept them. Was this another example of an unimplementable accord, or one which was never intended to be implemented? In 1989, *Lok Sabha* polling in Assam was once more postponed because, it was said, the voters lists were not ready. The postponement gave rise to new fears that the agitation might restart. (It had been the publication of voters' lists for the 1979 *Lok Sabha* elections, and the realisation by Assamese that they contained the names of many so-called foreigners, that had provoked the unrest and violence in the first place.) Clearly one of the main objectives of the original movement, the expulsion of non-Assamese immigrants, had not been achieved; in this respect, the accord had not been carried out. Rajiv's government also seemed quietly to have dropped the idea of building a barbed wire fence around Bangladesh to prevent further immigration.

In the meantime, the original Assam agitation had spawned further unrest as another sizeable tribal community, the Bodos, had started their own violent campaign to win their own state or territory separate from Assam. The AGP government of Assam accused Rajiv's Congress of sponsoring the Bodoland agitation in an effort to topple it from power. The Bodos may have also been inspired in part by the Gorkhaland movement which had campaigned successfully for more autonomy for the Nepali-speaking peoples of the northern West Bengal region around Darjeeling. Here, too, the Communist state government suspected that central government had colluded in the violent agitation as a destabilisation tactic. The Gorkha agitators had been pacified with the setting up of an autonomous hill council under an accord signed in August 1988, though a splinter group continued the fight for a greater degree of independence from West Bengal. Similar movements for separate statehood, like the long-standing one by the Jharkhand community who straddle the borders of Bihar, West Bengal, Orissa and Madhya Pradesh, seemed ever about to erupt into violence at the slightest provocation, encouraged by the successes of agitations elsewhere.

Rajiv's third major accord was with the Mizo people of Mizoram, another north-eastern state. Signed in June 1986, it brought to an end a twenty-year insurgency, also in pursuit of separate statehood. Certain concessions relating to tribal laws and customs, as well as trading rights, were granted to the Mizos, whose homeland was given full statehood for the first time. Rajiv made the former insurgent leader, Mr Laldenga, who had returned from exile in Britain to negotiate the accord, chief minister of the state. However, Laldenga and his Mizo National Front subsequently fell, after desertions from his party and Congress returned to power. From Congress's point of view, this was its most successful accord. It had paved the way for the laying down of arms by the Mizo guerrillas, thus ending their long agitation, and yet Congress returned to power after only a short interlude.

Rajiv also had to contend with political difficulties in the northern state of Jammu and Kashmir. The November 1986 agreement he signed was not really an accord but a deal under which Congress would share power in the state with Dr Farooq Abdullah's National Conference. What it had in common with the Punjab and Assam accords was that Rajiv had concluded the deal without consulting key Congress figures in the state, who could have pointed out its weaknesses. When the state Congress chief, Mufti Mohammed Sayed, who was also Rajiv's minister of tourism, heard about the deal, he protested that it would lead to Congress being wiped out in the state. The deal was the main factor which subsequently led to Mufti Mohammed Sayed's resignation from Rajiv's cabinet, and then from the Congress Party. (In due course he joined the Janata Dal, and became home minister in V.P. Singh's first National Front government.)

The Jammu and Kashmir power-sharing agreement had ended a messy period in Kashmiri politics. It had started with the underhand dismissal from power of Dr Abdullah two years earlier, whilst Indira Gandhi was still prime minister. Dr Abdullah and Rajiv were close friends, almost brothers, sharing as they did a Kashmiri Brahmin background. However, the power-sharing agreement did nothing to end the Muslim-separatist agitation which, especially during the last part of Rajiv's rule, increasingly took the form of attacks on the Congress-National Conference coalition. Dr Abdullah lost much of his backing in the state as a result of his agreement with Congress, which also – as Mufti Mohammed Sayed had predicted – did Congress's standing in the state much harm. Activists amongst Kashmir's majority-Muslim population had long challenged the right of Delhi to control the state, which has been disputed and divided between India and Pakistan since partition. With the substantial growth of anti-Indian sentiment during 1988 and 1989, Kashmir rapidly became as great a problem for V.P. Singh's government as Punjab had been for Rajiv's.

In tackling all these regional problems, Rajiv had shown an inclination to sign accords which conceded some of the agitators' demands.

Though his own ground rules had precluded negotiating with terrorists, every movement and many of the individuals to whom he talked had used or advocated violent means towards achieving their objectives. Just as meeting ransom demands risks encouraging kidnapping or hijacking, so Rajiv's tendency to concede demands through accords encouraged others to demonstrate their nuisance value in the hope that they too would be 'bought off' with concessions. None of the accords can be considered totally stable, and the terms of all were based more on hope than on realism when it came to putting them into effect. Rule by accord was turning out to be a dangerous means of quelling unrest, even before Rajiv tackled his biggest accord of all – involving a negotiating partner beyond India's shores.

CHAPTER SEVEN

The Neighbours

It has been said that because each of India's neighbours shares a language with at least one Indian state, it has never been easy for the Indian government to draw a clear distinction between domestic and foreign policy. This has caused it, for example, to see Pakistan as the troublemaker in Punjab and Kashmir, Bangladesh as the source of unwanted immigration into Assam and other north-eastern states, Nepal as a conduit for cheap Chinese goods which undermine India's industrial policy, and Sri Lanka as the source of an ethnic conflict which had led to an exodus of refugees to southern India, bringing with them the risk of a backlash by Indian Tamils, or a resurgence of India's own Tamil separatist movement of the 1950s and 1960s. There is some truth in each accusation, though perhaps not enough to justify India's unconventional means of treating the problems: a propaganda war against Pakistan, the threat to build a fence along the entire border with Bangladesh, the economic strangling into submission of land-locked Nepal and the training of a Tamil guerrilla army to fuel the ethnic war in Sri Lanka. In each case the remedy failed to solve the problem. Instead they enhanced India's reputation as the 'bully-boy' of South Asia where, in fact, it had wanted to establish its credentials as the keeper of peace in the region. Only in the Maldives, where India was the first to respond to calls for help in the face of a mercenary attempt to overthrow the government, did it merit the praise it received for altruistic peace-making.

Sri Lanka was clearly the main foreign concern when Rajiv came to power in October 1984. Years of simmering resentment by the island's minority Tamil community had flared into armed insurgency during 1983. The brutal and uncontrolled response of the Sri Lankan army to the insurgency had strengthened Tamils in their resolve to accept nothing short of an independent homeland, which they called Tamil

Eelam, in the northern and eastern parts of the island where they predominate. India had offered its good offices to help resolve the dispute, but had already earned the suspicion of President Jayewardene's government with the clandestine training it was giving the Tamil Tigers and other Tamil guerrilla armies. 'The only help we need is for you to stop exporting terrorism to Sri Lanka by training Tamil guerrillas,' was the gist of Jayewardene's response. Yet India refused to admit its undercover training role and, in the eyes of the world, its offer to help was taken at face value.

President Jayewardene was realist enough to appreciate that he had to accept India's help, whether he wanted to or not, especially after a mission to Washington and London failed to win him the help in suppressing 'international terrorism' for which he had asked in both capitals. He had presented the problem as an external threat, which was to ignore the fact that the militant Tamil groups had the sympathy, if not always the support, of most of the island's 3 million Tamils. He found a tacit acceptance by both Britain and the United States that tiny Sri Lanka, with its population of 17 million, lay within India's sphere of influence. Both powers hinted that Colombo should look to Delhi for help in solving its problem.

India's policy had in fact been part carrot and part stick – to train the Tamil insurgents lest the Sinhalese-dominated government be tempted to resume the patronising attitude previous governments had displayed towards this minority community, whose language did not even enjoy equal status with that of the majority Sinhalese; at the same time, India encouraged the government to devolve significant power from the over-centralised administration in Colombo to new regional units of government, modelled loosely on the Indian pattern. India was motivated as much by a desire to win favour with its own Tamil community of about 50 million, as by the concern that instability in Sri Lanka could spill over into India.

Rajiv's first statement on Sri Lanka came six weeks into his premiership, in December 1984, when he expressed his deep concern 'that the situation in Sri Lanka has rapidly deteriorated'. He regretted the food shortages in Jaffna, the main city in the Tamil-dominated northern part of the island, which had resulted from its virtual siege by the Sri Lankan army, and the fact that 'hundreds of youths are reported to have been taken into custody and shifted to unknown destinations'. He also complained of the harassment, killing and arrest of Indian fishermen in the Palk straits, the twenty-two-mile-wide channel that separates Sri Lanka from India. Stressing the need for a political solution within the framework of a united Sri Lanka, he appealed to the government in Colombo to defuse the present situation and give the lead to all-party talks on the crisis by finding a solution 'which meets the legitimate aspirations of the Tamils'.

A month later, after the all-party talks in Sri Lanka appeared to have broken down, Rajiv told an interviewer: 'This is a problem which really Sri Lanka must solve on its own. We will be ... having another look at this whole question, but we don't want to interfere in the internal affairs of Sri Lanka.' That answer concealed the fact that, by training Tamil guerrillas, India was already interfering in Sri Lanka, though Rajiv continued to deny giving any Indian support to Sri Lankan guerrillas. Over the coming months Rajiv was to state repeatedly: 'We have no intention to go into Sri Lanka.' The Sri Lankan government, which was acutely conscious of how the arrival of hordes of refugees from the eastern wing of Pakistan in 1971 had led India to declare war on Pakistan, did not take Indian assurances at face value. Rajiv was already referring to the refugees arriving in Tamil Nadu from Sri Lanka as a threat to India. The Sri Lankan government adopted a policy of compliance towards its powerful neighbour. President Jayewardene once said: 'I accept India as a great regional power; it is an undesirable fact.'

The first sign that President Jayewardene would accede to India's offer to help find a solution came when he flew to Delhi for talks with Rajiv in June 1985. The impetus for the talks had come from a particularly bloody attack by Tamil guerrillas on Sinhalese civilians in the northern city of Anuradhapura. President Jayewardene's first meeting with the new prime minister went cordially enough, with Jayewardene stating afterwards that he could 'do business with' Rajiv. The summit ended with an agreement that both leaders would take steps to defuse the situation in Sri Lanka. Later that same month, the Sri Lankan government began direct talks for the first time with representatives of the Tamil guerrilla groups. The Indian-sponsored talks took place in the capital of the Himalayan kingdom of Bhutan, chosen by India for its remoteness and the fact that India controlled the telecommunications links, which made it easy to keep journalists away. President Jayewardene's brother, Hector, headed the government delegation. The talks broke down two months later, but had been a significant episode in the search for peace. They were the first indication that the Sri Lankan government was willing to talk with those it had condemned as 'terrorists', and they were the first formal involvement of India in the peace process.

Over the next two years there were to be regular diplomatic missions between Delhi and Colombo. India was now firmly involved in the search for peace, which became more urgent as the warfare between Tamil guerrillas and the Sri Lankan army intensified. Rajiv appointed a string of special envoys to Sri Lanka whose main brief was to persuade the Sri Lankan government to concede a degree of autonomy to the Tamils. The implied inducement was that India would reduce its support to the guerrillas in return.

This period of negotiations between India and Sri Lanka coincided with the formation of a new regional organisation, the South Asian Association for Regional Cooperation, or SAARC, which grouped together India, Sri Lanka, Pakistan, Bangladesh, Nepal, Bhutan and the Maldives. SAARC was intended as a forum for promoting regional co-operation, and had been inspired in part by the neighbouring Association of South East Asian Nations. The main impetus had come from Bangladesh which, like India's other neighbours, was acutely conscious of the dominance of India in the region and wanted a forum in which the smaller south Asian nations could express their views on equal terms. There was an acceptance from the start that SAARC would focus on areas of potential multilateral co-operation and would keep contentious bilateral issues off the agenda.

For this reason, Rajiv studiously avoided any reference to the situation in Sri Lanka, or to India's role in attempting to mediate between the Sri Lankan government and Tamil guerrillas, in his speeches at the first SAARC summit, held in the Bangladesh capital, Dhaka, in December 1985. Behind the scenes, though, Rajiv spent a lot of time closeted with President Jayewardene. It was to be the same a year later when Rajiv was host to the second SAARC summit in the Indian city of Bangalore, becoming the association's chairman for the year.

By early 1987, the Indian government was increasingly angered by signs that the Sri Lankans had opted for a military solution in trying to bring Tamil insurgency in the north of the island to an end. A military blockade of the Tamil-dominated Jaffna peninsula was again giving rise to serious food and fuel shortages. India seized the opportunity to assert itself once and for all. Rajiv ordered that relief supplies be sent to the beleaguered Tamils of Jaffna. A convoy of Indian fishing vessels was turned back in the Palk straits by the Sri Lankan navy before it could enter Sri Lankan waters. Rajiv then turned to the fall-back plan and ordered that the food and medicines instead be air dropped onto the Jaffna peninsula, which Sri Lanka did not have the air power to prevent. On 4 June 1987, five Antonov-32 transport aircraft took off from Bangalore, escorted by Mirage 2000 fighters, to drop 22 tonnes of supplies onto the peninsula.

That ten-minute violation of Sri Lanka's air space had major implications for the regional balance of power. None of India's neighbours doubted that India, with 1.2 million men under arms, was the regional strongman, but now it was demonstrating for the first time since the Bangladesh war of 1971 that it would use its firepower to enforce its will. It was as if the Indian government were saying to its Sri Lankan counterpart: 'If you don't invite us in to sort out your crisis then we'll jolly well come in uninvited.' A helpless President Jayewardene explained: 'The Sri Lankan government had no means of resisting India's unilateral action physically, nor will it be able to do so in the future.' Nonetheless, there were reports that he immediately sent his national security minister on a secret visit to Pakistan to negotiate the purchase of surface-to-air missiles. If true, this attempt could have been an added motivation for India's subsequent insistence on the accord, which effectively denied Sri Lanka the right to seek military assistance from elsewhere.

Most of the world saw India's air drop of supplies as the humanitarian gesture it pretended to be. However, small neighbours like Bhutan and the Maldives expressed their profound concern at this territorial violation, which seemed to them to be against the spirit of SAARC as much as against the norms of international behaviour. Nonetheless, the Sri Lankan government immediately got the message. It signed an agreement permitting Indian vessels to deliver supplies to Jaffna, and intense diplomatic activity resumed between Delhi and Colombo to formalise a role for India in the search for peace in Sri Lanka.

The result was the 'Indo–Sri Lanka Agreement to establish peace and normalcy in Sri Lanka'. Rajiv flew to Colombo to sign the accord on 29 July 1987; with an upsurge in fighting on the island and a curfew imposed on the capital itself there were doubts till the last moment as to whether he would go. The absence from the signing ceremony of the prime minister, Ranasinghe Premadasa – who was later to succeed Jayewardene as president – was an indication of how unpopular the accord was amongst many Sinhalese, even before its full details became known. That fact was further underlined the following day when a sailor forming part of the naval guard of honour took a swipe with his rifle at Rajiv as he inspected the guard. Rajiv was unhurt, though not unnaturally rather shocked by the incident, which must have brought home to him what many people considered to be a major contributory cause of the Tamil insurgency: the indiscipline of Sri Lanka's overwhelmingly Sinhalese armed forces.

The accord required Sri Lanka to devolve unspecified powers to new elective provincial councils, one of which was to take power in the merged northern and eastern provinces, the area which Tamil guerrillas had designated for their separate homeland. A referendum was to be held to determine whether these two provinces remain merged. The accord also provided for the cessation of hostilities and the lifting of the state of emergency in the north and east of the island, and for the release of prisoners held under anti-terrorist laws. A further concession, and it was a major one reversing a thirty-year-old policy, was that Tamil was to become an official language once more, side by side with Sinhalese and English. For its part, India agreed to take steps to ensure its territory was not used for 'activities prejudicial to the unity, integrity and sovereignty of Sri Lanka', and to provide military assistance in implementing the accord 'in the event that the government of Sri Lanka requests the government of India' so to do.

At the time the accord was signed, nobody had realised the military assistance provision would be implemented so soon. Within twenty-four hours, before Rajiv had left Colombo, troops of what came to be known as the Indian peace-keeping force began arriving on the island. They were the first of a force that was to number 70000 at its peak. They had been invited, said President Jayewardene, to supervise the ceasefire and surrender of arms by the Tamil guerrillas, and would be withdrawing as soon as that limited objective had been completed.

There are those who argue that for India the accord was merely a device to introduce Indian forces into Sri Lanka, and to win international approval for doing so. Britain and the United States were amongst countries which praised India's peace efforts, though India's neighbours continued to have their doubts as to whether Indian motives were entirely altruistic. India's real gain lay not in the accord itself but in the documents which accompanied it. These provided what Rajiv was to describe to the Indian Parliament two days after the signing as 'measures to meet our mutual concerns and to strengthen our bilateral relations', a masterly understatement for documents that transformed the relationship between the two nations. An annexure to the accord provided for Indian observers to monitor the ceasefire, the elections to the north-eastern provincial council, and the referendum to determine whether the provinces remain merged. An accompanying exchange of letters between the two heads of government went further and effectively gave India a power of veto over Sri Lanka's free exercise of its foreign policy. They committed Sri Lanka to desist from three activities which had been upsetting India: using foreign military intelligence personnel (in one capacity or another Israeli, Pakistani and British personnel had been on the island helping Sri Lanka with its anti-guerrilla war); allowing facilities on the island to be used by foreign broadcasters, since India believed a new Voice of America relay station was listening in, or spying, on India at the same time as broadcasting; and no other nation was to be allowed to use the strategic east coast port of Trincomalee for military purposes. The exchange of letters is the testimony of the extent to which Sri Lanka's freedom to conduct its own foreign policy had been subjugated to India's interests.

Taken together, the treaty and accompanying documents established Indian hegemony over its small neighbour, with that neighbour's consent, rather as treaties with Bhutan in 1949 and Nepal in 1950 had done with those small neighbours. India's External Affairs Ministry regarded the Indo–Sri Lanka accord as a diplomatic triumph. President Jayewardene is said to have wanted the exchange of letters to remain secret; he may have been ashamed at being forced to grovel to India's will, the price India extracted for promising to bring peace to Sri Lanka.

Yet the Indo–Sri Lanka peace accord did not bring peace. The force which had come to supervise the ceasefire and keep the peace soon found it had in fact taken over from the Sri Lankan army – who were confined to their barracks in the north-eastern province – in fighting the war. The turning point in India's role in Sri Lanka, from would-be peace-maker to combatant, came in October 1987 when a group of Tamil Tiger guerrillas the Indian forces had captured, and were preparing to hand over to the Sri Lankan authorities, swallowed cyanide tablets. Twelve, including two commanders, died. The Tigers blamed the deaths on the Indians, who had not detected or confiscated the tablets which the Tigers were known to wear around their necks for use in case of capture. The Tigers' leader, Velupillai Prabhakaran, said his men were no longer bound by the ceasefire, so the nation which had nurtured them now took them on as their enemy. Other guerrilla groups who had acquiesced in the ceasefire felt hard done by and demanded their surrendered arms back when they came under fire from the Tigers.

In fact, though an unwilling Velupillai Prabhakaran had been forced by India to take part in pre-accord talks in Delhi, held a virtual prisoner in the Ashoka hotel, neither he nor any of the other guerrilla leaders had signed the accord. India had, in effect, signed on their behalf with Rajiv's government believing it had secured Prabhakaran's promise to comply with the ceasefire. Some arms were surrendered, but not many, and when, after a month or more, the Tigers did not seem to be getting their own way – not being granted enough seats to dominate the nominated interim north-eastern provincial council, for example – they withdrew the support they had given and took up arms again. However, this time the Tigers' enemy was the Indian army. Without the ceasefire and surrender of arms, it was going to be very difficult for India to implement the accord. It made it no easier for the Indian force in Sri Lanka that they seemed unable to find the Tigers' main base on the island from where Prabhakaran directed operations. The Tigers replenished their armouries through attacks on Indian patrols, and on what was left of the other Tamil guerrilla groups.

Whilst the accord failed to bring peace to the north, it also created a backlash in the south of the island where Sinhalese protested against the Indian-troop presence. President Jayewardene survived an assassination attempt inside the parliament building which killed one MP and wounded many more, including a senior minister. The attack, like others in the Colombo area, was blamed on the Sinhalese nationalist organisation, the People's Front, or JVP, who resented any concession being made to Tamil demands. Protests against the accord increased in the Sinhalese-dominated southern part of the island as the true import of the arrival of thousands of Indian troops on the island, and of two Indian frigates anchored provocatively off Colombo, struck home. There was a mood of indignation if not outrage that the government had 'sold out' Sri Lanka's sovereignty to India in this way. The JVP, which had been quiescent since the 1970s, was given a new lease of life as it launched a popular anti-accord and anti-India movement. In due course the campaign became a wave of terror and indiscriminate killing. It seemed as if the peace of the south of the island had been traded in the hope of ending the war in the north, except that the war in the north did not end.

In retrospect, it seems amazing that Rajiv could have signed an accord that he did not have the means to enforce. He misjudged the power he had over the Tamil Tigers, or at least his ability to bribe them into observing the accord. Many months later it emerged that the Indian government had paid money to the Tigers for their compliance, money that in all probability went towards buying more arms to fight the Indian army. It was a crucial failure not to have made them signatories to the accord, or at least ensured that India's hold over the Tigers, and thus its ability to deliver the promised peace, was greater than it turned out to be. History was repeating itself. Rajiv had himself recognised that the weakness of the Punjab accord was that it depended on a leader who did not have the total support of his party, yet, just two years later, he had signed another accord which promised peace, without the agreement of one of the parties to the conflict. It had certainly been premature for him to tell the people of Tamil Nadu three days after the signing that 'peace has come to Sri Lanka'.

The Indian and Sri Lankan governments reaffirmed their commitment to an accord that seemed less and less workable. It was clear that the proposed provincial elections, due by the end of 1987, the subsequent Indian troop withdrawal and the referendum on province merger due by the end of 1988, would all be way behind schedule. In a statement to Parliament, Rajiv blamed the Tamil Tigers: 'They went back on every commitment they had given us. They deliberately set out to wreck the agreement, because they were unwilling or unable to make the transition from militancy to the democratic process. While they promised us support to the agreement, they started a propaganda campaign against India and the agreement through meetings and through their illegal broadcasting facilities.'

From India's viewpoint, another essential ingredient for the successful implementation of the accord and discharge of the peace-keeping force's role disappeared when Jayewardene was replaced as president at the end of 1988 by his prime minister, Ranasinghe Premadasa. Premadasa had made clear his opposition to the accord and his dislike of India. Despite having no alternative solution to the disarray in the north and east, he ordered the Indians home, to the approval of his Sinhalese constituency. He also reached an under-standing with his former enemies, the Tamil Tigers, which united them as allies against the Indian military presence. However, India refused to withdraw its troops, saying the accord had not yet been fully implemented, which provoked another stand-off between India and Sri Lanka. Premadasa declared them an 'army of occupation', but his inability to make them leave only showed up his own weakness. A Sri Lankan journalist pointed out how little the rest of the world cared about India's military occupation: 'There are more Indian soldiers in Sri Lanka than Vietnamese troops in Cambodia or Syrian forces in Lebanon. Yet, no voices are raised in august assemblies, no resolutions passed. Not many tears are shed over Sri Lanka's killing fields.'[1]

The stand-off between the Indian and Sri Lankan governments remained unresolved when Rajiv's premiership came to an end. With the Indian general election in prospect, Rajiv had not wanted to be seen to be retreating in ignominy with peace still not achieved. Four months after V. P. Singh took office, the withdrawal of Indian troops was completed, enabling Sri Lanka's President Premadasa to declare: 'The affront to our sovereignty was removed with their exit.' The verdict on Rajiv's Sri Lanka accord can only be that it was a dismal failure. Even the part that had been implemented, the election of provincial councils, had yet to show any practical worth, except that it had brought some guerrillas in from the jungle. As long as others remained committed to fight, Sri Lanka would remain at war. India had no peace to show for its intervention, with or without honour. More than 1100 of its men had died in the operation. The souring of Indo–Sri Lankan relations had even had an impact on SAARC, as President Premadasa refused to host the summit which was scheduled to take place in Colombo in late 1989 because foreign troops remained on Sri Lankan soil.

While Premadasa had been campaigning for election as Sri Lanka's president, another episode took place which focused further attention on India's military role beyond its own shores. President Abdul Gayoom of the archipelagic Maldives sent requests to several nations for help in warding off a coup attempt by mercenaries, who had arrived

---

[1] Mervyn de Silva, editor of the *Lanka Guardian*, writing in the *Far Eastern Economic Review*, 31 August 1989 (before Vietnam withdrew its forces from Cambodia).

by sea from Sri Lanka. They turned out to be former Tamil guerrilla fighters who had been hired by a disenchanted Maldivian *émigré*. The coup attempt failed after Indian commandoes were flown into Male, the Maldives' main island, to secure it once more for Gayoom. An Indian frigate later apprehended a boatload of mercenaries in the Indian Ocean as they fled with hostages and the mercenaries were duly put on trial. It had been a swiftly executed Indian response to a plea for help, and earned the gratitude of President Gayoom as well as praise from Britain and the United States – both of which had been asked for help – and from the Commonwealth Secretary General. Indian troops remained on Male for a year until Gayoom felt secure enough for them to leave. India had shown itself a friend, and had at the same time reinforced its strategic philosophy of keeping non-regional powers out of the region, and regional powers (meaning Pakistan) at bay, by itself taking on the role of regional policeman.

Pakistan was the neighbour with whom India's relations had been most strained in the forty-odd years since Independence. The two countries had fought three wars, and dealings between Delhi and Islamabad were characterised by a high degree of suspicion when Rajiv became prime minister. When Rajiv became chairman of SAARC in late 1986, he accepted an invitation to visit Pakistan. No Indian prime minister had been received in the Pakistani capital for more than twenty-five years. But before Rajiv could do anything about repairing relations, new strains developed between the two which nearly led to another war. Early in 1987, India was conducting its largest ever military exercise in the deserts of Rajasthan, close to the frontier with Pakistan. As is usual, Pakistan had been given advance notice of the exercise. Pakistan was also exercising its forces, though its operations had been due to end by late 1986, whilst India's four-month long Operation Brass Tacks was to continue until March 1987. Suddenly Indian intelligence became aware that Pakistan's forces had not returned to their bases as expected but had instead regrouped at two very sensitive areas of their common frontier. One force was positioned close to the line of actual control, the *de facto* international frontier, in Jammu and Kashmir, the state which is disputed and divided between India and Pakistan and had twice been the cause of war between them. Another force was positioned opposite some of the most sensitive areas of India's troubled Punjab state. Pakistan said it had been concerned at the scale of Brass Tacks, but that India had done nothing to allay those concerns when requested. India's military establishment conferred over the Pakistani moves and briefed the cabinet, who decided that troops engaged in Rajasthan on Brass Tacks be immediately redeployed northwards to resist any Pakistani attack across the border into Jammu or Punjab. The troop movements took place on 23 and 24 January amidst speculation that Pakistan might choose 26 January, India's Republic Day and the day a big Sikh congregation was to take place in Amritsar, to launch an attack.

The Indian press were briefed by Arun Singh, who had become junior defence minister, and the chief of the army staff, General Sundarji. The briefing gave rise to lead stories in the following day's newspapers suggesting the two countries were nearer to war than at any time since 1971, the year when the last full-blown Indo–Pakistan war had led to the secession of Bangladesh from Pakistan. India was at least as much to blame as Pakistan for allowing the confrontation to reach such dangerous proportions. There are those who believe it was the outcome of a new military aggressiveness on the part of the Indian army commander, General Sundarji, which had also led to clashes between India and Pakistan on the 20 000-foot Siachen glacier. General Sundarji was accused of wanting to goad Pakistan into making an attack, and may well have been acting on his own initiative, without government approval. It was a dangerous exercise in brinkmanship between the two sides, neither of which would have much to gain from war at this stage. Since the creation of SAARC two years earlier, the trend had been towards normalising relations between India and Pakistan, though certain intractable obstacles were in the way – such as the disputed state of Jammu and Kashmir, suspicions over each other's nuclear intentions and Indian claims that Pakistan was training Sikh terrorists. It would certainly not have suited Rajiv, the would-be peace-maker in southern Africa and Sri Lanka, to go to war against his weaker neighbour.

After talks in Delhi between foreign ministry officials, the crisis was defused and a formula agreed for pulling back troops. Most of the blame for the crisis fell on the respective armies for allowing their exercises to get out of hand, or else failing to warn the other side of their true extent. The military hotline which was used to give advanced warning of military exercises seems not to have been used during the month leading up to the crisis. Amongst measures agreed was one to install an additional hotline so that foreign secretaries, as well as military commanders, could confer. There was plenty of suspicion on the Indian side of the border that the crisis had been contrived, or else the seriousness of the 'threat' had been exaggerated.

At the height of the crisis, there were two significant changes of senior personnel in India. V. P. Singh, the architect of Rajiv's economic policy and in particular his drive against corruption, was moved from the Finance Ministry to replace Rajiv as minister of defence. The crisis necessitated a full-time defence minister, explained Rajiv, which overlooked the fact that the minister of state Arun Singh had been defence minister in all but name. On 20 January, before Indian troops were moved north, Rajiv had addressed a televised news conference at which he was asked about relations with Pakistan. After expressing his concern at the failure of the Pakistani force to withdraw from the border after their annual exercises and saying he was trying to get in touch with Pakistan to see what the problem was, he was asked about his plan to visit Pakistan. Rajiv said he had no fixed plans for a visit. When it was pointed out that the permanent head of the External Affairs Ministry, foreign secretary A. P. Venkateswaran, had said during a visit to Pakistan a few days earlier that Rajiv would be visiting Pakistan as chairman of SAARC – which meant before November that year – he replied: 'You will talk with the new foreign secretary soon.'

Until that moment, A. P. Venkateswaran had no inkling he was about to be moved or sacked. He immediately offered his resignation. It was, by any standards, a remarkable way to be sacked, and it distracted attention from whether it was justified or not. A. P. Venkateswaran, who is not one to mince his words, had complained that the External Affairs Ministry was being by-passed in key decision making by the prime minister's office and the Congress Party hierarchy. He felt the crisis with Pakistan was the latest example of this. He is still convinced the prime minister intended to humiliate him in public. Rajiv denies this saying: 'I didn't intend it that way, it just happened' – overtones of the two-year-old Rajiv whose crying 'just comes', but no longer with a fountain to turn to! Rajiv accused Venkateswaran of disobeying instructions during his visit to Pakistan. There had been strains in relations between the two since before the prime minister appointed him to this senior post ten months earlier. A member of Rajiv's staff says that A. P. Venkateswaran could never understand that his role was to present policy options whilst leaving it for the minister to take the decision: 'He repeatedly transgressed the limits of his powers.'

For his humiliating dismissal, Venkateswaran won widespread sympathy, with Rajiv portrayed as the villain of the affair. Intended as a public rebuke or not, the incident showed Rajiv to be impulsive, and displayed the arrogance towards officials for which he was later to be much criticised. For the first time since taking office, Rajiv received a universally hostile press. *India Today* called it his 'most insensitive blunder, a public gaffe of such grave proportions that even his supporters were left stunned and speechless'. As Venkateswaran put it: 'My loss was nothing compared with his.' Relieved of the responsibility of having to toe the governmental line, Venkateswaran in due course became a strong critic of India's military involvement in Sri Lanka. As a Tamil, he was conscious of the unpopularity in his home state of the role of India's peace-keeping force.

Rajiv ended his year as chairman of SAARC without making the tour of SAARC capitals that had been expected. Possibly the Brass Tacks crisis had strengthened his resolve not to hurry to Islamabad. It was to be December 1988 before he went there, making the first visit to the Pakistani capital by an Indian prime minister since Nehru went in 1960. By the time of Rajiv's visit, General Zia ul-Haq had died in a plane crash, elections had taken place and Benazir Bhutto had become prime minister at the head of a minority government, the first truly civilian administration since her father, Zulfikar Ali Bhutto, was deposed in 1977.

Rajiv and Benazir, both offspring of political leaders who had followed their respective parents to power – he by way of Cambridge, she by way of Oxford – neither of them old enough to have experienced the social hiatus of partition and the lasting resentment it created, got on together extraordinarily well. So much so that Rajiv extended his visit, which had been prompted by the holding of the annual SAARC summit. They signed two important agreements – that they would not bomb each other's nuclear installations, and would abide by the accord that their parents had signed in Simla in 1972 after the Bangladesh war, which provides for the peaceful settlement of disputes between the two neighbours. But neither had been ratified by the time Rajiv left office a year later. Whether the latter agreement could help prevent a future war is questionable, since it has invariably been the absence of a will to settle differences through talking rather than the absence of machinery that led to previous Indo–Pakistan wars.

The pictures that flashed around the world of Benazir and Rajiv were a touching confirmation of the generational change that had taken place in the subcontinent. Rajiv made it clear that it was as much the restoration of democratic government to Pakistan as the personal rapport he established with his opposite number that had made his first official visit to Pakistan a success. One concrete demonstration of this was that India no longer opposed the re-admission of Pakistan to the Commonwealth – it had pulled out after Commonwealth members recognised Bangladesh in 1972. Pakistan was readmitted in October 1989.

Rajiv and Benazir met again the following July in Paris, where both had gone to help the French celebrate the bicentenary of their revolution. Once more these two young leaders of 900 million people were paired off, though each was again accompanied by a spouse. On the way home, Rajiv and Sonia accepted Benazir's invitation to stop-over in Islamabad for a truly bilateral visit, albeit a brief one. At that meeting, they endorsed an understanding between the two countries' foreign secretaries to try and defuse the tension that was regularly leading to fighting between their two armies on the Siachen glacier, the highest and most inhospitable part of the terrain disputed between India and Pakistan. With such personal amiability between Rajiv and Benazir, it was difficult to see why the problems of the past could not have been swept aside and a new era started. Perhaps the reason is that both scions of ruling dynasties bear the crosses of their forebears, making it no easier, and perhaps harder, for them to start afresh.

Benazir and Rajiv would have had another chance to demonstrate their new found friendship at the 1989 Commonwealth Conference in Kuala Lumpur. However, the day he had been due to fly to Kuala Lumpur, 17 October, Rajiv called the general election and cancelled his visit. It was, perhaps, just as well since by this time Benazir's galloping *détente* with India was becoming a stick with which her own Opposition were trying to beat her. She returned home from Kuala Lumpur to defend herself in Parliament on a motion of no-confidence.

Less successful than his dealings with Pakistan were Rajiv's relations with land-locked Nepal to the north, which deteriorated sharply during his last eight months in office. The treaties governing Nepal's trade with India, and allowing it to transit third country goods through India, had both expired in March 1989. India wanted a single replacement treaty whilst Nepal insisted on separate treaties on the grounds that transit was a right of land-locked states guaranteed in international law, whilst trade was a matter of bilateral agreement. There were other factors at issue in the strained relations. India was angered that Nepal had turned to China to buy weapons, including anti-aircraft guns which could have no other country's aircraft in its sights than India's. According to India, this purchase violated 'written covenants' between the two countries, believed to be a reference to a secret understanding, since the 1950 Treaty of Peace and Friendship specifically provides that the government of Nepal 'shall be free to import, from or through the territory of India, arms, ammunition or warlike material and equipment necessary for the security of Nepal'.

But Nepal may have been on weaker ground in imposing property and working restrictions on Indians living in Nepal, and in banning them from visiting areas of Nepal close to the border with China, since the 1950 treaty requires both governments to grant to nationals of the other country 'the same privileges in the matter of residence, ownership of property, participation in trade and commerce, movement and other privileges' as it does to its own nationals. India also accused Nepal of abusing the relative openness of their mutual border by allowing cheap goods of Chinese origin to be smuggled into India. During the stand-off which followed, India closed all but two border crossing points with Nepal and substantially increased duties on goods entering India from Nepal. Fuel rationing was imposed in Nepal and fresh vegetables were in particularly short supply.

While Nepal screamed, with the help of its public relations advisers, Saatchi and Saatchi, that 'its oldest and closest friend is now attempting to strangle us', India seemed in no hurry to settle the dispute, even after Rajiv met Nepal's King Birendra at the Non-Aligned summit in Belgrade during September 1989. Once more, India appeared to be flexing its muscles to the detriment of a weaker neighbour. India's own press were conscious of the reputation India was getting after first its role in Sri Lanka and then its treatment of Nepal were called into question. *The Illustrated Weekly of India* ran a story which asked: 'Is Super India emerging as the Big Bully?'

The Economist, London, had no doubts that it was. It editorialised: 'India is even bigger than it looks. Its soldiers control a large part of Sri Lanka and keep order in the Maldives. It treats Bangladesh as supplicant. It leans arrogantly across Pakistan to give support to the

Afghan government in Kabul, which is Pakistan's enemy. Now it is trying to turn Nepal into a vassal.' Unimpressed with the suggestion that India was merely being a good neighbour, *The Economist* went on to accuse Rajiv Gandhi of expansionism at a time when, it said, 'the real superpowers of the world are at least trying to look less menacing'. It questioned the motives for this behaviour: 'Some reckon India is flexing its muscles simply because Mr Gandhi's government faces a difficult election this year. Others', it went on, 'believe that any domestic advantage is peripheral to a long-term design for a greater India garrisoned by its army of 1.2 million men'.[1] *The Illustrated Weekly*'s writer, Bharat Wariavwalla, had his own opinion as to which theory was correct: 'This demonstration of might is not just intended to win votes in an election year; nor is it a result of errors of judgement or misperceptions on the part of the Rajiv Gandhi government. We assert by force because we want to be lords of the region.'[2]

Rajiv was not the first Indian prime minister to want to see India strong enough to assume the role of regional policeman and, just as important, prevent others from aspiring to that role. However, his policies towards three smaller neighbours suggested he was more ready than his predecessors to use the coercive power of India's military might for foreign policy ends. On the one hand he espoused the cause of regional co-operation, as represented by SAARC; on the other, he made sure that none of the neighbouring countries failed to appreciate that India considered itself to be the lord and master of the region. In India, people were beginning to talk of 'the Rajiv doctrine'.

---

[1] *The Economist*, 15 April 1989.
[2] *The Illustrated Weekly of India*, 11 June 1989.

CHAPTER EIGHT

Arming for Tomorrow

Whilst Rajiv preached peace and disarmament wherever he travelled abroad, at home he presided over the largest ever expansion in India's armed forces. Defence expenditure doubled during his five years in office as his government strove to maintain and modernise the armed forces, the fourth largest in the world, after those of the United States, the Soviet Union and China. All this for a country with a gross national product similar to that of a smaller European power, like Spain. During Rajiv's last two years in office, defence expenditure accounted for close to twenty per cent of government expenditure. Rajiv's defence minister from 1987 onwards, K. C. Pant, said defending India was bound to be costly, involving as it did the defence of high Himalayan frontiers, a long coastline and distant groups of islands, offshore oil installations and extensive Indian Ocean shipping lanes.

Also under Rajiv, India became the world's major importer of defence equipment, and was found by a World Watch Institute investigation to be the largest manufacturer of arms in the third world – almost all of them for India's own use. Unprecedented re-equipping of the armed forces involved the purchase from Britain of a second aircraft carrier, the purchase of howitzer guns from Sweden in one of India's largest ever defence deals, the joining of an exclusive club to become the first non-nuclear power to operate a nuclear-powered submarine with the lease of a vessel from the Soviet Union, and the joining of another exclusive club of nations capable of manufacturing intermediate-range ballistic missiles. The development of short- and medium-range missiles gave India an additional means, apart from aircraft drop, of delivering nuclear warheads should a decision ever be taken to join that other exclusive club of which India has been on the threshold for many years, that of nuclear bomb-possessing nations. India also had plans to build its own aircraft carrier, nuclear-powered submarine, battle tank and light combat aircraft.

Though Rajiv did not initiate the defence build-up, he did continue and accelerate it. He did not question why India needed such an awesome arsenal of weaponry, perhaps because he knew the answer. It lay in what became known as 'the Rajiv doctrine', a concept inspired by the Monroe and Brezhnev doctrines which have been used to justify or explain American and Soviet interventions abroad. The Rajiv doctrine is not written anywhere, but can be construed from what Rajiv said and did in the defence arena. Though the military operations in Sri Lanka and the Maldives were unconnected in their purposes, the fact that India engaged in operations beyond its own shoreline on these two separate occasions is the main evidence for its new 'defence' posture that goes beyond the strictly defensive. These operations led to questions in Parliament about where and in what circumstances India would intervene militarily abroad. MPs asked whether a request from the prime minister of Mauritius or the president of the Seychelles would merit Indian assistance, and if so in what circumstances, or whether India would consider responding to an appeal for help from U Nu, the former Burmese prime minister deposed by the army in 1962, who had been showing signs of wanting to return to power. By way of answer to these questions, Rajiv would only stress the importance of solving problems 'among ourselves without outside interference', without defining exactly who came within the orbit of 'ourselves' in this context.

The Sri Lanka and Maldives operations revealed a willingness to fight battles abroad. Encouraged by his foreign ministry, Rajiv was emulating the late Shah of Iran, who had wanted to be the 'policeman' of the Gulf region. However, India's 'policeman's beat' potentially encompassed the entire Indian Ocean. Whilst laying the foundation stone for a new naval base at Karwar in Karnataka – described as the biggest and most sophisticated in South Asia – Rajiv said: 'If we have to remain independent, we must look to the south and the Indian Ocean for safety and security.' India stands committed to a policy of making the Indian Ocean a zone of peace. 'Unfortunately,' said Rajiv, whilst inducting India's first nuclear-powered submarine, INS *Chakra*, into the navy, 'the Indian Ocean has been militarised and infested with nuclear weapons flouting the overwhelming sentiment in the region in favour of establishing a zone of peace'. On another occasion, he told a gathering of Asian statesmen in Delhi that 'uninvited military

15 Having committed himself to politics, Rajiv used to visit his parliamentary constituency of Amethi as often as possible. Here he is with Sonia during the campaign for the 1984 elections.

16 Rajiv, the international statesman, struck up a rapport with the Soviet leader, Mikhail Gorbachev. Here they are signing the Delhi declaration to work together for nuclear disarmament.

17 In Downing Street with the British prime minister, Margaret Thatcher, during Rajiv's first visit to London as prime minister.

18 Visiting Pakistan on the first visit there by an Indian prime minister for twenty-eight years, Rajiv got on well with the prime minister, Benazir Bhutto. They reaffirmed an accord that their respective parents, Indira Gandhi and Zulfikar Ali Bhutto, had signed in 1972.

19 Rajiv with Sonia on the Great Wall of China. This was another epoch-making visit after a long breach between the two countries.

20 Rajiv enjoys anything to do with technology and flying. Here he is aboard one of India's aircraft carriers watching a flying display.

21 The signing of an accord with President Jayewardene of Sri Lanka in July 1987 led to India assuming a peace-keeping role in Sri Lanka.

22 Rajiv's relations with President Zail Singh cooled mainly because he excluded the president from negotiations over Punjab, preferring to work through his home minister, Buta Singh (**right**).

23 The Bofors gun. This Swedish-made howitzer became Rajiv's most serious political embarrassment when it was claimed that illegal commission payments had been made in connection with its purchase.

24 On the campaign trail. Rajiv campaigned exhaustively in state and national elections.

25 Security around Rajiv was always tight especially, as here, on his rare visits to Punjab.

26 The 1989 election campaign coincided with celebrations of the centenary of the birth of Rajiv's grandfather, Jawaharlal Nehru. There was criticism that the Congress Party exploited the centenary for electoral benefit.

27 Rajiv was conscious of the importance of religious ceremonial, but anxious not to identify too closely with any particular religious community. Here he and Sonia take part in a Hindu ceremony.

28 The disputed shrine at Ayodhya in Uttar Pradesh which became a contentious issue in the 1989 election campaign. Muslims claim it as the Babri mosque, but Hindus say the mosque was built on the site of the birthplace of their god, Ram.

29 After the defeat of Rajiv's Congress Party in the 1989 elections, President Venkataraman (**second from left**) swears in V. P. Singh as India's seventh prime minister. Also in the picture are Vice President S. D. Sharma (**second from right**) and Devi Lal, who was sworn in as deputy prime minister.

presences in our area have grown and assumed increasingly dangerous proportions'. He went on: 'The challenge before us is to put an end to all outside intervention and interference and not allow our countries to become the cockpit of conflicts engineered from outside, at the behest of others and in the interests of others.'

The essence of the Rajiv doctrine is clear: to exclude other powers from the region. This was implicit in the exchange of letters which accompanied the signing of the Indo-Sri Lanka accord which, amongst other things, secured a promise from Sri Lanka that neither the United States, nor indeed any other power, would be allowed to use the strategic port of Trincomalee for military purposes. The logic of the doctrine was that India would itself handle policing and peace-keeping needs in the region. Rajiv was especially pleased by the way India's operations in Sri Lanka and the Maldives were praised by the United States, as this signalled Washington's endorsement of at least the 'policing' aspect of the doctrine.

From the increasing proportion of defence expenditure committed to the navy, it seemed that the Rajiv doctrine applied to the sea approaches to India's 3800-mile-long coastline to a greater extent than to the approaches across 9500 miles of land frontiers. Rajiv explained why at the induction of INS *Chakra*: 'The defence of India requires our undisputed mastery over the approaches to India by the sea ... While those who have conquered India by the land routes were eventually absorbed and assimilated into our society, those who conquered us from the sea ruled as alien masters and therefore had to be rejected. If we are to keep the destiny of India in our hands, we must have full control of the waters around us and the thousands of kilometres of shoreline which stretch along the Arabian Sea and the Bay of Bengal and abut upon the Indian Ocean.' This was hyperbole aimed at a naval audience, and intended to justify the massive naval expenditure which was beginning to draw resentment from the other services. In this day and age, it is unthinkable that anyone should contemplate trying to conquer India – by land or by sea. The 99 naval vessels in service, including 2 carriers, 12 submarines, 5 destroyers and 21 frigates, would certainly be enough to deter any seaborne invasion.

India's preoccupation with controlling the Indian Ocean dates from 1971 when, during the Bangladesh war, the United States' aircraft carrier *Enterprise* sailed into the Bay of Bengal in threatening posture. This episode infuriated India and became the justification for the expansion of its naval force into what it calls a 'blue-water' navy, capable of operating hundreds of miles from India's shores. The lease from the Soviet Union of the INS *Chakra* – which is nuclear-powered but not nuclear-armed – is part of that capability. Nuclear-powered submarines do not need to surface or refuel as frequently as conventionally powered ones, which gives them a much longer 'reach' away from home base. It is said that the Soviet Union wanted India to operate the submarine to confuse American surveillance systems, which could detect the presence of a submarine in the Indian Ocean but could not distinguish an Indian-operated one from a Soviet-operated one. When this was put to K. Subrahmanyam, the former director of the Institute of Defence Studies and Analysis who had negotiated the lease, he said: 'That is what I told the Soviets to persuade them to lease us the submarine!' With INS *Chakra*, India had become the sixth nation to operate nuclear-powered submarines. India is hoping eventually to build its own nuclear-powered submarines, which explains why it regards INS *Chakra* as a training vessel, 'to give our seamen experience of using the equipment', according to Rajiv.

The purchase from Britain of the aging Falklands war-tested carrier, HMS *Hermes*, was also part of the blue water naval policy. Its arrival in service with the Indian navy in 1988 as INS *Viraat*, a sister ship for the existing carrier, INS *Vikrant*, finally gave India a 'round-the-clock blue-water navy [providing] greater capability to withstand any onslaught that may occur against India's maritime interests', in the words of the then Chief of Naval Staff. The plan was that one carrier should patrol each of India's coastlines; both carry British-built Sea Harrier jump jets and various types of helicopter. By the time INS *Vikrant* reaches the end of its active service, towards the end of the century, India hopes to have designed and built its own carrier, a project currently at the planning stage.

When two-thirds of India's naval fleet were anchored in Bombay harbour in early 1989 for the President's review, one newspaper reporter wrote of 'the happy affirmation that the maritime neglect of our pre-independence days is over'. According to the same unnamed reporter, even President Venkataraman – a former Congress defence minister – spoke of 'the maritime renaissance' the country was going through after 'half a millennium of neglect', as if no greater reason were needed for building India's navy into the eighth largest in the world. Indian defence analyst Ravi Rikhye is probably near the truth when he writes: 'Navies are symbols of power. We want to be a world-class power, so we must have a world-class navy.'[1] Rikhye argues that a coastal navy is what India needs to ensure that its territorial sovereignty is respected, so the decision to opt for a blue-water navy suggests a more ambitious objective.

India's naval build-up under Rajiv had little if anything to do with perceptions of threats from the country's traditional enemies, Pakistan and China, the only nations it has fought wars against since winning Independence. To defend against the possibility of attack from these directions – or, as Rajiv's government put it, to match their weaponry – India invested a great deal of money in improving the quality of its artillery, and in developing an indigenous programme for the design and manufacture of guided missiles. The purchase from Sweden of towed howitzers was claimed to be a response to recent Pakistani acquisitions; however, in value terms, India's howitzers were worth much more than any artillery Pakistan possessed. Another plan sanctioned by Rajiv's government during 1988 was to replace Soviet-designed Indian-built T-72 tanks with an all-Indian battle tank, the Arjun.

Some experts argue that there is no need for a new tank and that the plan to develop the Arjun at a cost of tens of millions of dollars derives from a preoccupation with proving its domestic design and manufacturing capability rather than from need. As with all areas of Indian life, from food production to the most sophisticated weaponry, there is a tremendous stress on self-sufficiency. More than forty years ago, Nehru said that 'no country can be truly independent unless it is independent in matters of its defence equipment'. Neither his daughter nor grandson have seen fit to revise that fundamental principle of Indian defence strategy. It's not enough, in the eyes of successive Indian governments, to operate advanced weapons: the target always is to make them, or at least assemble them, in India. Yet even the Arjun will not be totally home-made. It will be based around an engine imported from West Germany, though most other parts will be developed by India's own considerable defence and research organisation. The plan is to have around 1500 Arjun tanks in service by the end of the century.

Another major domestic defence research programme, this time into

[1] *The Illustrated Weekly of India*, 30 October 1988.

guided missiles, had been initiated by Mrs Gandhi in 1983, and the fruits of its success were tasted during the latter half of Rajiv's premiership. Two short-range missiles, the Trishul surface-to-air missile and the Prithvi 160-mile-range, surface-to-surface missile, were tested during 1988 and 1989, and are expected to be brought into military service. A few months later, an intermediate-range missile with a range of 1500 miles, the Agni, was successfully tested. This was a proud moment for India, bringing it into the club of intermediate-range missile manufacturers whose membership consists only of China, France, the United States, the Soviet Union and Israel. Rajiv has taken a close interest in the development of Agni, which means 'fire' in Hindi. Whilst sharing the national excitement at its successful test launch and congratulating the many scientists in the fifty-three separate institutions which were involved, Rajiv told Parliament that Agni is 'not a weapons system' but a demonstration of technology, a research and development system.

It may have been true that no immediate military application was planned for Agni, not even the carrying of a non-nuclear warhead, which Rajiv conceded it has the ability to do. What he did not say was that Agni gives India the capability of delivering a nuclear warhead, should such a warhead be developed. With the relative accuracy of the present generation of micro-processor guided missiles, Agni is capable of delivering a nuclear payload that would otherwise take four aircraft to deliver on any target in Pakistan or southern China, at much less risk and at much less cost. India's main argument for developing its own intermediate-range missile was that China already had such missiles. However, the awareness that the United States could easily target its submarine-launched missiles on India must also account for something. K. C. Pant insists that developing missiles of its own could well turn out to be India's cheaper defence option.

The development of Agni, the fifth and by far the most sophisticated product of India's guided-missile programme, owes everything to the theory of deterrence. India is particularly proud to have produced for itself a missile which, in technology terms, is comparable to the American Pershing missile, though with a range closer to that of the Cruise missile. Somewhat contradicting his assertion that Agni is not a weapons system, Rajiv spoke at its test launch of 'a major achievement in our continuing efforts to safeguard our independence and security by self-reliant means'.

There was satisfaction too, that, since Agni is entirely Indian-made, it does not have to be submitted for scrutiny under the 1987 Missile Technology Control Regime agreement. India regards this agreement as another example of a restrictive practice by the technologically advanced nations – similar to the nuclear non-proliferation treaty – to protect their monopolies over advanced defence technology. Such agreements are anathema to Rajiv. He believes that science belongs to all mankind, so such agreements act as a spur towards self-sufficiency with the specific purpose of evading restrictions on technology. This attitude explains why Rajiv's government was so annoyed by the initial United States reluctance to sell India a super-computer which it wanted for non-military purposes. After the test launch of Agni, concern was expressed in the United States that India had crossed another threshold towards becoming a major military power, and there were calls for the administration to end discussions with Delhi about coupling defence purchases with the transfer of technology for indigenous production.

India usually insists that arms purchase agreements do include arrangements to transfer the technology, though it has not always been able to open domestic production lines, especially in the case of aircraft. The Soviet MiG-27 and European Jaguar fighters are partly manufactured in India, but the option was not pursued, for example, in the case of the computerised French Mirage 2000, possibly because it is so sophisticated. Foreign-designed frigates and submarines are being built at Bombay's Mazagon dockyard and India now plans to build its own advanced tactical fighter, making use of technology purchased from American and European companies. Despite the criticism over Agni, it is a sign of improved defence co-operation with Washington that the United States Air Force is to have a consultancy role in the project. The aircraft is described as 'a fighter pilot's dream' and is intended to match the best in the world with some of the most advanced technology available, yet weighing only eight tonnes as a result of using carbon fibre. It is due to go into production by 1995, though cuts in the defence budget during 1989 make the timescale, and indeed the entire project, look vulnerable.

India's desire to be self-reliant is coupled with a sense of national pride in being at the forefront of technology, which in turn owes something to the nation's drive towards industrialisation. That is certainly a sentiment endorsed by the technologically minded Rajiv, who had warned: 'We must remember that technological backwardness also leads to subjugation.' When the Defence Secretary, T. N. Seshan, was asked whether Agni would be produced for India's armed forces, he said he was anxious not to increase the defence budget unnecessarily because he thought it would 'send the wrong signals to people around the world'. On the other hand, he added, 'we don't want to waste the technology', a remark which seems to demonstrate that the pursuit of advanced technology in weaponry has a momentum of its own, if it has not actually become the end in itself. Another point of view espoused by the military establishment, which probably has Rajiv's support too, is the one which says: 'If we must have a military machine then it should be the best that money can buy.' Even so, there are many who would argue that the current annual level of defence spending of Rs 130 000 million (£5000 million) is excessive for a country where poverty, disease and illiteracy are endemic, and where the majority of the population are still a long way from having piped water or basic sanitation.

Most indigenous weapons production is entrusted to one or other of the eight public corporations or thirty-four ordnance factories dedicated to supplying the armed forces. India's defence industry, particularly the 'high-tech' parts of it like Hindustan Aeronautics and Bharat Electronics, has demonstrated an ability to manufacture some very sophisticated equipment. When concern at the level of defence spending led to a budget freeze in 1989, Rajiv's cabinet took a decision to encourage defence corporations to try to sell their produce abroad. Mainly for ideological reasons, India had not previously wanted to be seen to be an arms exporter at the same time as it was promoting the cause of disarmament internationally. Under Rajiv, the pressure of paying for the arms which India imports forced a decision to try to push the country up from its low position at number thirty-eight on the league table of arms exporters. Before long, Agni and other guided missiles may well be 'on sale', since India has noted the fact that China became a major arms exporter – reputedly the fourth largest in the world – mainly through supplying guided missiles to Middle Eastern countries, including Iran and Iraq whilst they were at war with each other. The lesson was not lost on Rajiv's government that China's arms exports were the main source of finance for its 'four modernisations' programme. Yet for India to move from being a manufacturer of arms for its own self-defence to becoming a purveyor in the international marketplace further undermines the cause of peace and disarmament that Rajiv was so fond of promoting.

Some credit, or perhaps blame, for encouraging the escalation of defence expenditure under Rajiv has been laid at the door of General Krishnaswami Sundarji, chief of army staff between 1986 and 1988, though his naval counterpart, Admiral Tahiliani, probably deserves his share too. It was General Sundarji who coined the theory of 'coercive diplomacy' which may have been the reason for the Brass Tacks crisis with Pakistan. He was allegedly trying to demonstrate that India's armed forces could fight wars on two fronts at once: Operation Brass Tacks was followed by military exercises close to India's north-eastern frontier with China, where there had been a dangerous escalation in tension the previous year when India discovered China had built a helipad in disputed mountainous terrain. *India Today* tells how General Sundarji was outlining his two-wars-at-once theory to the cabinet's political affairs committee when one senior minister responded: 'This warlike talk of taking on two powerful neighbours is not going to get us anywhere.' Yet many people believe the fact that General Sundarji was allowed to pursue his hawkish philosophy is an indication that he had the tacit approval of the cabinet; at any rate, they did not restrain him. Thus Sundarji's defence policy became the government's; Rajiv had appointed him chief of army staff, and saw no reason to dismiss him before his term of office was completed. *India Today* said of General Sundarji that no previous army chief had matched his ability 'to influence so markedly, by the sheer force of his personality, the political leadership in the country'.[1]

Underlying Rajiv's defence policy, and the Rajiv doctrine, lay his government's somewhat ambivalent 'near nuclear' policy, a policy followed by all previous prime ministers of India. Since India exploded a nuclear device in 1974, it has been content to preach nuclear disarmament whilst retaining a capacity to 'go nuclear' if provoked. India professes not to have the nuclear bomb and not to have any intention of developing it. At the same time, it is widely believed in India that Pakistan already has the bomb or is very close to acquiring it. Rajiv often said that if Pakistan did not desist from 'going nuclear', then India would reconsider its decision not to develop its own bomb. It is a policy based on the very theory of deterrence that Rajiv rejects,

[1] *India Today*, 15 May 1988.

though his line has always been that India would 'go nuclear' as a response to others and would not lead the way. Many defence analysts believe the difference between India having the technology to develop nuclear weapons – which nobody disputes it has – and having the weapons themselves is a matter of days or even hours, though Rajiv insists it is much longer than that. Under Rajiv, the government secretly imported heavy water, an essential ingredient for its power stations. To have done so openly would have meant subjecting its nuclear plants to international scrutiny, something India is anxious not to do lest it foreclose its nuclear weapons' option.

With its sophisticated fighter aircraft and now its equally sophisticated array of soon-to-be-in-service guided missiles, India has alternative means to deliver nuclear warheads. To this extent, there is a clear contradiction of a nation which, on the one hand strives to win others over to the cause of nuclear disarmament – and has set the year 2010 as a target date for the total elimination of nuclear weapons – and, on the other hand, makes its own use of the theory of nuclear deterrence by allowing the world – and especially its neighbours – to believe it is only a political decision away from possessing and perhaps deploying the nuclear bomb. Rajiv's dual-track approach revealed a determination to remain in the forefront of the worldwide campaign for nuclear disarmament, without sacrificing what he regarded as India's sovereign right to exercise the option of developing nuclear weapons at some stage to meet a perceived threat from Pakistan.

Given that China undoubtedly has nuclear weapons, it must be doubted whether, if Pakistan convincingly demonstrated that it has no plans to develop its own bomb, India would do likewise, or would allow international inspection of its facilities. It is widely believed in India that China has provided technological assistance for the development of Pakistan's nuclear bomb, just as it has provided help with Pakistan's missile programme.

Adverse international reactions to India's missile programme, as well as other aspects of its pursuit of self-reliance in defence spending, forced Rajiv's government on to the defensive. Although public criticism of the Indian army's role in Sri Lanka may not have mattered too much, even in Tamil Nadu – foreign and defence policy have never been electoral issues – indications that some senior members of India's armed forces were unhappy about what they saw as the Sri Lanka quagmire, the involvement in an unwinnable war, may have been of greater concern to the government. Rajiv was defensive in tone when he told military commanders in Delhi: 'We do not aspire to be a regional power, and we do not want to be described as one.' The United States, Britain and the Soviet Union had all tacitly accepted India's involvement in Sri Lanka, believing it to be in the pursuit of peace. Yet criticism in America of the Agni programme had led to calls for new restrictions on the supply of technology to India restrictions no longer based on the fear that such technology would reach the Soviet Union but on the increasing power of India itself. These criticisms coincided with pressure on Capitol Hill for India to be included on a blacklist of nations engaging in protectionist trade policies, and caused unease in Delhi which had been working hard to improve relations with Washington.

India's weapons' build-up is scaring others, and itself fuelling an arms race. Under Rajiv, India was beginning to be seen as a war-mongering nation spending massive amounts on sophisticated weapons, rather than as a peace-loving nation which favoured nuclear disarmament, the image which Rajiv worked tirelessly to promote. Rajiv may say he was only matching Pakistan's acquisition of weaponry but, by matching it, India fuelled demands in Pakistan for newer, more sophisticated weapons to match Indian fire power. Even Indonesia, by no means an enemy of India, had responded to the naval build-up with plans to build its own new naval base in Sumatra. What has been going on between Pakistan, India and China is a classic arms race. Rajiv would claim that India was the victim rather than the cause of that race, a race which perhaps began when China acquired its nuclear bomb in 1964, and accelerated when China demonstrated its intermediate-range missile capability. Rajiv's visits to both China and Pakistan, during December 1988, made no appreciable difference to defence thinking, though tension and troop strengths on India's border with China were reduced. 'Be prepared' continued to be the motto of Rajiv's government, and the 1989 defence-spending freeze was presented as a necessary economy rather than as the outcome of a reappraisal of the level of threat. No major defence programmes were cut as a result.

The aggressive image of India was brought home to many people abroad when *Time* magazine ran a cover story under the title 'Super India'.[1] It showed how India was spending enormous amounts on

---

[1] *Time* magazine, 3 April 1989; the following quotations are all taken from that report.

weaponry and seemingly preparing itself for war. The *Time* article aired the views of a number of critics of Rajiv's defence policy. The director of Asian studies at John Hopkins University and former National Security Council member, Thomas Thornton, said India's military 'build-up has taken on a momentum of its own, and India is increasingly pushed to find a threat and rationale to justify its military strength'. An unidentified Australian naval officer, asked about India's naval build-up, replied: 'We have no objection to a country the size of India building such a large military establishment. But the question is: What do the Indians want to do with it?' Indian defence analyst Ravi Rikhye believes the military build-up is not a reaction to external threats, saying: 'Ever since independence, India has dreamed of being a major military power.'

Indian defence planner, K. Subrahmanyam, one of the advocates of the blue-water naval strategy, sees the defence build-up as a means of persuading the world to give India what he regards as its rightful place in international diplomacy. He says: 'One out of every six people in the world is an Indian. In any democratic structure, India would have an effective say. But you in the West devised a world order in which the second largest country isn't even a permanent member of the United Nations Security Council. That's a big omission.' This echoes an opinion commonly expressed in India that China only acquired world power status after it exploded its nuclear bomb. The danger is that this type of reasoning – that India should spend a lot on weapons to advance its diplomatic standing – has a logical extension that Subrahmanyam has already articulated: 'If you are living in a world of nuclear-weapons powers, then you must have the bomb. If the world can live with five or six nuclear powers, it can live with eleven or twelve.'

CHAPTER NINE

Scandal

The first half of 1987 found Rajiv beset with almost every imaginable difficulty. The year had started with the very real risk of war with Pakistan and continued with a series of rows and scandals which reflected adversely on Rajiv's leadership, culminating in the resignation from the government, and subsequent expulsion from the party, of Rajiv's most trusted and respected colleague, V. P. Singh. Rising discontent within the Congress Party was further filled by the electoral defeats in several important states. The most serious of these, in Haryana, led directly to calls for a change of party leadership. These calls came to nothing after the potential alternative leader, V. P. Singh, refused to join the anti-Rajiv movement, at least not by way of the sort of presidential coup that the dissidents were contemplating.

Operation Brass Tacks and the near war with Pakistan contributed in their own way to Rajiv's difficulties. They had provided the pretext in January for transferring V. P. Singh from the Ministry of Finance, which he had headed for two years, to Defence. The ostensible reason was that the Defence Ministry needed a full time head at a moment when the country felt itself threatened by Pakistan. However, it was widely believed that the true significance of V. P. Singh's transfer lay in his removal from Finance and not in his arrival at Defence. V. P. Singh had become the bane of industrialists who resented the increasingly strident investigatory raids which he had authorised in a zealous pursuit of tax evasion, foreign exchange violations and other financial wrong-doing.

Rajiv's repeated denials that V. P. Singh had been moved at the insistence of aggrieved industrialists were not entirely convincing, and became less so in the light of later developments. V. P. Singh had earned the reputation as a powerful and effective finance minister who had succeeded in controlling inflation as well as raising tax revenue by more efficient collection and by tightening controls on evasion. He had brought the country's economic growth to a healthy five per cent. A public opinion poll by the MARG organisation, reported by *India Today*, found an overwhelming majority of respondents believed V. P. Singh's departure from the Ministry of Finance was a victory for the business houses who had demanded his transfer. A similar majority refused to believe assurances that the anti-corruption drive of the ministry would continue with the same impetus. At this stage, V. P. Singh remained a loyal member of Rajiv's cabinet. Rajiv said later: 'He thought that I was dumping him from Finance, but I had to have someone good in Defence.'

Barely was the Brass Tacks crisis over and conflict with Pakistan averted than another brewing crisis began absorbing national attention. It had been apparent for some time that Rajiv was not on good terms with the president. Zail Singh too had gradually come to resent the way Rajiv excluded him from affairs of state to the extent of virtually ostracising him. Rajiv believes that the estrangement was a direct result of his decision to keep the president out of negotiations over Punjab. 'I did not want him to be involved in Punjab because I felt that I could not move ahead if he was,' recalled Rajiv. Nevertheless, Zail Singh did interfere; according to Rajiv it was compulsive rather than a deliberate attempt to undermine the negotiations. Rajiv denies holding Zail Singh responsible for creating the Punjab problem in the first place, as has been suggested, but says that by handling it the way he did as home minister he had 'made it much more difficult to resolve'. It was as home minister that Zail Singh had once ordered the release of Bhindranwale after he had been detained on suspicion of involvement in murder.

Not surprisingly, Zail Singh sees things differently. He says he does not know what happened in his relationship with Rajiv, but is inclined to blame it on a lobby amongst those around Rajiv who 'tried to create a rift' between the prime minister and himself. He of course had strong views on Punjab, believing it was not a dispute between Punjab and Haryana, as it sometimes seemed to him it was being regarded, but a dispute between Punjab and the central government about three things: water, Chandigarh, and Punjabi-speaking districts that needed to be returned to Punjab by adjoining states. In other words, he considered it to be essentially a territorial dispute, and denies he wanted a Sikh state. Of the Punjab accord, Zail Singh says it was a good idea but defective and therefore unimplementable. 'I did not say anything, but I believed the government did not want to implement it,' recalls Zail Singh. In his view, the Congress Party, of which he had once been a staunch member, had itself undermined the Punjab accord. If the accord itself was the cause of the first major break between Zail Singh and Rajiv, its non-implementation became a stick the president used to beat the man he continued to regard as his young protégé.

The former president was also upset at being told by Rajiv to praise Punjab chief minister Barnala in his presidential speech opening the 1987 budget session of Parliament, a time when Barnala did not have the support of the majority in the Punjab assembly. 'Three times I said to Rajiv: "Don't make me praise Barnala," but he insisted.' Three months later, Zail Singh had been asked by the prime minister to dismiss Barnala and declare President's Rule again in Punjab. Zail Singh says: 'I could see no reason for dismissing him as he had majority support in the Punjab assembly by then. I wrote a note for the file – it must still be there – saying that it is not understandable that you asked me to praise him when he was in a minority and now he is in a majority you ask me to dismiss him.' It is clear from both men that differences over Punjab were the crucial cause of their falling out, though not the only one – perhaps those differences led to others.

Amongst other things, Zail Singh harboured grievances at the government's delays in approving his visits abroad, and indeed, his visits to Indian states, which are normally cleared in advance by the government. He felt they were not following a consistent policy in appointing judges, a matter on which he had sought 'clarification' from the Law Ministry. There was also a family grievance: that Zail Singh's nephew had not been granted a 'ticket' to contest the Punjab assembly elections for Congress.

One letter from the prime minister to the president gives an insight into how far their relations had deteriorated. The president had rebuked Rajiv for signing the accord over Mizoram, of which he strongly disapproved. Rajiv wrote back justifying the accord, saying his government was trying to solve the problems which he had inherited from 'the time when you were home minister', implying that Mizoram was one such problem.[1] This response from Rajiv provoked the president into further criticism – of both that particular accord and

[1] *India Today*, 28 February 1987.

of the failure of the prime minister to consult him before signing all such accords.

Rajiv had seldom called on the president since becoming prime minister, or even spoken with him on the telephone. The two men tended to meet only at formal occasions, such as award ceremonies or when receiving visiting heads of state. Another damaging incident occurred when one of Rajiv's ministers, K. K. Tewari, made a reference in Parliament to supporters of Khalistan residing in Rashtrapati Bhawan, the presidential residence. The president demanded and was granted his dismissal, though Rajiv later brought him back into government. Zail Singh privately accused Rajiv of bringing the office of president into disrepute.

Towards the end of 1986, Zail Singh began to assert himself in one of the few ways open to him under the constitution, which gives the president much stature but very little power: he delayed signing a bill into law. The purpose of the Indian Post Office (Amendment) Bill was to give legislative effect to the recommendations of the law commission. Amongst other things, the commission had recommended that the right of the authorities to intercept personal mail, which had existed since 1898, be restricted to avoid transgressing the fundamental rights of the individual protected by India's constitution. However, when the government introduced its new bill, the circumstances under which private mail could be intercepted were wider than those the constitution listed as justifying the withdrawal of fundamental freedoms and rights (circumstances such as war and threats to public safety or the security of the state). The Postal Bill allowed for the interception of mail during 'the occurrence of any public emergency', a wide-ranging provision which, Zail Singh believed, gave the government too much power since it was the arbiter of what constituted a 'public emergency'. The president stopped short of sending the bill back to Parliament for further consideration as he is entitled to do but which no Indian president had ever done. Instead, he delayed signing it and demanded an explanation from the Communications Ministry as to why the precise proposals of the law commission had not been implemented.

The president may have chosen to delay this bill to demonstrate his unhappiness at the way he was being treated by Rajiv's government. However, he also felt strongly about the matter because he believed Mrs Gandhi had ordered the interception of his mail and the tapping of his telephone when she suspected he was sabotaging her negotiations with the Akali Dal in Punjab. At any rate, his choice of the Postal Bill gave the impression he was concerned about fundamental rights, and won him the support of those who saw him as a libertarian trying to check the power of government. However, both the delay in signing the bill and its reference to the Communications Ministry, which were regarded by the prime minister as unwarranted interference in the process of government, had the effect of worsening relations between the two and bringing the looming crisis to a head.

During a parliamentary debate on the Postal Bill controversy, an opposition parliamentarian questioned whether the prime minister was fulfilling his constitutional responsibility of keeping the president fully briefed on all government decisions. Rajiv's reply – that he always kept the president fully briefed on all important matters – provoked widespread discussion as to what the responsibilities of the prime minister towards the president were.

It also provoked another move by Zail Singh, who wrote to Rajiv, taking issue with the assurance he had given Parliament and pointing out instances where he said he had not been briefed by the prime minister. He specifically cited what he said was Rajiv's failure to follow 'certain well-established conventions' that a prime minister brief a president before and after he made visits abroad and he specifically mentioned Rajiv's visits to the Soviet Union and the United States. Zail Singh reminded the prime minister that he had asked him for a briefing when they met during a banquet held for a visiting head of state, saying that Rajiv had agreed, but the briefing had never taken place. He also repeated his complaints that, despite requests, Rajiv had not consulted or briefed him about the Punjab, Assam and Mizoram accords. Furthermore, he demanded to know why he had not been allowed to see the unpublished finding of the commissions of enquiry into Indira Gandhi's assassination and into the killings of Sikhs which had followed it.

The president's letter to Rajiv was published in the *Indian Express* on 20 March, creating an uproar in Parliament as the opposition exploited fresh evidence that the prime minister was not fulfilling his constitutional obligation to the head of state. A few days later, Zail Singh gave what amounted to an interview to the *Illustrated Weekly* news magazine, though it did not quote him directly. It was a thinly-veiled attack on Rajiv Gandhi's premiership, though the prime minister was never actually mentioned. Zail Singh spoke of the cloudy future of Indian democracy and referred to parties whose inner democracy had been destroyed by leaders wanting to impose their own personality on everything. He even seemed to be lecturing the prime minister when he said that humility and political wisdom to know the common man do not come easily to those who are arrogant – 'he who rules by arrogance falls by it'. Continuing his attack, but apparently preferring to forget the role he himself had played in maintaining the Nehru-Gandhi dynasty in power, Zail Singh said: 'This country does not belong to any party or any particular family, however much they may have contributed to its political history. India belongs to the common man.'[1]

The effect of this extraordinary outburst was to fuel the controversy. Since the chairman of the *Rajya Sabha* and Speaker of the *Lok Sabha* had both rejected demands for parliamentary debates on the president's leaked letter, arguing that it was not in the national interest to debate communications between the president and prime minister, the debate took place mainly in newspaper columns. The key issue was: had the prime minister failed in his constitutional obligation to keep the president informed on all matters of state, and thus demeaned the office of president? Conversely, had the president abused his office by publicly entering into the realm of controversy in leaking his letter and giving a magazine interview?

By this time, Rajiv was seen to be making amends. Since January, he had regularly called on the president and spoken to him by telephone. He was briefing him on various matters, including the unfolding defence commission scandals in which the president was particularly interested. On one occasion, Rajiv took his entire family to lunch at Rashtrapati Bhawan, and was photographed helping Zail Singh celebrate his birthday. However, as subsequent actions made clear, the president did not appear mollified. He started entertaining Opposition politicians and Congress Party dissidents. Some of them urged him to dismiss the prime minister on the grounds that he had failed to keep the president fully briefed, which he is obliged to do under article 78 of the Constitution. Another group was inclined to believe the accusations by then being made in the newspapers and Parliament that the prime minister had received commission payments

[1] *Illustrated Weekly of India*, 22 March 1987.

in connection with a major arms deal, and wanted Rajiv to be dismissed for that reason.

The emergence of Zail Singh as a key figure in a developing anti-Rajiv conspiracy coincided with the end of his five-year tenure as president. On 24 July he was due to step down and make way for his successor, unless he could win support for a second five-year term. That support was clearly not going to come from Rajiv Gandhi and the Congress hierarchy, so he was canvassing the support of Congress dissidents and Opposition MPs. Many of them promised to support Zail Singh if he would agree to dismiss Rajiv Gandhi's administration. They believed the constitution implicitly gave a president the right to dismiss a prime minister, since article 75 lays down that 'ministers shall hold office during the pleasure of the president'. Most constitutional lawyers believe, however, that entreaties in the previous article, which oblige the president to follow the advice of the prime minister, effectively preclude any possibility of a prime minister being dismissed by a president, unless he has lost his majority support in Parliament. Though most of this political drama was being played out behind the scenes, and only subsequently became widely known, the fact that around forty Congress dissidents were discussing such matters with the president indicated the extent to which Rajiv had lost the backing of a significant number of his MPs.

Ironically, it was the continuing loyalty to Rajiv of V. P. Singh – who had been ousted from government and was well on his way to being ousted from the Congress Party too – that helped avert a constitutional collision. By refusing to support Zail Singh's bid for a second term as president and declaring his support for the official Congress candidate for president, Vice President Venkataraman, V. P. Singh effectively blocked the moves to unseat Rajiv, of which he may not have been fully aware. This, together with the decisions of the Opposition Bharatiya Janata Party not to take part in the presidential election, and of the Marxist Communist Party not to endorse Zail Singh's candidacy, resulted in the collapse of the coup attempt. Shortly after nominations closed, Zail Singh told Rajiv he would not be seeking re-election and would retire gracefully from office.

Though it is far from certain that an attempt by the president to dismiss Rajiv would have succeeded, Zail Singh's decision to bow out avoided both the constitutional crisis and the humiliation of the prime minister that would have resulted from any attempt to do so. Rajiv described moves to dismiss him as an attempt to 'subvert the constitution'. In rebuffing those attempts, Rajiv effectively disposed of one more potential rival, and strengthened the pivotal role of the prime minister under India's constitution. But the episode had further eroded Rajiv's standing in that post. In due course, Vice President Venkataraman became India's ninth president when members of India's central and state parliaments, who constituted the electoral college, gave him an easy victory.

In the meantime, more serious storm clouds were gathering. Some had already exploded in March with disastrous electoral performances by Congress in state assembly polls in Kerala, where Congress was ousted by a Communist-led alliance, and West Bengal, where another Communist-led alliance which had ruled the state for ten years increased its majority at the expense of Congress. Rajiv was criticised for both defeats, having personally campaigned extensively, especially in West Bengal where he had been advised – badly as it turned out – that Congress could win. But greater humiliation was to follow in Haryana where voting had been delayed until June. Despite the dismissal of the elected government of neighbouring Punjab, seen as a cynical attempt to win favour in Haryana, Congress was heavily defeated, retaining only five seats out of ninety in an assembly it had previously dominated. The result was taken to be a vote against the Punjab accord, under which Haryana would have had to give up its claim on Chandigarh, the capital it shared with Punjab. The Haryana result was also considered to be a personal vote against Rajiv Gandhi, who once more had led an active campaign in the state.

Though fresh parliamentary elections were not due for two and a half years, Congress members were undoubtedly troubled by Rajiv's consistent record in losing elections – both assembly polls and parliamentary by-elections – over the previous two years, causing them to question his continued leadership of the party. As well as being a test of opinion on local issues like the Punjab accord, the Haryana poll was the first opportunity any of India's vast electorate had to express their views on Rajiv's public exchanges with the president and the series of scandals that were now unfolding in Delhi which had led to the ouster of V. P. Singh.

The first scandal to explode was the Fairfax affair. News leaked out that V. P. Singh, whilst still finance minister, had approved the appointment of an American detective agency, the Fairfax Group, to investigate the affairs of a number of Indian industrialists to see if they were holding money in bank accounts abroad against India's strict foreign currency regulations. This was in line with the government's attack on corruption, of which the Finance Ministry's raids on suspected tax evaders and foreign exchange regulation violators was a major plank.

What made the appointment of the Fairfax Group suspicious was that it appeared to be on the advice of a chartered accountant who had himself been exposing the alleged wrong-doings of one prominent business house, Reliance Industries, in a series of articles in the *Indian Express*. When police raided *Indian Express* premises on 20 March, it was thought at first that the raids were in response to the publication in the paper that day of the letter President Zail Singh had sent to Rajiv Gandhi. It later transpired that the raids related to the paper's investigations of Reliance which, it was claimed, indicated the paper had access to confidential government files. The government was particularly embarrassed by the revelation that Reliance's rival textile manufacturer, Bombay Dying, had been a source of some of the confidential allegations against Reliance featured in the *Indian Express* articles. Bombay Dying's own dealings with the Fairfax Group pre-dated their selection by the Finance Ministry to investigate the overseas assets of the owners of Reliance and other industrial houses.

It was another supposedly leaked letter that brought the Fairfax investigation to public notice, except that this one turned out to be a forgery. It had purported to show that the Bachchan brothers were amongst those whose affairs the Fairfax Group had been asked to look into. Amitabh Bachchan is a well known film-star and a close friend of Rajiv Gandhi. Since 1984, he had also been a politician having, at Rajiv's instigation, contested and won the parliamentary seat of Allahabad for Congress. His younger brother, Ajitabh, had recently settled in Switzerland, raising questions in the newspapers as to how the family had acquired its wealth. Hence the mere suggestion that Fairfax were looking into the affairs of the Bachchans put a new perspective on the transfer of V. P. Singh from the Finance Ministry in late January. Had he been transferred to halt the investigation into the affairs of the Bachchan brothers? The Fairfax revelations seemed to strengthen the popular belief that V. P. Singh had been transferred as a direct result of the pressure senior industrialists were exerting on the prime minister, rather than because of the crisis in relations with Pakistan.

When V. P. Singh confirmed to Parliament that he had authorised the hiring of the Fairfax Group, fellow Congress MPs criticised his decision. They said he should have sought the prime minister's approval before hiring a foreign agency, particularly an American one which, they suggested, had former CIA operatives on its staff. V. P. Singh justified his action which, he said, was within his power as finance minister and in conformity with the government's policy of tracking down economic offenders. V. P. Singh pointed out that the prime minister had often endorsed this policy. 'How does this enquiry embarrass the government or the party?' asked V. P. Singh.[1] The man who had earlier endured the anger of India's business community, now found himself taking on the might of the Congress party, of which he was still a member, though his time was running out. Whatever the reason for the removal of V. P. Singh, and the following transfer of the two senior officials overseeing the Fairfax investigations, the government subsequently 'went soft' on its campaign against tax evasion and foreign currency manipulation after Rajiv himself took over as finance minister.

Next to explode was the scandal over the purchase some years earlier of submarines from the West German Howaldt Deutsche Werke shipyard at Kiel. Here again it was V. P. Singh, by now at Defence, who played the crucial role, setting the seal on his departure from the government, and ultimately from the party too. As far back as December 1981, just after Rajiv Gandhi had been elected to Parliament for the first time and whilst his mother was defence minister, India had signed a contract to buy four submarines – two to be built in Kiel and two more in Bombay. HDW was selected after the expert team charged with the task had visited two West German shipyards as well as the Kockum shipyard in Sweden. The government was now, in 1987, negotiating a follow-up deal with HDW to buy two more of the same class of submarine.

As defence minister, V. P. Singh had received a telegram from the Indian ambassador to Germany informing him that a seven per cent commission had been paid out of the price of the original deal with HDW. This had come to light when India pushed for a lower price on

---

[1] *India Today*, 30 April 1987.

the follow-up order. The manufacturers were unwilling to lower the price because they were committed to paying the same commission again. The original deal had been worth Rs 4300 million (around £286 million), so a seven per cent commission would have brought its recipient the equivalent of Rs 300 million (£20 million). After receiving the telegram, V. P. Singh ordered an enquiry into the possibility of tax evasion or foreign currency regulation violations on the commission, saying 'he could not compromise the lives of *jawans* (soldiers)'. Subsequently, the departmental enquiry was asked to investigate the alleged commission payment itself since, even if it was not illegal at the time, the alleged amount of the commission on the HDW contract exceeded Ministry of Defence norms. By the time V. P. Singh ordered the enquiry, Rajiv's government had introduced a rule that defence contracts should not involve middlemen or commission payments, but should be negotiated directly between supplier and government.

The HDW enquiry was the final straw for Congress MPs already outraged by V. P. Singh's initiation of the Fairfax investigation. V. P. Singh's 'error', in their eyes, was that once again he had acted on his own initiative without seeking the prime minister's approval for his action. He seemed to them to be pursuing a one-man crusade against corruption by ordering enquiries without stopping to think what they might unearth. The HDW submarine deal had been signed by a Congress government in which Rajiv's mother was both prime minister and defence minister. The follow-up contract was also being negotiated by a Congress government, and V. P. Singh, whilst properly involved as defence minister, had become involved at a relatively late stage. His Congress critics accused him of being unwilling to leave behind the investigatory zeal of his previous job as finance minister. They clamoured for his blood. His enquiry into the HDW affair was also criticised within the cabinet. Three days after announcing the investigation, V. P. Singh took the only course open to him and delivered his resignation letter to Rajiv Gandhi. Rajiv made no attempt to dissuade him. The parting of the ways had become inevitable.

Rajiv had cut another political colleague down to size. He had once again shown who was in charge, though in the process had created a potential rival around whom party dissidents could group. V. P. Singh was the most senior, and the most respected, member of Rajiv's government. Three months later, Rajiv expelled V. P. Singh from the Congress Party, on the trumped-up charge of engaging in anti-party activities, thus completing the process of his estrangement from the man who had seemed to be both his ablest minister and his most loyal colleague. The breach had resulted entirely from V. P. Singh's determination to attack corruption, tax evasion and other forms of black money. The whole affair had created the impression that V. P. Singh was much more committed to this anti-corruption drive than Rajiv.

With V. P. Singh forced out of office, the parliamentary Opposition as well as much of the press believed they now had their proof that the government was corrupt. It was the increasingly anti-Rajiv *Indian Express* which expressed it most forcefully, declaring in a front page editorial that 'the decision of the Prime Minister to force Mr Singh out removes all doubt that Mr Rajiv Gandhi, or someone dear or near to him either living or dead, has received a financial kickback'. Through the mere whiff of scandal, yet without any substantiated proof of his involvement, Rajiv had lost his reputation as 'Mr Clean'. Simultaneously, V. P. Singh, who had five years earlier resigned as chief minister of Uttar Pradesh on an issue of principle, had further enhanced his own reputation as a tireless crusader against corruption in public life.

The Fairfax enquiry reported towards the end of the year. Several months earlier, the government had cancelled the agreement with Fairfax. The report was variously described as a 'whitewash', a 'non-report' and a 'truly pathetic document that settled nothing'. It concluded that the agreement to hire Fairfax was inconsistent with national security. The report had nothing to say about the alleged currency violations that Fairfax had been asked to investigate. V. P. Singh himself said the report provided evidence that economic offenders were being allowed to go free whilst their pursuers were punished and he called it 'a monument of injustice'.[1] The outcome of the Defence Ministry enquiries into allegations that commissions were paid during the purchase of HDW submarines was even less satisfactory. A year after V. P. Singh had set it in motion, his successor as defence minister, K. C. Pant, closed the enquiry, telling Parliament: 'The allegations have been found to have no basis.' His announcement attracted little

---

[1] *Frontline*, 26 December 1987.

attention because by that time Parliament and the nation had become enthralled by a much bigger defence scandal which made the submarine commission payments seem insignificant by comparison.

CHAPTER TEN

A Tangled Web

On 16 April 1987, Swedish Radio reported that millions of dollars had been paid in bribes to Indian officials and members of the Congress Party by the Swedish Bofors arms company in connection with a contract for the sale to India of 155 mm howitzer guns. The contract for 410 howitzers had been signed a year earlier, in March 1986, the culmination of a long search by India to replace aged Second World War artillery with sophisticated modern weaponry which was as good or better than that which had recently been acquired by Pakistan. For Sweden, the contract was the country's largest ever export sale. It brought job security for six years to about 1500 workers at Karlskoga, the small town near Sweden's border with Norway dominated by Bofors and its sister companies, which together form part of Nobel Industries. The contract was worth 8410 million Swedish kroner or Rs 14367 million (£815 million) and had been won against fierce competition, especially from the French Sofma company. Bofors' managing director, Martin Ardbo, had hoisted the Indian flag over the Bofors works when the Indian contract was signed.

The Indian government was quick to issue a denial of the Swedish Radio accusation of bribery. It called it 'one more link in the chain of denigration and destabilisation of our political system', without explaining who was meant to be behind such an attempt. It stressed that, during the lengthy negotiations to buy the gun, the Indian government had made clear to all contenders that middlemen were not to be involved. The Bofors company also denied the charges, even though there was nothing illegal under Swedish law about paying commission. It was Indian law, or maybe just Indian ethics, that had allegedly been breached.

The allegations were not so easily dismissed. The parliamentary Opposition were already on the warpath because of the resignation a few days earlier of the defence minister, V. P. Singh, and debates had been scheduled in both houses of Parliament into the allegations that had caused his resignation – that commission payments were made on the West German submarine deal. Those debates were now used to demand fuller details of the circumstances of the much bigger Bofors deal. It was as if the government, already forced to its knees by one blow, was knocked completely to the ground by a massive kick.

Just how Swedish Radio obtained the evidence that money had been paid to middlemen, or why it chose to reveal it at a moment which would cause maximum embarrassment to Rajiv Gandhi's government, has never been made clear. There have been suggestions that the allegations were an attempt to embarrass Sweden's already troubled arms industry, rather than to cause a political crisis in India. Swedish Radio, a much respected institution which has the monopoly of radio broadcasting in Sweden, is run by a public corporation which is itself controlled by various non-governmental groups. The dominant voice belongs to voluntary organisations, cooperatives, trade unions and the churches, though some power is also wielded by newspaper proprietors and business houses.

Part of the reason why the Bofors charges had such an impact in India was that Rajiv Gandhi was himself defence minister at the time the Bofors deal was signed. At an early stage, soon after winning the election, he had reaffirmed the existing government policy that no middlemen were to be involved in defence contracts. A few days before the Bofors charges were made, the 'no middlemen' policy had been reiterated in Parliament by the junior Defence Minister, Arun Singh, in response to questions about the West German submarine deal and the possibility that commissions might have been paid on that. The policy that Arun Singh had outlined says specifically that foreign firms were not to use Indian agents when negotiating with the Indian government.

As a result of the parliamentary clamour, the government asked the Swedish government for help in determining whether middlemen had been used. The Swedish government's response was to ask its National Audit Board, the NAB, to examine the transactions made by Bofors in connection with the Indian deal, and to report by the end of the following month, May 1987. Indian parliamentarians, who had not reduced their demand for a public enquiry, awaited the outcome of the NAB report with interest. When it came, it confirmed that payments totalling 32 million Swedish kroner had indeed been paid into numbered bank accounts in Switzerland, but stated that the Bofors company had said that these were reimbursement for consultancy services within the areas of marketing and counter purchase, and the winding up of agency agreements. Bofors had told the NAB that no payments 'of the kind alleged by the media' had been made, and reiterated its denial that any middlemen or agents had been used to win the Indian contract. It did concede, though, that agency agreements had been terminated after the Indian government had made clear that the deal should be concluded directly between the company and the government, and that this had necessitated the winding up of existing agency agreements. According to Bofors, winding up payments were therefore made.

For reasons of commercial confidentiality, Bofors were unwilling to name the recipients of the payments, and the NAB had not seen fit to press them to do so since there was no evidence of Swedish law having been broken. According to the NAB, however, none of the money had gone to any Indian company or citizen, except for a regular monthly payment of 100000 kroner that Bofors had admitted making to an Indian company, Anatronic General Corporation, for administrative services. Bofors had said that the company did not have an agent or representative 'especially employed in India for this project'. The NAB report confirmed that so-called 'winding up' charges amounting to between two and three per cent of the value of the order, or about 170–250 million kroner, had been agreed, and that 32 million kroner had been distributed by the end of 1986.

By the time the NAB reported, Indian newspapers had begun weighing in with their own suggestions as to who the recipients of the commission payments might be. A press that has little to fear from the laws of defamation had many suggestions to make. In early June, the Madras-based *Hindu* newspaper published the name of a company it said had received the largest share of the Bofors payments. The government, after consulting opposition leaders, asked the Speaker of the *Lok Sabha* and chairman of the *Rajya Sabha* to institute a committee of both houses to enquire into the Bofors contract and, in particular, to determine whether the Bofors company had violated the terms of the contract by using middlemen. Rajiv Gandhi told journalists that the payments Bofors had admitted making were in respect of its agents' global commission and may not have had anything to do with the Bofors deal itself. However, the allegations in the press continued and a few days later, before the Joint Parliamentary Committee had been set up, Rajiv had been forced to deny the innuendos being made by telling the *Lok Sabha*: 'I categorically declare in this highest forum of democracy that neither I nor any member of my family has received any consideration in these transactions. That is the truth.'

On 28 August, the Joint Parliamentary Committee of both houses was constituted, but was boycotted by all opposition parties. They were dissatisfied with the committee's terms of reference, and had in any case favoured a commission of enquiry under a Supreme Court judge instead of a parliamentary enquiry. This decision to boycott was to weaken their criticism of the commission's report when it appeared, and to lay them open to the charge of having failed to co-operate with a genuine attempt to get to the bottom of the Bofors charges.

The Joint Parliamentary Committee report was laid before Parliament the following April. After what appeared to be a thorough investigation into the circumstances of the Bofors contract, committee members concluded that the elaborate evaluation and negotiation procedure leading to the signing of the contract had been sound and objective. It found the Bofors gun met all the necessary technical requirements, that it had been chosen in the face of keen competition which had enabled the government to secure it at the lowest price and on the best financial terms, and that the decision to award the contract to Bofors 'was purely on merits'. It concluded that 'no extraneous influence or consideration such as kickbacks or bribes ... affected ... the selection and evaluation of the gun systems or the commercial negotiations'. According to the report, the payment by Bofors of 'winding up charges' to companies with which it had agency agreements, was necessary to fulfil the Indian government's wishes that no middlemen or agents should be involved in the gun contract, though it had been unable to inspect the termination agreements with these companies, which it named as Pitco, Svenska and A.E. Services. It upheld the Bofors company's claim that the payments made to Anatronic General Corporation were for administrative services and that the firm had not acted as a middleman. It concluded that there was no evidence of the involvement of middlemen at the time the Bofors contract was signed, or to substantiate allegations of kickbacks or bribes having been paid to anyone. Therefore, said the parliamentary committee acquitting the Indian political and bureaucratic establishment of all charges, the question of whether or not Indian citizens or companies had received payments did not arise.

One of the thirty members who served on the committee, Aladi Aruna of the Tamil Nadu-based AIADMK party, dissented from its conclusions. It is significant that the AIADMK had been an alliance partner of Congress in Tamil Nadu when the Joint Parliamentary Committee was established, and so had not joined the Opposition boycott. However, before the committee's report was published, the AIADMK–Congress alliance had come undone. Aladi Aruna had told his fellow committee members: 'I will not be a party to the cover up,' and he went on to claim, in a dissenting minority report, that the committee had not taken serious steps to identify the persons who received the huge amounts through what he called 'spurious agents'. He said the story that there had been no middlemen involved in the deal and no commission payments made was unbelievable. He also questioned what he called the 'extraordinary interest' which the prime minister had taken in the Bofors deal, as revealed in the documents made available to the committee, and added, in regard to the choice of the Bofors gun as opposed to the French gun, that 'the wind began to blow in a different direction after Mr Rajiv Gandhi, our prime minister, took over the portfolio of defence'. Opposition members seized on Aladi Aruna's minority report as providing evidence of Rajiv's personal involvement in the alleged commission payments. It provided no such thing, and had pointed out little that could not be put down to the proper exercise of the role of a prime minister, who also happened to be defence minister throughout the period in question, in connection with a major arms deal.

Notwithstanding Rajiv's denial to Parliament that he had benefited from the deal, the focus of the very public inquisition now underway in the press switched to address the theme: Had Rajiv Gandhi himself been responsible for overturning the originally preferred French-made gun in favour of the Bofors gun, and if so what factors had influenced him? Also, what was the significance of the prime minister himself insisting that no middlemen be involved in the deal? This stipulation had been communicated to all the contending companies in May 1985, though Bofors said that word had not reached them till November 1985. This was shortly after Rajiv Gandhi had personally spoken with the Swedish prime minister, Olof Palme, at the United Nations General Assembly. The two prime ministers, who had become friends through their joint participation in the Six Nation disarmament initiative, were to meet again in Delhi in January 1986. On that occasion, Rajiv told Olof Palme that a decision on which gun was to be chosen was imminent. Two months later, the deal with the Bofors company was signed. The Joint Parliamentary Committee (JPC) report pointed out that although the non-involvement of middlemen, and particularly of Indian agents, was the clearly stated policy of the Indian government, they had not thought it necessary to make this a condition of the contract.

In many people's eyes, the JPC report raised more questions than it answered. Whilst it found the procedure which had led to the choice of the Bofors gun to have been 'sound and objective', it threw no light on why the French Sofma gun, which had been the army's choice continuously for three years, and which was named as its preference on six occasions, was relegated to second place in favour of the Bofors gun during the last two months of the lengthy negotiating process. Also, whilst the report found that a number of companies had at various stages in the negotiations acted as middlemen, earning commissions ranging between two per cent and five and three-quarter per cent of the contract value, it threw no light on why so many intermediaries were needed for a relatively straightforward contract. The enquiry team believed that such commission agreements had been terminated before the contract was signed.

Another problem with the JPC report was that it was rapidly overtaken by other revelations. Even before it was published, the *Hindu* newspaper had started to expose details of the winding up agreements that the parliamentary committee had been unable to find. Its first exposure showed a direct link between one of the companies which had received commission, Pitco (later known as Moresco), and a well-known Indian business family based in London, the Hinduja brothers. Though the Hindujas have consistently denied that any of the brothers was involved in the howitzer deal, they do not deny having inside knowledge about the deal and its aftermath, knowledge that caused G. P. Hinduja, one of the brothers, to tell the *Hindu*'s associate editor, Narasimhan Ram, that the government of Mr Rajiv Gandhi would fall if the real truth behind Bofors surfaced. The Hindujas defended their refusal to reveal details on the grounds that they were pursuing Indian 'national interests' in preventing the destabilisation that they believed would result from the fall of Rajiv Gandhi. The Hindujas were to demonstrate their access to high places in Sweden when they arranged for correspondents of the *Hindu* to interview Olof Palme's successor as prime minister, Ingvar Carlsson. After the interview took place, the Hindujas had miraculously obtained a transcript and they tried unsuccessfully to influence the way it was reported by asking N. Ram to make various alterations to both questions and answers, to make the former sound less tough and the latter more confident (according to N. Ram). G. P. Hinduja also offered further exclusive interviews to the newspaper, including interviews with George Bush (then vice president) and the Chinese premier. But N. Ram refused to make even minor changes saying that to have done so would have been unprofessional.[1]

It was now the press, and in particular the *Hindu,* which effectively took over the Bofors enquiry with one exposure after another. Documents obtained by the newspapers purported to show that the payments made by Bofors were directly related to the Indian contract, and thus were in effect commissions rather than winding-up costs. They showed that Indians had been recipients, or at the least conduits, for the money, contradicting another finding of the JPC report. They showed that the sums of money paid into Swiss bank accounts were much higher than the JPC had found, amounting to a total of at least ten per cent and possibly as much as fourteen per cent of the value of the contract. And they indicated that the payments had been continuing right up to the time that the scandal broke, and doubtless would have continued long afterwards, casting further doubts on the claim that they were merely winding-up charges.

Though none of the newspapers came up with any evidence that Rajiv or his family had received Bofors money – though there were plenty of allegations to that effect – the documents that were revealed pointed to a cover-up involving Bofors and the JPC with the connivance of both the Swedish and Indian governments. As the *Hindu* itself put it: 'The story of "termination negotiations" and "winding-up costs" – trotted out by Bofors and accepted as reasonable . . . by the government of India . . . and the Joint Parliamentary Committee – was a concoction and a cover-up strategy for the management of a crisis after the scandal surfaced.'[2] Rajiv denied there was a cover up as forcefully as he denied

[1] *Hindu*, 10 November 1989.
[2] *Hindu*, 22 June 1988.

receiving any commission on the deal. Yet the way he changed his position – at first declaring no commissions were paid, then, when it was shown that they were, denying that any Indian had received any payment – dealt a severe blow to his credibility.

While all this was going on in India, Bofors was involved in another scandal in Sweden. Evidence had come to light that the company was supplying arms to countries in the Gulf in direct contravention of Swedish law, which banned arms sales to countries at war or in regions of conflict. Having been refused an export licence by the government to sell its laser-guided RBS-70 missile to Dubai and Bahrein, out of a fear that they might find their way to one of the Gulf war combatants, Iran or Iraq, Bofors nonetheless illegally went ahead with shipments. The company was experiencing difficult times and redundancies would have become inevitable unless it could secure new markets for this technologically advanced missile.

Details of the illicit exports came to light when a Singapore-based intermediary was found guilty of forging end-user certificates, forcing Bofors' president Martin Ardbo to resign. This was in March 1987, shortly before the scandal over the Indian deal broke. After a lengthy investigation, Ardbo and two other senior managers were put on trial, accused of smuggling 300 anti-aircraft missiles to Dubai and Bahrein and ammunition to Oman. Their defence was that they had the tacit approval of the Swedish government to proceed with the sales. Neither of the two men who could confirm this defence was able to give evidence in their support. The head of the government's war materials inspectorate, Carl Frederick Algernon, had mysteriously fallen under a Stockholm underground train. The other person who would have had to approve any major arms sale abroad was the prime minister at the time the deal was concluded, Olof Palme, who had been shot dead in a Stockholm street on 28 February 1986, just a month before Bofors' Indian contract was signed.

The three Bofors managers were eventually convicted of arms smuggling and given suspended prison sentences. The trial was a devastating blow to Swedish innocence and self-righteousness, with its revelation that a country so committed to peace and disarmament was secretly fuelling international conflict as a major arms exporter, a revelation of national hypocrisy that some Swedes found difficult to accept. Quite what the role in the affair was of Olof Palme and his Social Democratic government, which whilst supporting disarmament was also committed to full employment, remains unclear. Given the difficult times Bofors was encountering in finding markets for its products there is no doubt that the Indian deal came as a relief to the company.

Martin Ardbo's diaries were later to form a key by which Indian newspapers were able to identify the recipients of commission payments. If anyone knows the full details of who, if anyone, took back-handers on the sale of Bofors howitzers to India, it is Martin Ardbo. So far, he has been unwilling to tell what he knows. He has admitted, though, that if Bofors had ended its use of business agents, as the Indian government had apparently expected it to do, then it would not have got the Indian contract. In other words, Bofors secured the contract because it was willing to pay commissions.

One of the more intriguing puzzles raised by the newspaper disclosures over the Bofors deal concerned the role of the British company, A. E. Services. Its agency contract with Bofors had been signed on 15 November 1985, just three weeks after Olof Palme and Rajiv Gandhi met at the United Nations, and after Bofors had been told that there were to be no middlemen. It was the only commission agreement to have been signed by Martin Ardbo himself, and the agreement specified that it remain secret. A. E. Services' commission of three per cent (which was to come from money previously destined to be paid to another recipient, Svenska) was conditional on the contract for the howitzers being signed before the end of March 1986. The contract was signed on 24 March. A. E. Services themselves say they had no role in concluding the agreement, though without explaining just how they did earn their three per cent. They are coy about revealing their precise role, and the full name of A. E. Services' holding company, the Liechtenstein-based Consortium for Information Assimilation and Output Unit, hardly makes it any clearer. A. E. Services' founding director, Major Bob Wilson, had served in a Gurkha regiment of the Indian army. After retiring, he trained as a lawyer and subsequently specialised in defence contracts. He appears to have played an important role at a high level in Bofors' Indian contract. Because of its late entry into the fray, the size of its cut, and the fact that it was deregistered as a company, and its Swiss bank account closed, soon after the JPC investigation, A. E. Services was the commission recipient most suspected of being a front for an Indian beneficiary or beneficiaries.

An entry in Martin Ardbo's diary for 2 July 1987 reported: 'Bob has talked with Gandhi truste (sic) lawyer', the only mention of the name

Gandhi to have appeared in any of the published documents. Rajiv denies knowing anything about a Gandhi trust. Two months later, Bob Wilson features again in the Ardbo diary when the two men met. According to the entry, Wilson promised to sort out what was said between 'P and R', which has been interpreted as meaning Palme and Rajiv. The two prime ministers were known to have discussed the Bofors deal on at least two occasions before it was concluded – in October 1985 at the United Nations and when Palme visited Delhi in January 1986. During that visit, Palme had a meal with Rajiv at his home: Sonia and the children were present. According to one of Palme's aides, the howitzer contract and Rajiv's ban on middlemen was discussed over lunch. Martin Ardbo seems to have been in Delhi at the same time, and flew back with Olof Palme.

The day before Ardbo's meeting with Wilson in September 1987, there is an entry in his diary which bears an uncanny similarity to G. P. Hinduja's claim that the government of Rajiv Gandhi would fall if the real truth behind Bofors surfaced. Ardbo had written: 'Palme's involvement, if it will become known, will most likely bring the Swedish government down. Everyone is afraid that I shall tell the whole truth.'

In November 1988, Rajiv Gandhi spoke about the Bofors scandal in an interview with the news magazine, *Sunday*.[1] It was the first time he tacitly accepted that middlemen had been involved in the deal and that payments had been made to them. He said that so far the government had not been able to establish whether money had come to any Indian, but it was trying very hard to find out. Nor was he certain that the money paid out constituted commission payments: 'If it was paid for some genuine work that was done for Bofors, then we cannot question it ... genuine work gathering information against the French weapon ... that is industrial espionage. You can't grudge them that.' The prime minister was asked why he had not cancelled the contract when revelations about commissions payments had become known. He said the Defence Ministry had been strongly against cancelling the contract because they feared it would be at least a year before another howitzer contract could be negotiated. As for asking for the Rs 640 million commission money to be repaid, the prime minister was concerned about India's credibility in the international market place: 'Manu-

---

[1] *Sunday,* 13 November 1988.

facturers would be reluctant to sell us weapons if they felt that a controversy would lead to a cancellation and heavy costs on their side,' he said. He repeated his belief that India had got the best gun and said that to the best of his knowledge money had not been used to influence the decision-making process.

Rajiv conceded to his interviewers that he had 'taken a beating' from the Bofors controversy, but repeated: 'I have personally done no wrong, and we are clean on that. It doesn't affect me as an individual. It is better that I take a beating than the nation take a beating.' The most obvious demonstration of the political beating the affair was causing Rajiv and the Congress Party came at the polls in June 1988. The party was badly defeated in a series of by-elections to the *Lok Sabha* and state assemblies in which the Bofors scandal was clearly a factor. Most humiliating for Rajiv was the victory of his former finance and defence minister, V. P. Singh, contesting on behalf of the newly-formed Jan Morcha, or People's Front, from Allahabad. The by-election in this traditional Congress safe seat had been caused by the resignation of Rajiv's film star friend, Amitabh Bachchan, after he was accused, though without evidence, of having benefited from the West German submarine contract. Congress put up Sunil Shastri, the son of the former prime minister, Lal Bahadur Shastri. V. P. Singh defeated Sunil Shastri by more than 120 000 votes after a campaign in which the issue of corruption in public life featured prominently. The Bofors gun seemed to be his unofficial campaign symbol. Pictures and models of the gun adorned the streets of Allahabad, the home city of the Gandhi family. With his election to parliament, V. P. Singh had formally usurped Rajiv's title as the 'Mr Clean' of Indian politics. Congress began to have major worries about its ability to win re-election.

Those worries increased as more and more exposures appeared in the newspapers. Bofors had become a crusade in which the strongly anti-Rajiv *Indian Express* aspired to play the leading role, even though the *Hindu* secured the better documents. However, the journalists and editors who were engaged in the crusade were as frustrated by their own failure to produce definite evidence of wrong-doing on the part of the government, as the government and prime minister were confounded by the gathering momentum of what had become an all-consuming political campaign. Rajiv's credibility was suffering badly. He needed a success if he was to recover in time for the election, which was due by the end of 1989, and he also needed to shake off the Bofors charges.

For a while the Opposition's campaign seemed to falter, though V. P. Singh's success at Allahabad had been followed by the forging of an unexpected degree of Opposition unity. Towards the end of 1988, four Opposition parties including the Jan Morcha merged together to form the Janata Dal, or People's Party. It was a call to the spirit of 1977 when the former Janata party had become the only party ever to oust Congress from power in Delhi. At the same time, it was a reminder, and one of which Congress were to make great play, that the Janata government had fallen from power after two and a half years when rivalry and bickering amongst its would-be leaders led it to lose its parliamentary majority. That had provided the opportunity for Congress to return, and Mrs Gandhi had been re-elected triumphantly in January 1980. Most members of the new Janata Dal were former members of Congress who had left of their own volition, or else been expelled. The creation of the Janata Dal under V. P. Singh's leadership prepared the way for the replay between Congress and Janata in 1989.

However, before Bofors became an electoral factor, the central role the press had played in exposing details of the Bofors affair gave rise to two sideshows. Goaded by the accusations that were appearing almost daily in certain newspapers, many of them accusing him directly of accepting bribes, Rajiv introduced a bill into the *Lok Sabha* in August 1988 which he said was intended to protect the individual from defamatory writings, speeches and actions. It was an attempt, he said, to reconcile the rights of the individual with the freedom of the press. What angered the press most about Rajiv's defamation bill was that it put the onus of disproving a defamation charge on the publication against whom the action was brought. Editors were also annoyed that they had not been consulted before the government introduced its controversial proposals, which considerably tightened existing rules on defamation. The bill sailed easily through the *Lok Sabha,* but was withdrawn before it came before the *Rajya Sabha* after an outcry from the press, who held strikes and demonstrations to get across their staunch opposition to the bill. The government had also received indications that some Congress members of the upper house would vote against the bill, possibly resulting in its defeat. It had been an ill-considered – though not entirely unjustified – measure, and opposition to it had resulted in a humiliating climb-down by the prime minister.

The second newspaper fallout from the Bofors scandal, which came many months later, was a domestic dispute within the family which owns the respected Madras-based daily, the *Hindu*. The paper had for many months led the field in exposing details of the alleged Bofors payoffs. One day, in October 1989, its associate editor, Narasimhan Ram, suddenly presented himself before a hastily summoned Delhi press conference to complain that he was being prevented by his uncle, the paper's editor, Gopalan Kasturi, from publishing any further Bofors materials. Ram claimed the government had put pressure on the paper by stopping government advertising and encouraging state-owned corporations to do likewise as well as by increasing the rates for facsimile transmission, on which the paper relied to produce its Delhi edition. It was these actions, he alleged, which had caused his uncle to block the publication of further Bofors materials. The family row, however, had the opposite effect from that which the government may have hoped, for Ram announced that henceforth the *Hindu* would be sharing its key exposés with other like-minded newspapers and journals.

On the political front, 1989 had started badly for Congress. It was heavily defeated in elections to the Tamil Nadu state assembly, losing its last foothold of power in southern India. Then there were problems within the Congress leadership in Bihar, Madhya Pradesh and Rajasthan, all of which took some sorting out. It seemed that the defeat in Tamil Nadu had prompted a mood of revolt against the party's high command. On the Bofors front, all was quiet for a time. Some commentators believe that what they called 'Bofors fatigue' had set in. The public was tired of the detailed intricacies of documents purporting to establish wrong-doing in high places, but not actually proving it. There was a feeling that the campaign to make Bofors a key issue in the forthcoming elections was running out of steam for lack of any conclusive proof that Rajiv or any of his family or associates were directly implicated. Then came two further blows to the prime minister and the ruling party.

Firstly, the conclusions of a new enquiry into the affair were laid before Parliament. It was by the Comptroller and Auditor General, or CAG, an officer of state whose post is established under the constitution for the purpose of keeping a check on governmental expenditure. The incumbent is answerable to India's president rather than to the government of the day, though the president is obliged to lay his reports before parliament. Whilst the Joint Parliamentary Committee enquiry had given most emphasis to the payments made in connection with the Bofors contract, the report by the CAG, former senior civil servant T. N. Chaturvedi, explored in some depth the procedure followed in selecting the Bofors gun, and found it wanting. It criticised the technical evaluation of the gun, deplored the fact that no field trials had been held since 1982, and concluded that the recommendation of the negotiating committee which led to the Bofors contract had not resulted from an evaluation of the gun's performance against what was needed – which is normal practice – but was based on the recommendation of army headquarters, which had preferred the French gun until the last minute when it changed its preference in favour of the Bofors gun.

The CAG had been unconvinced by the explanation given to the JPC that the main reason for the late switch of preference from the Sofma to the Bofors gun was because of its superior 'burst fire' and 'shoot and scoot' capabilities, following the realisation that Pakistan had recently acquired more accurate radar for its artillery. The CAG also criticised the purchase procedure in a number of further respects, including the credit arrangements and currency involved, which it said went directly against advice earlier received from the Department of Economic Affairs. And it charged the Ministry of Defence with delaying for two years in providing documents that the CAG had asked for in connection with its audit. The CAG also questioned why the government's ban on the use of agents had not been included in the contract signed with Bofors.

Though the CAG found no evidence that the payments made by Bofors involved a violation of Indian law, or had been made to Indian officials or politicians, the effect of his report was, as one columnist put it, 'that the JPC now stands exposed with its pants down'. The same writer went on: 'The way in which the Bofors deal has been handled by the Indian government is similar to the manner in which the Watergate was handled by Richard Nixon. One lie was covered by another lie, and so it went on until a nation, sick of the stalling tactics of a criminal president, finally decided to call for his indictment.'[1]

The CAG report was a gift to the Opposition in election year. When it was placed before Parliament on 18 July, they demanded the prime minister's resignation saying he had no moral right to continue in

---

[1] M. V. Kamath writing in the *Indian Post*, 26 July 1989.

office. Pandemonium reigned in Parliament, causing proceedings in both houses to be suspended on several occasions. Opposition MPs were heard to mutter: 'The CAG report proves Rajiv Gandhi is a thief.' In fact, the report did no such thing, and hardly even referred to the issue of whether or not bribes had been paid on the contract. For three days, proceedings in both houses were stalled by Opposition MPs clamouring for Rajiv Gandhi's resignation, or at the least a parliamentary debate on the CAG report. A resolution passed unanimously by Opposition parties said the CAG report had finally exposed the stone-walling tactics, shifting positions, clumsy cover-ups and plain lies that the prime minister and his colleagues had been resorting to during the last two years in order to suppress the truth of Bofors payments.

Then Opposition MPs, who had surprised themselves at how united they were in demanding Rajiv's resignation, hit on their master-stroke. At the suggestion of N. T. Rama Rao, whose Telegu Desam party was the largest Opposition party in the *Lok Sabha*, almost the entire Opposition membership of the house – a total of seventy-five members – resigned their seats. Members of the upper house, the *Rajya Sabha*, also walked out in protest, though in their case they did not actually resign their seats. The effect of the protest was to leave the government with virtually empty Opposition benches in both houses, though members of the *Rajya Sabha* later returned to take part in important debates. It had been an unexpectedly successful *coup de grâce* by the Opposition, the most dramatic political event of Rajiv's premiership and one which administered it another severe jolt. His large majority in the lower house had in any case rendered the Opposition largely impotent, but it did his government's standing no good to be deprived of Opposition altogether. Congress accused the Opposition of 'murdering democracy with this cheap election stunt'. One Opposition politician defended the mass walk-out saying: 'Parliament is an arena of public accountability. If the government decides to violate norms on the strength of its majority, the opposition must dissociate itself from this.'

The CAG report had concluded that it was army headquarters that effectively chose the Bofors gun, rather than the negotiating committee set up for that purpose. This might have pointed the finger of suspicion at the army chief, General Krishnaswami Sundarji. He took over as chief of the army staff just sixteen days before the decision to buy

Bofors was made. However, it was General Sundarji himself who dropped the second pre-electoral bombshell. In an interview with the news magazine, *India Today,* in September 1989, long after he had retired, he effectively contradicted Rajiv's assertion that the service chiefs had been against cancelling the Bofors contract. General Sundarji said that he had himself recommended that Bofors be threatened with cancellation to force them to reveal the names of those who had acted as its agents. He felt the two-year delay that cancellation would cause to the acquisition of the gun 'was an acceptable risk from the point of view of the totality of circumstances'. The advice was not followed. Indeed General Sundarji said he had been told by a Defence Ministry official that his advice was 'awkward' in the light of a decision the government had taken. He was asked to consider modifying it. Instead, he took back the paper on which the advice had been given, but re-submitted it at a later date when told the prime minister was upset that the Defence Ministry had not provided the assessment he had asked for on the implications of cancelling the Bofors contract. Despite this further blow to the government's position, which increased talk of a cover-up, General Sundarji stood by the choice of the Bofors gun which he insisted was 'the best gun'. General Sundarji's evidence directly contradicted Rajiv's assertion that he had considered cancelling the Bofors contract but had met opposition from the army chiefs.

If the main casualty of the Bofors affair was the prime minister's credibility, a lesser casualty was his long-standing friendship, through school and Cambridge days, with Arun Singh. Arun Singh had helped Rajiv organise the Asian Games in 1982. A year after Rajiv became prime minister, he made Arun his minister of state for defence, or junior defence minister, when he took the defence portfolio himself. Arun found himself having to defend in Parliament his ministry's record over both the submarine and the howitzer contracts, and defending the reputation of his close friend. It was a particularly difficult time for him.

Three months after the Bofors scandal broke, Arun Singh suddenly announced his resignation from the government. There was speculation that, as the minister most involved in the Bofors deal, and having accepted responsibility for failing to write a 'no middlemen' clause into the contract, he was finding his position increasingly untenable. There were at least two particular issues which may have prompted his decision to go, both arising out of the Bofors scandal. Early in July

1987, he had accepted an offer by Bofors that a team of their top officials visit Delhi to clarify details of the payments made. Returning on 4 July from an overseas visit, Rajiv held a meeting at his house with Arun Singh and other senior defence ministry officials. The visit by the Bofors team was then cancelled at short notice, which was subsequently to evoke much criticism.

General Sundarji's belief is that Arun Singh, who was his boss, 'had a very big dust-up with the PM. He was torn between his loyalty to the man and what he felt was right'. General Sundarji believes Arun's resignation a few days later was directly connected with the advice he had given that Bofors should be threatened with cancellation of the contract. However, Arun Singh had already made plain his resentment that he had not been called to give evidence to the JPC, though members of the ministry that, for all intents and purposes, he headed had been summoned without his approval. He may also have resented the way Rajiv had appointed cabinet ministers – first V. P. Singh and then K. C. Pant – over him, when he had effectively been running the Defence Ministry for two years as minister of state. Arun's resignation could have been prompted by these sleights, or it could have been, as he said at the time, for purely personal reasons. It coincided with the break up of his marriage. He later resigned his membership of the *Rajya Sabha* and left Delhi to live on a remote farm in the Kumaon hills of Uttar Pradesh, where he has maintained a discreet silence and loyalty to Rajiv over what he knows about the Bofors scandal.

CHAPTER ELEVEN

After the Honeymoon

Rajiv had won re-election in December 1984 amidst a greater sense of euphoria than had followed any previous election victory in India. It deserved to be compared with the sense of triumph surrounding his mother after she had led her country to defeat Pakistan in the Bangladesh war, resulting in her comparison with the Hindu goddess Durga, a many-armed figure associated with power and the triumph of good over evil. In a strictly electoral sense, Rajiv too had defeated his foes. But in all other respects, he was seen as lacking the strength and the ability to perform many tasks at once that were essential to his mother's Durga image.

For the first eighteen months after his election triumph, Rajiv hardly seemed to be able to put a foot wrong. He had a superb press, and even the Opposition found it difficult to criticise his actions and were instead reduced to criticising his style. Then the bubble burst. Rajiv himself has commented on the ending of his honeymoon in the video *India's Rajiv*: 'First there was nothing I could do that was wrong – then there was nothing I could do that was right. Of course, neither was true.' He was to add, perhaps rather presumptuously, in that same interview: 'Criticism doesn't affect me.' The euphoria had heightened expectations, but Rajiv was subsequently unable to deliver all that he had promised. Some of the problems he encountered from mid-1987 were of his own making, and could perhaps have been avoided. Others were not, and it hardly seems fair that he was blamed. They combined with the unproven corruption charges to tarnish his reputation; no longer was the 'Mr Clean' image paramount. Instead he acquired the pejorative nickname 'the boy', intended to draw unfavourable comparison with his mother, who seemed with hindsight to have been as well endowed with political judgement and wisdom as Rajiv was lacking. 'Is the boy really up to the job?' was the theme of newspaper editorials and Delhi drawing room conversation alike.

One of the strongest pieces of evidence that he was not came from the frequency with which he reshuffled his cabinets – altogether nearly thirty reshuffles in five years, an average of one change every two months. Some were dictated by desertions of people like Arun Nehru and Mufti Mohammed Sayed, not to mention the effective expulsion of V. P. Singh, but others sometimes seemed to defy explanation. Each time he switched ministers, he was inevitably reducing the expertise which should have been building up. It can hardly have promoted continuity in foreign policy that five different ministers held the portfolio of External Affairs over five years, including Rajiv himself who held it for two stints of around a year each. One minister, Shiv Shankar, combined External Affairs with the Commerce portfolio.

The career of one of Rajiv's main troubleshooters, Arjun Singh, further illustrates the point. He came to Rajiv's attention as chief minister of Madhya Pradesh at the time of the Bhopal disaster. Rajiv subsequently made him governor of Punjab, where he was joint architect of the ill-fated Punjab accord. He was brought into cabinet as commerce minister, only to be transferred days later to supervise the intended reform of Congress as party vice president. Less than a year later, with the reforms still unimplemented, Rajiv brought Arjun Singh back to cabinet at the Communications Ministry. Subsequently he was reappointed chief minister of Madhya Pradesh, only to be forced to resign some months later after being implicated in a corruption scandal.

Arjun Singh's mobility may have been exceptional, but frequent reshuffles of ministers and chief ministers were not. Rajiv's excuses seemed rather lame: 'I cannot find good ministers.' On his tendency to drop previously trusted ministers, he explained: 'I went wrong in my assessment of their being able to cope with power.' To this extent Rajiv at least took the blame himself for appointing them in the first place. He can also claim to have warned them, having said, after the swearing-in of his first post-election cabinet, that he would be watching cabinet members' performance closely, and those found wanting would be replaced. The trouble was that, almost without exception, those he found wanting and dismissed had considerably more direct political experience than he did. Arguably his was the greater loss, especially when members of his A-team like V. P. Singh, Arun Nehru and Arun Singh left his service, though the two Aruns had never held cabinet rank. Many of his ministerial changes gave the impression he was putting a higher value on political loyalty than on ministerial ability.

Rajiv had as much difficulty with his non-ministerial aides, his 'inner coterie' as they became known. They were not only his closest advisers, his hand-picked men, but also controlled access to the prime minister, determining who could see him and who could not. Mrs Gandhi had one key adviser, R. K. Dhawan, her special assistant for twenty-two years. Rajiv had several advisers on whom he came to depend. They eroded the power of his ministers and, of course, they were not accountable to anyone for their advice, or for their mistakes, as the ministers were. Senior ministers resented the way these unelected officials came between them and the prime minister. The expansion of the staff in the prime minister's office mirrored Rajiv's growing suspicion of his ministers, whom he used to suspect of plotting against him.

Satish Sharma, Rajiv's former Indian Airlines pilot colleague to whom he gave the responsibility for looking after his parliamentary constituency of Amethi, had the reputation of not understanding politics. He became a liability for Rajiv when questions were asked about his allegedly extravagant life style. In an interview with a news magazine in late 1987, Rajiv found himself having to defend Satish Sharma from accusations that he had imported Italian marble and tiles for his swimming pool, which was in any case a costly acquisition for a former airline pilot. Rajiv's remark, suggesting that it was quite normal for Indian Airline pilots to build themselves swimming pools, is remembered much more than all that he had to say about the state of the economy in that interview. Incidentally, Satish Sharma was entrusted with another important task. It was his responsibility to remind Rajiv whenever his pilot's licence was about to expire, so he could catch up on his minimum annual flying hours, or have his routine medical check-up. Rajiv had no intention of allowing his flying licence to lapse just because he was, for the time being, otherwise engaged at being prime minister.

Another controversial aide and fellow 'Dosco' was Mani Shankar Aiyar, who saw himself as Rajiv's Bernard Ingham, his press spokesman and public relations adviser. He first joined Rajiv's staff as a speech writer on secondment from the foreign service. On the eve of the 1989 election, he resigned in order to devote himself full-time to the task of securing Rajiv's re-election and played a leading role in organising Rajiv's hectic election programme. Having failed in the re-election strategy, he stayed on with Rajiv in opposition, contributing articles to the press on the inevitability of Rajiv's return to office.

It may have been partly the fault of his aides that Rajiv began to acquire a reputation for inaccessibility and arrogance. He was criticised for keeping chief ministers waiting, and they in turn blamed the aides. It was probably not true, as some have suggested, that this behaviour showed Rajiv's contempt for politics and politicians. In any case, it was not only politicians who saw this supposedly arrogant side of Rajiv. Bureaucrats too experienced his short-temper and his tendency to insult or publicly humiliate officials he thought had not carried out his instructions. The public humiliation of the foreign secretary A.P. Venkateswaran enhanced this reputation for arrogance and imperiousness towards senior officials, of which there were already many examples. Rajiv had been known to describe an entire ministry as 'useless' for sending the confidential information for which he had asked in an unsealed envelope, and repeatedly blamed the bureaucracy in general for frustrating his economic reforms.

Even before Rajiv became prime minister there were two very public reprimands which are particularly remembered. As Congress general secretary, he severely rebuked the chief minister of Andhra Pradesh in 1982 for laying on an elaborate welcome ceremony at Hyderabad airport. The incident is also remembered as a demonstration of Rajiv's dislike of sycophancy. The following year, he publicly admonished the commissioner of Delhi police, in the presence of his subordinates. Rajiv had arrived to supervise a fire-fighting operation, and thought the police chief was not doing a good job. The fit of temper he displayed came from a man who, at the time, held no government office, only a party post, though he was the prime minister's son. Many other officials were to experience Rajiv's short-temper after he became prime minister, including one security official who was transferred from his post for telling the prime minister not to drive too fast because the security escort could not keep up!

Another area of criticism by midterm was Rajiv's fondness for taking New Year holidays in seemingly exotic locations. It was perhaps reasonable that someone who worked as hard as he did, and kept such long hours, deserved a break. But India is not a country where a holiday is regarded as a right. At the end of his first full year in office, Rajiv took a party which included his Italian in-laws and his film star friend, Amitabh Bachchan, to the tiger reserve at Ranthambhor in Rajasthan. The main criticism was that such a large security apparatus had to follow him. Two years later, he was to be similarly chastised for the high security costs of another excursion into Rajasthan when he decided, for the first time ever, to hold a cabinet meeting away from the capital.

The year after the Ranthambhor New Year party, Rajiv chartered a ship to take his family and friends to the Andaman Islands, which lie in the Bay of Bengal close to the Malay peninsula. At the end of 1987, a similar party met in the Lakshadweep Islands to the south-west of the Indian mainland. Whilst these elaborate wildlife-orientated holidays could be seen as exercises in national integration, for they gave Rajiv the opportunity to get to know the remotest parts of the country, the press preferred to harp on about the high costs involved, particularly after it became known that warships and submarines had been involved in maintaining a security cordon around the prime minister and his party. At the end of his fourth year, Rajiv took an altogether more modest holiday at Corbett Park, another wildlife reserve just a few hours' drive from Delhi.

Not all Rajiv's midterm problems were political in origin, or of his own making. Aside from the year's other problems, 1987 brought one of the most severe droughts this century across a large swathe of the country. Its main cause was the near total failure of the south-west monsoon, though Rajiv blamed widespread deforestation, especially in Rajasthan, for having contributed to the expansion of the western Indian desert, and thus to the rain failure. There had been no rain for three years in many parts of Gujarat and Haryana, whilst some areas of Rajasthan and Maharashtra were enduring their fourth year of drought. The seriousness of the 1987 drought was in its extent: it affected eleven states, or nearly a third of the 470 administrative districts into which India is divided. In population terms, a quarter of all Indians were affected. The shortfall in food grain production was around 23 million tonnes. Fortunately India maintains a foodgrain buffer stock, and there was enough in the stock to meet shortages. Other foodstuffs, like edible oils and pulses, had to be imported. Apart from the immediate effects on agriculture and rural life, the shortage of water affected the generation of electricity, which in turn slowed down industry.

Rajiv took personal charge of a massive relief effort, cancelling a planned visit to Europe at short notice. As well as distributing food and drinking water to areas that had neither, the government launched employment schemes to cope with the loss of work – and thus of income – in areas where crops had been destroyed. As a result of his government's relief programme, it was Rajiv's proud boast that nobody had died from starvation. The cost to the exchequer was high and most areas of government had to make savings to help pay for the distribution of food and water, extra food imports – including the replacement of buffer stocks – and employment schemes. Prices of basic foods increased even in non-affected areas. In weighing the successes and failures of Rajiv's government, the response to the drought was undoubtedly a major success.

There is a very poignant moment in Simi Garewal's video, *India's Rajiv*. Four commentators are asked what they think was the worst crisis Rajiv faced as prime minister. They are equally divided; two are quite sure it was the Bofors scandal and the other two are equally certain it was the dispute with president Zail Singh, which almost resulted in Rajiv's dismissal. Then Rajiv himself is asked the same question. He has no doubt at all that it was the drought, which is perhaps a more honest answer than it appears because the drought was a real crisis facing the nation whereas the other two were political crises facing Rajiv in particular.

On the political side, nothing better illustrates the quagmire into which Rajiv was sinking midway through his term than the fate of the two commissions of enquiry set up following the assassination of Mrs Gandhi. The Thakkar commission had been appointed within days to enquire into the circumstances of the killing and determine whether it could have been prevented. It was also charged with investigating whether anyone else, apart from the immediate assassins, had been involved. The one-man commission submitted its final report in February 1986, but its contents remained secret for a further three years. Then a newspaper published some of its findings and indicated that it would publish more if the government did not. The fact that the report had been concealed even from Parliament, as well as from former President Zail Singh, fuelled the suspicion that it implicated prominent people in an assassination conspiracy. Names being mentioned included those of President Zail Singh, and Mrs Gandhi's former special assistant, R. K. Dhawan.

By telling parliament one day that the report would not be published, and the next day that it would, Rajiv gave the impression he was only laying it before Parliament out of fear that more of its details would appear in the press if he did not. When it was published, it was greeted with accusations of 'eyewash'. Like the report of the Warren commission into the assassination of John Kennedy, it raised more questions than it answered. By failing to prove that Mrs Gandhi's assassination was a conspiracy, or that anyone other than Beant Singh and Satwant Singh were involved, the report inevitably raised new doubts about the conviction of Kehar Singh who, together with Satwant Singh – the surviving assassin – had been hanged in January 1989 for his role in the assassination.

Mr Justice Thakkar's report did implicate R. K. Dhawan, though on slender grounds. These included the fact that he had rearranged the timing of the television interview Mrs Gandhi was about to give when she was shot, and that he had countermanded security instructions that Sikhs be removed from her bodyguard after Operation Blue Star. This latter move was, according to Dhawan, at Mrs Gandhi's own insistence. To most people it was inconceivable that Mrs Gandhi's most trusted aide of twenty-two-years standing could have been involved in her assassination. No less absurd was the rumour that Sonia Gandhi was also involved.

However, by delaying the report's publication for so long, and keeping Dhawan out in the cold for more than four years, Rajiv had allowed the speculation as to Dhawan's involvement in the assassination to grow to totally unnecessary proportions. Had it really taken so long to clear his name? Rajiv had passed special legislation through Parliament in order to keep the Thakkar commission conclusions secret. Yet he did not explain why it had been necessary to suppress the report. After the report was published, Rajiv told Parliament that a special investigation team had cleared Dhawan of any involvement in the assassination. He had, by that time, reappointed him to the prime ministerial staff. R. K. Dhawan, while asking publicly who had encouraged Mr Justice Thakkar to point the 'finger of suspicion' at him, was generous enough to say that, in reappointing him, Rajiv was fulfilling a promise made at the time he had been dismissed. The truth was that Rajiv had second thoughts. After initially accepting advice that Dhawan be excluded from his new team, Rajiv found by early 1989 that he badly needed his expertise on party affairs. That hardly justified the long shadow cast over Dhawan's loyalty to Rajiv's mother.

R. K. Dhawan believes he was himself the victim of a political conspiracy.

After his recall, R. K. Dhawan became Rajiv's access man on party affairs, the man for aspiring Congress candidates, or those who wanted to become chief ministers, to see. He understood the workings of the Congress party much better than Rajiv. His reappointment was closely followed by the return of several chief ministers whom Rajiv had earlier dismissed. Rajiv's critics accused him of bringing back the 'power brokers' and party 'old guard' whom he had so roundly criticised at Congress's centenary meeting.

Despite the report's failure to establish a conspiracy or produce conspirators, Rajiv continued to insist there was a conspiracy whose objective, he said, was 'clearly a Khalistan'. He maintained that the murder of his mother had been 'not only the murder of an individual' but was an attempt 'to sabotage our integrity ... wreck our secularism ... subvert our self-reliance ... and destroy our democracy'. The conspirators, he told Parliament, were still at large. Three days after the Thakkar commission report was published, and almost five years after the event, charges of involvement in the assassination were brought against Simranjit Singh Mann, the former policeman who had resigned after Operation Blue Star, and four others. The dropping of the charges eight months later, when Mann was elected to Parliament from a Punjab constituency with a massive majority, gave rise to serious doubts about the soundness of the charges. This was the final nail in the coffin of the Thakkar commission's conspiracy theory, and a further blow to the credibility of Rajiv, who had for so long endorsed the theory.

The other main enquiry arising out of Mrs Gandhi's assassination was handled in a similarly clumsy fashion. It was six months before Rajiv bowed to pressure and appointed a commission to investigate allegations that the riots in Delhi following the assassination had been organised. He did so as part of a package of measures aimed at solving the Punjab problem, rather than on its own merits. Supreme Court Judge Raganath Mishra was appointed to carry out the enquiry. Within four weeks of the killings, the report by civil liberty groups, 'Who Are The Guilty?' had concluded the riots were organised, and named 227 people, including police and Congress Party workers, whom it said were implicated. When the Mishra commission report was published two years later, it implicated 19 Congress workers, though found no evidence against the most senior ones, including a cabinet minister, who had been mentioned in the report by the civil liberty groups. Yet progress towards indicting anyone for the post-assassination killings was notoriously slow. By the time Rajiv stepped down, one murder case, out of an estimated 3870 in Delhi, had been cleared up. In that one case, six people had been sentenced to life imprisonment. Defendants in ten other cases had been acquitted. This was not a record that brought any comfort or reassurance to those Sikhs who lost breadwinners or other family members, or indeed to the Sikh community at large.

The handling of the electronic media, in particular television, was another issue that diminished the credibility of Rajiv's government. Under the control of Bhaskar Ghosh, the Indian state television service, Doordarshan, had acquired something it never had before: a degree of independence from government. According to regulars, Doordarshan was, for a brief period, really watchable, especially the news bulletins. Rajiv had himself helped the process by encouraging his ministers to appear on a television programme in which they were confronted by members of the public who had grievances or who wanted to criticise some of their actions. The programme, *Janvani*, commanded huge audiences. It was said that Rajiv himself was a regular viewer: perhaps that was what he meant when he said he would be 'watching cabinet ministers' performances closely'!

Then suddenly this period of liberal television ended, and ministers as a whole became less accessible to the media. It was as if Rajiv's own version of *glasnost* had come to an end. Bhaskar Ghosh was transferred to become the senior bureaucrat in charge of culture at the Broadcasting and Information Ministry, and a new minister was put in charge of broadcasting. Rajiv had been persuaded to act after several of his ministers thumped the table at a cabinet meeting, complaining that Doordarshan had not been covering their every activity. Even the president was troubled that he has not getting much coverage on television. The change of leadership had the desired effect. Doordarshan, once again under close supervision from the ministry, devoted so much space to the affairs of the government, and the prime minister in particular, that it was dubbed 'Rajivdarshan'. By contrast, the activities of Opposition leaders, and particularly of V. P. Singh, who was increasingly being seen as the main alternative prime minister, received hardly any television coverage at all. The new Broadcasting minister, K. K. Tewari, unashamedly admitted that he considered it to be the role of Doordarshan to promote the government.

Part of Rajiv's problem in arresting the slipping credibility of his government was that so many problems arrived simultaneously, mostly during 1987. The departure of V. P. Singh coincided with the very real threat that President Zail Singh might try to dismiss Rajiv. By the time that crisis had passed, he was faced with the major challenge of severe drought. The greatest problem afflicting Rajiv also dated from this midpoint in his premiership; the taint of corruption. However much he denied receiving commission payments from Bofors, or from any other deal, many people believed he was implicated. The newspapers had shown convincingly that someone had received commission payments. Rajiv, as many people's prime suspect, was expected to prove his innocence, even though nobody had been able to establish his guilt. On corruption in general, Rajiv had to admit that he had 'found it harder to clean up corruption than when you are on the other side, talking about it rather than having to do it'. His failure to make inroads in checking the ubiquitous corruption of Indian daily life did as much harm to his 'Mr Clean' image as did the specific charges laid against him.

Of these charges – that he had benefited from commission paid on the Bofors howitzer and HDW submarine deals – there is a theory that Rajiv was the victim of a system that had been put in place many years earlier. It is suggested that, around the time of Mrs Gandhi's return to power, her son and political aide, Sanjay, had decided to institute a system whereby Congress received a set commission on all sums paid on defence and other deals. Sanjay was apparently tired of the practice of calling on Indian industrialists to make their regular contributions to party funds.

By the time Rajiv came to office, the system may have been well established. Yet it seems that the commission paid on the HDW submarine purchase never reached its intended recipients. Sanjay had been involved in the negotiations, but died before the deal was concluded. If such a system of routine commission payments was in operation, then commissions were probably paid on the purchase of the Mirage 2000 and Harrier jump-jet fighters, as well as non-military aircraft like the Westland G-30 helicopters and Airbus Industries A-320, and probably on many other deals as well. It remains unclear to what extent private, Indian-owned industrial houses were involved, whether as conduits or for their own benefit as well.

If the secret of the commission payments was indeed that they went to finance the Congress Party, then Rajiv may have been the largely innocent victim of a financial scandal for which his brother, and possibly his mother, were ultimately responsible. Rajiv himself is adamant that this was not the case, at least as far as Bofors was concerned, just as he is adamant that no members of his family received commission payments. He says: 'I am absolutely sure that our party got nothing from Bofors. I can say that categorically. I am not protecting anybody.' But he agreed, during his November 1988 interview with *Sunday* magazine, 'that parties have to run, and parties run on donations. They run on donations from individuals and they run on donations from companies. That is the democratic system as it functions in every part of the world.'

Accepting party donations from companies is not illegal in India. But the system of political donations does underline the difficulty of trying to do what Rajiv's government was initially trying to do – crack down on illegalities and irregularities in company affairs. For, if a company which had given funds to the ruling party came under suspicion of having evaded taxes, or having stashed money abroad in an illegal account, the government's scope for punishing the illegality would be diminished, unless it was also prepared to reveal the political contribution. Companies in India, as elsewhere, prefer to keep their political donations secret, just as politicians prefer to keep quiet about who may be helping finance their re-election campaigns.

Rajiv found himself presiding over a system that encouraged corruption. It is widely recognised that one of the main attractions of political life in India is the power of patronage that it bestows. The system was not kind to Rajiv, who was either unwilling or unable to play according to the rules. If he had a genuine desire to clean up politics, it came undone after the Bofors scandal broke and he was himself accused of violating the standards that he purported to follow. As Rajiv himself puts it: 'From that time onwards we've had a very rough ride.'

CHAPTER TWELVE

Hindu India

Rajiv is the son of a Hindu mother and a Parsi father. When Feroze Gandhi died, he was at his own wish, cremated according to Hindu rites, rather than being offered to the vultures according to Parsi practice. Thus, in the eyes of the common man, Feroze Gandhi died a Hindu.[1] It was Rajiv who lit the pyre at his father's cremation, as he did twenty years later at the cremation of his brother, Sanjay. Neither Rajiv or Sanjay had been brought up to follow any particular faith. Sanjay had married a Sikh at a ceremony which, for convenience, was held at the home of a Muslim family friend. Rajiv had married a Roman Catholic in a strictly non-denominational ceremony presided over by a magistrate.

It may have been Rajiv's misfortune to have inherited command of India at a time when the notion of secularism was increasingly under siege – from Hindus as much as from Sikhs and Muslims. However, his critics say he did not do enough to reassert secularism, and even tried to harness religion for his own political purpose. India's constitution enshrines secularism as a pillar of the nation, notwithstanding the fact that the vast majority of Indians – some eighty-two per cent – are Hindus, or that Hinduism is 'the backbone, the heart and the soul of Indian civilisation'.[2] Followers of India's other religions – Islam, Christianity, Sikhism, Buddhism, Jainism and Zoroastrianism are the main ones – are all guaranteed 'equal protection of the laws' under the constitution.

Both Rajiv and Sanjay, like their mother before them, had been imbued with the secularism of their grandfather. Nehru's secularism meant that none of India's many faiths had a pre-eminent position;

---

[1] *Nehru: the Making of India*, Akbar.
[2] According to Tully and Masani in *From Raj to Rajiv*.

there was no state religion, like Islam in Pakistan for example. It was similar to the Western belief in keeping Church and State broadly separate from one another. For Nehru personally, secularism meant being neutral; not favouring one religious community at the expense of another. The communal violence of partition had made Nehru and all of his generation acutely conscious of what could happen when followers of one religion set upon those of another. Twenty years before partition, he had declined to mediate in a Hindu–Muslim dispute saying: 'Who would I represent? The Hindus are not going to accept me, and why should the Muslims do so?'[1] In that way Nehru had come to stand above religion. He had been born into the Hindu priestly Brahmin caste, but privately admitted to being agnostic, if not actually an atheist. Nehru's initial opposition to Indira's inter-religious marriage was because he felt Feroze was not of the same class as the Nehrus and lacked wealth, rather than because of his Zoroastrian faith.

Christian educationalists had played as great a role as Hindu ones in Indira's upbringing. Nehru had made it his duty to teach her about all religions. The fact that she chose a marriage partner from another faith perhaps reveals that religion was not important to either her or Feroze. In office, Indira continued the Congress tradition as protector of the minorities as well as the outcast Hindus, the Harijans. Congress had come to regard both the Muslims, the largest religious minority, and the Harijans, as important sources of electoral support. However, many Muslims believe Indira effectively departed from the secular path during the Emergency, between 1975 and 1977, and that in order to win re-election in 1980, she openly pandered to Hindu nationalism. In later life, Indira became more religious, and on several occasions worshipped at Hindu temples. She consulted astrologers before taking important decisions, such as announcing election dates or swearing in new governments. She also made several visits to seek the blessings of an 'ageless' Hindu sage, Devraha Baba, who lived on a wooden platform raised on stilts six feet above the ground – to avoid human vibrations, it is said – on the banks of the river Jumna at Vrindaban, to the south of Delhi. Muslims were not the only minority who believed Indira showed a less secular and more Hindu face during her second term as prime minister. It was one of the grievances of Sikhs that

[1] Quoted in *Nehru: the Making of India*, Akbar.

her government had become a Hindu government, especially after Operation Blue Star, which many Sikhs considered to be an attack on their faith.

Rajiv says he is not an agnostic and believes in religion, but not in any particular one. Sonia, though born a Roman Catholic, is not religious. According to Rajiv, she had not been to church 'since long before I met her'. Rajiv also professes to be as committed to the notion of a secular India as his mother and grandfather had been. He reconciled these two beliefs during a September 1988 visit to Punjab: 'Religion is important in everyday life, but it is also necessary that religion should be kept out of politics. The two should not be mixed. This is our secularism.' However, there was some surprise when this young technocrat, who had shown no sign at all of being superstitious or being guided by faith, followed the example of several fellow Congress politicians in visiting Devraha Baba on the eve of the 1989 elections. Earlier Rajiv and Sonia had made offerings at a Hindu temple at Ambaji in Gujarat where, ten years earlier, his mother had prayed before beginning her successful campaign for re-election. After visiting the temple, Rajiv told a rally that his mother had got her strength from the Ambaji temple before going on to win the elections. Clearly he hoped to do likewise. Both devotional visits were criticised since they came at a time when communal sentiments of Hindus and Muslims had been aroused by a dispute between the two communities over a shrine at Ayodhya to which both religions laid claim. That dispute was to flare into a key election issue.

Rajiv fought and won the 1984 election on an anti-Sikh tide. Subsequently he tried to regain the confidence of Sikhs, though without much success. A year into his premiership, Rajiv found himself having to arbitrate on a religious issue that was not between Hindus and Sikhs or between Muslims and Hindus, but between Muslims and Muslims. The Supreme Court had upheld the ruling of a lower court granting maintenance of Rs 500 a month (about £20) to a seventy-three-year-old woman, Mrs Shah Bano, who had been divorced by her husband according to Muslim, or *shariat,* law. Orthodox Muslims were outraged because, they said, Muslim personal law should have been applied rather than the Criminal Procedure Code under which the award was granted. They argued that Muslim law provides for a lump sum to be paid on divorce, but nothing thereafter. Muslims believe that a divorced woman should be looked after by her blood relatives, who can expect to inherit her property, or else by a Muslim charitable trust. They believe – and Muslim law reflects this belief – that a husband's responsibility for his wife ends on divorce, and that it would in any case be demeaning for a wife to continue to accept money from a husband who has discarded her in this way. (The right to divorce under the *shariat* is heavily in the husband's favour.) What outraged orthodox Muslims more than the judgement itself were comments made by the five Hindu judges hearing the case which suggested that Islamic law does not give women a fair deal.

The case provoked controversy beyond the Muslim community too. There was resentment amongst Hindus that Muslims were not bound by the same civil laws to which they were subject, and were bound instead by the *shariat,* which was often at variance with statute law. Nehru had taken a conscious decision not to draw Muslim personal law into line with statute law on such matters as monogamy, divorce and inheritance. He felt he was protecting this minority community in a secular society, but others have seen it as a failure to provide Muslim women with the 'equality before the law' promised in the constitution. The Shah Bano case reopened a controversy about the failure of successive governments to introduce a common civil code, as the authors of the Indian constitution had intended they should. It also focused attention on the uneasy relationship between God-given law, which can be interpreted but not changed, and statute law, which is capable of being adjusted to suit the times.

Orthodox Muslim opinion maintained that no civil jurisdiction was entitled to interfere in the God-given law which Muslims follow in family matters, and that the intervention of the courts – which had been at Mrs Shah Bano's instigation – had violated the basic canon of the *shariat* that it is for Muslim judges, or *ulemas,* to interpret and apply the law in such matters. Muslim law itself lacks an authoritative, codified version – and indeed there are differences between the four main branches of Islam – rendering it open to differences of interpretation, which added to the confusion as to precisely what the *shariat* did say on the subject and who was entitled to interpret it. Progressive Muslims argued that the Supreme Court judges had correctly interpreted the *shariat,* which specifically lays down that 'fair provision' should be made for the divorced. According to them, the court had merely determined what constituted fair provision in this case. They hailed the court's decision as a progressive application of the law in keeping with the times.

Orthodox Muslims were in no doubt that the judgement had transgressed the limits of the legitimate concerns of the state. They demonstrated in the streets against the Supreme Court judgement and petitioned the government to reverse it. The controversy also aired itself within government where two of Rajiv's Muslim ministers took opposing sides. Minister of state for power, Arif Mohammed Khan, strongly backed the Supreme Court, whilst the minister of state for the environment Ziaur Rehman Ansari was one of those who petitioned Rajiv to introduce legislation to reverse the effect of the Supreme Court ruling, rather than allow the court to get away with what he considered to be interference in the *shariat*.

What may have weighed strongly with the prime minister in deciding how to react to the judgement were indications that Congress had lost the so-called 'Muslim vote' in a number of by-elections around the country following the Supreme Court ruling. At any rate, as a result of consultations with prominent Muslims, he decided to reverse the judgement by introducing the Muslim Women (Protection of Rights on Divorce) bill. Its effect was to exclude Muslim women from the provisions of section 125 of the Criminal Procedure Code under which the maintenance award in the Shah Bano case had been made. Minister of state Arif Mohammed Khan promptly resigned from his government post in protest at what he considered to be the appeasement of fundamentalist Muslim opinion. He was later to leave the Congress Party and join the Janata Dal.

Muslim fundamentalists were placated by the legislation, though they considered the episode had represented a serious threat to their religion. They were particularly concerned at the renewed demands for the drawing up of a uniform civil code for Indians of all faiths, since they believed that such a code would undermine or supersede the *shariat*. Indian Muslims are notoriously paranoid about anything which might be construed as an attack on their faith. The Shah Bano judgement had come soon after the signing of the Assam accord, another move which they saw as anti-Muslim because it discriminated against Muslim immigrants from Bangladesh. However, Hindus were resentful at the reversal of the Supreme Court judgement and the exclusion of Muslims from another provision of the Criminal Procedure Code. The belief that the government was pandering to Muslim orthodoxy doubtless played its own part in the revival of the fortunes of the Hindu Bharatiya Janata Party, for whom it is an article of faith that concessions to minority communities be opposed at all cost. Aside from the Hindu sentiments that the legislation aroused, there were many who considered the worst thing about the act was that it was anti-secular.

Critics accused Rajiv of introducing the bill as a direct appeal to the Muslim vote, on which Congress had traditionally counted. Electoral wisdom has it that Muslims tend to vote *en bloc,* and have traditionally voted for Congress. Research has indicated that collectively Muslims can have an important impact on the result in at least 100 *Lok Sabha* constituencies. Four years later, after Rajiv had been voted out of office, one of his former ministers, Vasant Sathe, identified the introduction of the Muslim Women's bill as 'the turning point in Rajiv's fortunes'. Speaking in an interview with the *Sunday Observer,* Vasant Sathe said that Rajiv's 'gut reaction' had been to abide by the Supreme Court judgement, but that veteran Congress leaders, including many Muslims, had advised Rajiv to reverse the judgement.[1] The pity of the matter was that Rajiv originally thought he was taking a secular course of action. He was later to admit privately that he had changed his mind after realising what a sensitive subject personal law was to Muslims: 'In a secular society,' he reasoned, 'it was best not to trample on the religious convictions of a minority'. Vasant Sathe, however, believes that the reversal of the judgement lost Rajiv's government credibility with both Hindus and Muslims: 'We ourselves are responsible for giving credence to this communal feeling because, in the name of secularism, we ourselves were not too secular. In the name of pragmatism, the government had succumbed to fundamentalists.'[2]

In the same month that the Muslim Women's bill was introduced into Parliament – February 1986 – another, unrelated, judgement was made which was to have even more far-reaching implications for India's Muslims, and for Rajiv's government. In response to a Hindu petitioner, a district judge at Faizabad in eastern Uttar Pradesh had

---

[1] *Sunday Observer,* Delhi edition, 4 March 1990. Sathe mentions Mohammed Kidwai, Z. R. Ansari, Khurshed Alam Khan, Mehmooda Begum, Buta Singh, M. L. Fotedar and Arun Nehru as those who had advised Rajiv to reverse the judgement.

[2] There is an irony in that two cases decided before the Kerala High Court in 1988 have demonstrated that, far from reducing the right of Muslim divorcees to claim maintenance before the courts, the Muslim Women's Act has in fact strengthened their rights to do so.

authorised the unlocking of a mosque at the town of Ayodhya. Hindus say the mosque was built at a place which they believe to be the birthplace of their god, Ram. The effect of the judgement was that Hindus were permitted to worship at the shrine, which also contained Hindu idols, but that Muslims could not, as the result of a previous court ruling which had ordered the mosque to be locked.

The dispute has a long pedigree dating back to 1528 when, it is claimed by Hindus, the Mughal Emperor Babar halted in the town and decided to build a mosque there. This he did, so the legend has it, by demolishing a Hindu temple which stood on the very spot of Ram's birthplace. This version is contested by Muslims who say there is no evidence that there had been a Hindu temple on the site before Babar built his mosque. It would have been unlikely, they say, since Babar was known to be accommodating towards Hindus and visited many of their temples.

The Babri mosque stood undisturbed and in use as a place of worship until 23 December 1949, when two Hindu idols suddenly appeared inside the mosque. According to Hindu fundamentalists, they were placed there by Ram himself, though the district magistrate of the time reported that around fifty Hindus had entered the mosque at night, breaking the lock on the compound gate, and placed the idols there. It was the culmination of a nine-day recital of Hindu scriptures outside the compound. The district magistrate ordered that the shrine be locked to prevent a breach of the peace, but sixteen months later Hindus were granted the right to worship outside it whilst the seventy or so Muslim families of Ayodhya were not. Muslims were reported to have felt terrorised by the incident, with many moving away from Ayodhya as a result. This was just two years after the partition of the subcontinent, which had led to the largest mass slaughter of Hindus by Muslims and Muslims by Hindus ever seen there.

The granting of the petition in February 1986 to have the shrine reopened brought this long-standing dispute into the open, and subsequently into the political arena. The Hindus' case rested on the twin assertions (neither of which were proven) that the mosque occupied the birthplace of Ram, and that a Hindu temple had been demolished to make way for it. The Muslim case rested on the antiquity of the mosque in which they had worshipped more or less undisturbed for 400 years. Indeed, until 1949, Muslims and Hindus had worshipped side by side, the latter using a small shrine outside the mosque. The

petition for Hindus to gain admission to the mosque itself had been
backed by the Hindu fundamentalist organisation, the Vishwa Hindu
Parishad. It later won the support of the Bharatiya Janata Party, or
BJP, one of the main Opposition parties. In response to this fresh attack
on their religion, Muslims formed the Babri Mesjid Action Committee.
On 30 March 1987, an estimated 300000 attended a rally in New Delhi
in pursuit of their objective to recover control of the mosque. It was
the largest gathering of Muslims since Independence and signalled a
new politicisation of the community. A prominent Hindu politician,
Subramaniam Swamy, called the Muslims' programme to regain
control of the mosque 'a declaration of war against Hindus'.

Rajiv became involved in the Ayodhya saga at an early stage. According to his former Congress colleague, Arun Nehru, who later joined
the Janata Dal, a decision had been taken by the Congress high
command in early 1986 to 'play the Hindu card' in the same way that
the Muslim Women's bill had been an attempt to 'play the Muslim
card'. According to Arun Nehru, Ayodhya 'was supposed to be a
package deal ... a tit for tat for the Muslim Women's bill'. In an
interview in August 1989 with a Delhi Urdu newspaper, *Akhbar-e-
nau*,[1] Nehru hints that Rajiv played a key role in carrying out the
Hindu side of the package deal by such actions as arranging that
pictures of Hindus worshipping at the newly unlocked shrine be shown
on television. Arun Nehru, whose interest in showing his erstwhile
colleague in a bad light at this pre-election juncture must be allowed
for, says of this 'Hindu card' strategy: 'I knew it was a dangerous thing
to do and I did not agree.'

The Ayodhya dispute polarised India's two largest religious communities as never before, and revived a debate about the nature of
Nehru's secularism. Did it just mean keeping one's own faith out of
politics, or did it – as many Hindus argued – mean that minority
communities should acknowledge that India is a Hindu nation, and
that as minorities they should not seek special privileges or protection?
Hindu fundamentalists believe in a Hindu *rashtra,* or nation, with
Muslims, Sikhs and other minorities accepting that they share a
common heritage with Hindus, of which the god Ram forms a part.
This argument does not reassure Muslims, who have too often felt

---

[1] Quoted in the article 'The Babri Mesjid-Ram Janmabhoomi Question' by A. G. Noorani in
Economic and Political Weekly, 4–11 November 1989.

threatened by the assertion of Hindu nationalism.

Since early in Rajiv's premiership, Indian television had been winning mass audiences for its Sunday morning dramatisation of the *Ramayan*, the great Hindu epic in which the story of Ram is enacted. The appeal of the series, which was in due course followed by the other great Hindu epic, the *Mahabharata*, cut across community barriers. It was thoroughly good television which attracted some of the largest audiences ever. But in some people's minds, the showing of the two series heightened a sense of Hindu nationalism and encouraged a reassertion of Hindu beliefs that non-Hindus found worrying. Nor was the Congress Party above exploiting the popularity of the series for its own ends. The actor who played the part of Ram campaigned for Congress against V.P. Singh in the 1988 Allahabad by-election. However, some members of the party were conscious of the dangers of identifying too closely with the Hindu epics. For example, Rajiv's campaign manager in his Amethi constituency, Satish Sharma, believes the televising of the *Ramayan* and *Mahabharata* was the major factor behind a leap in support for the Hindu-based BJP at the 1989 election.

The escalation of the Ayodhya shrine dispute in early 1987 coincided with one of the most severe outbreaks of Hindu–Muslim violence since partition. The town of Meerut to the north of Delhi, remembered as the place where the Indian mutiny (or first war of independence) broke out in 1857, lies at the opposite end of the state of Uttar Pradesh from Ayodhya. Uttar Pradesh is home to the majority of India's 100 million Muslims. In Meerut, poor Muslims provide the work force in Hindu-owned textile mills. As is so often the case, the incident was sparked by an insignificant land dispute. Over the course of a few days, a frenzy of communal violence had led to the deaths of dozens of people. Shops and petrol pumps were burnt, and the violence had spread to neighbouring areas, including the old city of Delhi. Uttar Pradesh's Provincial Armed Constabulary, or PAC, were sent in, but this only exacerbated things as the PAC themselves took on the task of massacring Muslims. In one particularly gruesome incident, at least fifty Muslims were butchered in the Meerut suburb of Maliana. Two young Muslims survived to tell how the PAC had set about systematically killing Muslims and disposing of their bodies in a nearby canal. The Uttar Pradesh chief minister later defended the PAC, though he did promise to restructure the force and improve its training programme 'so that the policemen acquire a secular outlook', a tacit admission that they did not at the time have such an outlook.

By the time order was restored in Meerut, at least 300 people, the majority of them Muslims, were dead. Rajiv visited the city to be greeted by cries of 'PAC Zindabad', or 'Long live the PAC', showing how this force had become the heroes of the Hindus. There was strong resistance to suggestions that the force be withdrawn. M. J. Akbar, one of India's best known Muslims, a former newspaper editor and now a Congress MP, wrote: 'It is when the so-called guardians turn into communal armies that order begins to crumble. To allow guilty police to escape is to condone a police state.'[1] Yet many guilty police-men did escape justice. The failure to punish provoked the same sense of outrage amongst Muslims that Sikhs had felt after the 1984 Delhi killings. In both cases, the bringing to justice of those with blood on their hands would have done more than anything else – such as rhetorical assurances that 'Sikhs and Muslims are Indians too' – to restore the trust of the minorities that they do enjoy the 'equal pro-tection of the laws' for which the constitution provides.

In such a frenzied atmosphere as that at Meerut, Indian Muslims are often accused of being Pakistani fifth columnists, which somehow is taken to justify the assault on them. Similarly, after the assassination of Mrs Gandhi, all Sikhs were instantly considered to be Khalistanis by those bent on exacting their revenge by teaching the Sikhs a lesson. As in Delhi in early November 1984, the authorities in Meerut took an inordinately long time to bring the situation under control. It was many days before the full extent of the massacre became apparent as bodies were recovered as they floated down the canal. Meerut was not the first serious outbreak of Hindu–Muslim violence after Rajiv became prime minister, but it seemed to demonstrate how the dispute between the communities over the Ayodhya shrine had caused a polarisation in politics along communal lines. There was no doubt that the position of Muslims had become an issue in Uttar Pradesh and that Hindus were starting to feel threatened by this minority community. Com-munalism, the antithesis of secularism that Indians fear, had become a real threat.

Rajiv should have been working hard to uphold his government's commitment to secularism; and indeed, in speeches, he did attack communalism. When addressing the National Convention Against

[1] M. J. Akbar's collection of reports published as *Riot after Riot*, p. 154.

Communal and Divisive Forces in October 1988 he said: 'The battle against communalism is not a battle that can be fought strictly and only through constitutional, legal, policy or administrative means ... [it] has to be fought primarily in the minds of the people.' Communalism, he suggested, took hold where one relatively well established group suddenly finds that another group which was much weaker and more economically depressed is surging ahead. He said the simplest solution for the politician was 'to grab at the communal straw'. He warned against allowing any section of society to feel insecure or to feel that they were not getting their rights because, he said, in such circumstances 'tensions build up. If we answer those tensions with police action, it doesn't relieve the tension, it only increases the tension.' He went on to advocate a 'judicious mix' of just, unbiased police action together with 'the human touch with the softness which makes those who are feeling disenchanted with whatever system they are facing accept the system and come into the mainstream'.

Unfortunately, the evidence is that Rajiv's own government encouraged communalist or other sectarian sentiments for political advantage, by exploiting the disaffection of both religious and ethnic minorities. Claims that Congress had encouraged the Bodos of Assam or the Gorkhas of West Bengal in a deliberate attempt to make difficulties for the non-Congress governments of those states may not be fully proven, though the suspicion is strong. The evidence that Rajiv's mother and brother were involved in promoting Sikh separatism in Punjab is much stronger, though it cannot be said with any certainty that Rajiv himself was involved. Yet his failure to implement the accord that he had authored to solve the Punjab problem reeks of political self-interest and an anxiety not to alienate Hindus.

The same conclusion must be reached from the shocking failure to bring to justice those responsible for the anti-Sikh communalism in 1984, on which matter Rajiv stands accused of the additional charge that members of his own party were involved in the killings. Had justice been done, a large part of the Sikh sense of alienation would have been removed, and Rajiv would have enhanced his claim to be a secular, rather than a Hindu, ruler. The main charges against Rajiv of 'playing the Hindu card', as well as some of the worst communal incidents of his premiership, were to come during the run up to the 1989 elections, when the issues of communalism and secularism really came to the fore.

CHAPTER THIRTEEN

Elections

On 17 October it was announced that the 1989 elections would take place on 22, 24 and 26 November. Four days earlier, constitutional amendments designed to give effect to Rajiv's much-vaunted programme of 'power to the people' were defeated in the upper house. The Panchayati Raj and Nagarpalika bills failed by just three votes to win the requisite two-thirds majority in this latest parliamentary challenge to Rajiv. Needless to say, he had no trouble getting the legislation through the lower house; Congress's massive majority combined with the fact that almost all opposition MPs had resigned in August, after the Comptroller and Auditor General's report had criticised the Bofors howitzer contract, ensured the bills an easy passage.

Rajiv's decision to call the election seven weeks before he had to – most observers were expecting the poll in early January – was based on a number of factors. There was undoubtedly concern amongst his advisers that there would be more embarrassing disclosures in the Bofors affair. Five days before the polls were announced, the associate editor of the *Hindu* newspaper had accused the government of bringing economic pressure to bear on his paper in an effort to prevent further disclosures. Another fear was that prices would rise sharply over the next few weeks – despite a favourable monsoon, which was expected to result in a record grain crop, prices of some other staples had rocketed. The price of sugar in particular had shot up. After a poor crop, the government had been slow to arrange for supplies to be imported to meet the shortfall. By the time the election was called, sugar (one of the most widely used foodstuffs in India) was fetching Rs 12 a kilogram, double its price when Rajiv came to power five years earlier.

Rajiv also had worries about a resurgence of communalism with the threat by militant Hindus to march to the disputed shrine at Ayodhya to build a temple on the site of the Babri mosque. The way in which religious passions had been aroused was highlighted when severe communal rioting broke out at Bhagalpur in eastern Bihar within days of the announcement of the elections. Many hundred Muslims died in more than two weeks of communal blood-letting. Though not directly connected, there was a feeling that the politicisation of the Ayodhya issue and resulting communal polarisation had played their part in unleashing communal forces at Bhagalpur.

However, it was Congress's assessment of the extent to which Opposition parties could maintain their fragile unity that was the major factor in the decision to go for early polls. The Panchayati Raj and Nagarpalika bills had been narrowly defeated in the upper house by a coalition of Opposition interests which, beside the middle-of-the-road National Front alliance – dominated by the Janata Dal – included the Communists and the Hindu nationalist Bharatiya Janata Party, or BJP. Despite their shared objective of ousting Congress from power, it was becoming abundantly clear that the Communists and the BJP would not co-operate in an election. Furthermore, the Communists were saying that if the Janata Dal formed an electoral alliance with the BJP they would not support it. Since the Opposition's hopes of throwing Congress out rested on their degree of unity – the extent to which they did not contest against each other at the hustings but fielded common candidates – this represented the best hope Congress had of retaining power.

Indeed, differences between the parties which comprised the Opposition were not the only weakness on which Congress hoped to play. Bickering was continuing within the National Front itself, especially within the electorally important state of Uttar Pradesh, over who should hand out the election 'tickets'. The announcement that elections to state assemblies would take place at the same time as the *Lok Sabha* polls in five states, including Uttar Pradesh, for the first time since 1967, was further evidence of an attempt by Congress to catch the Opposition off their guard. It hoped, with good reason, that the simultaneous polls would bring the National Front leadership bickering to the fore, and would test the state level organisation of the newly formed alliance against the Congress Party organisation.

In fact, by the time nominations had closed and the time for withdrawal of nominations had passed, the Opposition parties had achieved a high degree of unity. This was mainly the result of agreements between the two dominant Opposition forces, the Janata Dal-led National Front and the BJP, not to contest against each other in around eighty-five per cent of the seats where the two would otherwise have fielded candidates. The National Front also reached a smaller number of seat-sharing agreements with one or other of the Communist parties.

Before the campaign commenced, Congress suffered another setback. Defence minister K. C. Pant learned on the final day for filing nominations that he was not being allowed to contest from the Nainital constituency in Uttar Pradesh that he regarded as his family seat. He declined two other constituencies offered him and declared he would not contest the election. At a press conference, he complained that the party apparatus had fallen victim to 'state bossism', a return to the days when party leaders in the state rather than in Delhi handed out electoral 'tickets'. He also complained of the role of 'inexperienced and unelected coteries' whom he accused of interfering in political decision making. Mr Pant was criticising, and in a very public manner, the small group of political aides on whom Rajiv depended, people like R. K. Dhawan, Mani Shankar Aiyar and Satish Sharma, who had come to play a key role in political decision-making. This criticism from one of Rajiv's longest-serving ministers, who had been moved from the Steel and Mines Ministry to Defence when V. P. Singh was forced to resign, was the most public indication that morale in the Congress Party was low. Another senior minister admitted off the record that Rajiv was 'a negative factor' in the Congress campaign, adding: 'We should have got rid of him, but it's too late now.'

By the time the campaign opened on 5 November, observers who had been predicting a narrow Congress victory – perhaps the largest party in Parliament without necessarily gaining an overall majority, they said – were giving the two sides even chances of victory. Everything would depend on the campaign itself. What was evident from the beginning was that there was no 'electoral wave', like the sympathy wave that had swept Rajiv to power five years earlier, shortly after his mother's assassination, or the anti-emergency wave that had swept his mother out of power twelve years earlier. There were few national issues, though the sharp rises in prices was the main one. The Opposition tried hard to make Bofors and corruption in public life an electoral issue, with pictures of the Bofors gun used as part of their election advertising. The single word 'Boforsgate' in Hindi greeted visitors to V. P. Singh's Fatehpur constituency in Uttar Pradesh, proclaimed from a banner straddling the road near the railway station.

To an extent the bid to make corruption a key election issue succeeded. Much of V. P. Singh's own following were derived from his campaign against corruption and a belief that he really would try to clean up public life, in the way that he had started to as Rajiv's finance minister. His campaign against black money, which he described at election meetings as 'robbing the poor', earned him much respect, rather as Rajiv's father, Feroze, had won widespread support and respect for his own parliamentary drive against corruption in the 1950s.

This was also the election in which the Nehruvian concept of secularism was on trial. The BJP, in particular, made it a central part of its campaign, asking 'Why should we not be proud of our Hindu heritage and why should we pander to Muslims and other minorities?' Anyone who doubts the effectiveness of this argument has only to look at how the BJP, in alliance with another Hindu fundamentalist party, the Shiv Sena, increased its parliamentary seats at this elections from two to eighty-eight. At any rate, Congress seem to have lost the Muslim vote from an early stage; probably due to the feeling that the party was backing the fundamentalist Hindu line over Ayodhya. However, the failure of the Congress government to protect Muslims from being killed at Bhagalpur, whilst the election campaign was underway, was also a factor in bringing about the Muslim alienation from Congress.

It was at the insistence of the Uttar Pradesh chief minister, N. D. Tiwari, that Rajiv went to seek the blessing of the Hindu holy man, Devraha Baba, three days before the foundation stone of the Hindu temple was to be laid at Ayodhya. Rajiv says Devraha Baba 'sent me a message asking me to come to see him, indicating that he had convinced the various groups not to precipitate the Ayodhya issue'. He says he called on the holy man in an effort to defuse the Ayodhya dispute, and prevent it leading to violence.

Devraha Baba, who died in June 1990, used to speak of India being a home for followers of all religions, but he was undeniably a Hindu holy man, living as he did on the banks of the river Jumna, close to the birthplace of another Hindu god, Krishna. He would not reveal what passed between him and Rajiv at their hastily arranged meeting, but said people came to seek his guidance for the well-being of the country. If there was a message of peace and reconciliation over Ayodhya, Rajiv did not share it. He made no effort to ban the laying of the foundation stone of the Hindu temple at a ceremony in which thousands of bricks brought from all over India were blessed. Nor did he condemn the action, which was bound to cause concern to all India's Muslims that Hindu nationalism was on the march again. Indeed, about the only positive thing that can be said about Rajiv's role in the Ayodhya dispute is that he turned down a suggestion that he himself lay the temple's foundation stone, a suggestion that reportedly emanated from his own home minister, Buta Singh. Buta Singh had several meetings with the Vishwa Hindu Parishad in the period leading up to the foundation stone ceremony on 9 November. That may have been a legitimate role for a home minister, but it strengthened the belief that Congress were quietly supporting this provocative enterprise. Was Rajiv really putting into effect a Congress decision to exploit the dispute at Ayodhya for political advantage, a decision which, according to Arun Nehru, had been taken nearly four years earlier? The suspicions grew ever stronger.

Launching his election campaign at Ayodhya's district capital of Faizabad, Rajiv claimed that only Congress could restore 'Ram Rajya'. Mahatma Gandhi had first coined this concept of India's Golden Age. He had in mind a land in which minorities of all sorts were protected by the existence of perfect justice, tolerance, equality and freedom. But, in an age where religious fundamentalism was on the verge of becoming religious bigotry, the notion of 'Ram Rajya' was all too easily misinterpreted to mean the rule of the god Ram, in other words, Hindu rule. It was a dangerous appeal to introduce into the election campaign, and one which risked further alienating Muslims who had already been alienated by the Bhagalpur communal massacre. Congress has always regarded the Muslim vote as a 'vote bank' on which it could depend, though the beliefs that Muslims vote *en bloc* for one party, or that Congress deserve to be regarded as the main protectors of Muslims and other minorities, are both open to question.

If Congress was 'playing the Hindu card', it seems to have backfired. The foundation stone ceremony on 9 November passed off peacefully thanks to a heavy police presence. But this dangerous appeal to Hindu sentiment did not appear to win Congress any support, and may indeed have helped lose Congress the election. The Janata Dal picked up the mantle of secularism, and with it the votes of the minorities. Voters who were of a Hindu fundamentalist persuasion rejected Congress in large numbers in favour of the BJP.

Rajiv himself kept a punishing schedule during the four-week campaign, addressing 170 meetings in as many constituencies. The choice of constituency visits was made on the strength of a computer assessment of the challenge to Congress. Rajiv would leave Delhi well before dawn on the air force Boeing which, for reasons of security, the Election Commissioners had allowed him to use, though the costs of operating the Boeing and the fleet of helicopters, which took him to locations without air strips, were charged to Congress. The prime minister took light meals only *en route*, and availed himself of shower facilities on board the Boeing allowing him to arrive at meetings even late in the day still looking fresh and relaxed. He also kept pretty closely to the timetable. A typical day took him to three or four states, addressing two or three meetings in each. Two fleets, each of three Soviet-built helicopters, had gone ahead, practising their landings in sometimes difficult locations on the previous day. His last meeting of the day would be well after dark, and after midnight he would take off by Boeing for the first port of call of the following day, catching a few short hours' sleep on the aircraft, or else in the circuit house on arrival. Only someone with Rajiv's stamina could have kept it up.

Towards the end of the campaign, some of Rajiv's scheduled meetings were cancelled. This was because of indications that large crowds could not be guaranteed to turn up – something which was already being exploited by the anti-Congress press – rather than because Rajiv was flagging. Opposition leaders had criticised the ruling that only Rajiv could use government aircraft, especially since they found their own movements by air were limited by the effects of a strike by Indian Airlines' engineers. Nor did it necessarily enhance Rajiv's image in the eyes of the people. As one of his political opponents asked: 'How can he know what's happening on the ground while he's moving around in the sky?'

As Rajiv travelled the length and breadth of the country, accompanied on at least one tour by his son, Rahul, Sonia and daughter Priyanka campaigned in his constituency, Amethi. It is a prospering constituency of 1½ million people, clearly showing the benefit of having the prime minister as its MP. Most roads are metalled and most villages have both drinking water and electricity. There had also been a mini industrial boom with many small factories setting up there. Sonia was the main attraction for curious villagers, anxious to see this foreigner who always wears a sari, and speaks good Hindi. She preferred to enter homes and talk to people at the roadside rather than address public meetings. She handed out Rajiv stickers and badges, and, to the ladies, caste marks to stick on the forehead in the shape of the Congress election symbol, the hand. Sonia's message was to point out how the situation in the villages of the constituency had improved since Rajiv became Amethi's MP eight and a half years earlier, and to appeal in Hindi: 'Brothers and Sisters, if you want our work to continue, vote for my husband.' She moved quickly between villages, earning herself the title 'the whirlwind of Amethi'. Explaining away her foreignness, Sonia told the electorate: 'I may be a daughter of Italy, but I am the daughter-in-law of Amethi.'

Rajiv made several fleeting visits to Amethi, campaigning as much for the Congress candidates in the state assembly elections, which were taking place in Uttar Pradesh simultaneously with the parliamentary poll. Though he was confidently expecting to be re-elected, the Janata Dal had chosen as its candidate the grandson of Mahatma Gandhi, Rajmohan Gandhi, which introduced both a rival dynastic appeal and a confusion of names into the electoral battle. Rajiv had entrusted the organisation of his campaign in Amethi to his pilot friend, Satish Sharma, who is sure that religion was an important factor in the constituency. He believes the BJP took advantage of the heightened Hindu awareness, promoted by the *Ramayan* and *Mahabharata* on television, whilst Congress lost the Muslim vote because Muslims were 'confused' about the party's position over Ayodhya and as a result of the Bhagalpur massacre which was, he says, 'a big factor'.

Cassettes and videos were widely used to help candidates put their message across. The major parties had special election songs composed and had them recorded by well known singers and movie stars. Candidates had themselves filmed meeting important people, and then showed the videos from the backs of campaign vehicles to enhance their appeal to an electorate that is addicted to films and television. Loudspeakers also blared forth political messages at street corners. Walls were bedecked with colourful posters displaying the party symbols – a hand for the Congress party and a wheel for the Janata Dal – which appear on the ballot paper to help illiterate people cast their votes. Posters of Rajiv, his mother and grandfather demonstrated that Congress considered the dynastic factor to be a plus point in their favour. They took advantage of the fact that the centenary of Nehru's birth and the 72nd anniversary of Indira's birth both fell during the campaign period. One of Rajiv's campaign slogans was *Mera Bharat*

Mahan, or 'My India is Great'. Both the slogan and Congress's use of Nehru and Indira Gandhi as campaign symbols were criticised by the Opposition, who resented the implicit suggestions that India belonged to Congress, or that Congress had a monopoly on patriotism.

V.P. Singh's face was noticeably absent from Janata Dal and National Front posters, probably because neither the party nor the alliance had been able to agree for sure that V.P. Singh was their candidate for prime minister. Had they done so, it might have improved their electoral prospects. Opinion polls suggested that an overwhelming majority of those planning to vote for the National Front wanted V.P. Singh to become prime minister, rather than any other National Front leader. In many respects, the election was a personality contest between Rajiv Gandhi and V.P. Singh.

All large parties are entitled to television airtime for election broadcasts. However, there was a row when Doordarshan, the television service, refused to allow a broadcast which mentioned Bofors. Opposition parties argued that Doordarshan had no legal right to censor or edit campaign broadcasts, and most of them decided to boycott television. In its own election coverage, Doordarshan showed a remarkable degree of balance, considering how unbalanced it had been over the previous few months. It was by now subject to additional rules on impartiality imposed by the Election Code. Significantly, all major parties, including Congress, were making much of their plans to reduce government controls over radio and television by granting the broadcasters greater autonomy. Inevitably, Opposition parties wanted to know why, if Congress believed in autonomy now, it had not already loosened the government's control over the electronic media.

Polling itself was an elaborate affair with just under 500 million people entitled to cast their votes. This included about 35 million who had newly gained the franchise with the lowering of the voting age from twenty-one to eighteen. Three and a half million officials were deployed to staff 589 449 polling booths in the largest exercise of democracy anywhere in the world. It was an awe-inspiring thought that the entire process took place on three days, with two rest days in between. The Election Commission, which is entrusted with organising elections, estimated the total bill was around Rs 1600 million (£66 million), not including what the political parties spent on their campaigns. In the circumstances it was more surprising that voting passed off peacefully at the vast majority of booths than that repolling was ordered at around 1200. It was, in fact, the most violent election India has ever had, with over 100 people killed in poll-related violence. There were many examples of 'booth capturing', especially in Bihar and Andhra Pradesh, with thugs employed by one party literally to capture polling booths and either mark all the ballot papers in favour of their candidate, or only allow known sympathisers to cast their votes.

What shocked many people was the extent of the violence in the prime minister's own constituency of Amethi, from where there was little doubt that Rajiv would be re-elected. It caused V. P. Singh to remark that the last action of the ruling party was to kill democracy. A prominent member of the Janata Dal and relative of V. P. Singh, Sanjay Singh, who was contesting for a state assembly seat from Amethi, was shot and badly injured in the stomach. Rajiv's Janata Dal-rival for the Amethi *Lok Sabha* seat, Rajmohan Gandhi, refused to accept the election result, pointing out that both the Returning Officer and the superintendent of police were implicated in attempts to rig the polls, and were transferred before the repolling took place. He brought an election petition which, if successful, would result in the Amethi result being declared null and void, and repolling ordered. This had happened to Indira Gandhi in 1975, prompting her to declare the Emergency rather than bow to the court ruling. The rigging and violence in the prime minister's constituency left a stain on the 1989 electoral process. According to Rajiv's campaign manager, Satish Sharma, it was unnecessary anyway since Rajiv had a clear lead over his nearest rival and namesake.

It was apparent to those reporting the campaign that many people were planning to cast their vote for negative rather than positive reasons. Many were rejecting Congress rather than endorsing the National Front alternative. This was especially true in traditional Congress territory like Bihar, where the party's almost universal renomination of its sitting MPs backfired. Voters showed their dis-satisfaction with the sitting MPs' performances by voting them out. In south India, where Congress did well in a reverse of the trend in the north, the biggest single factor seemed to be that people were casting their votes against the ruling state governments. There, it was not so much a pro-Rajiv or anti-V. P. Singh vote but rather it was a vote against the ruling DMK government of Tamil Nadu, or ruling Telegu Desam government of Andhra Pradesh, that allowed Congress to retain a majority of southern seats at the same time as it was losing most seats in the north.

It was clear as soon as counting started that no party would gain an overall majority of the 525 seats being contested. Indeed, the opinion polls were predicting that for the first time ever India would have a hung Parliament. What was less easy to anticipate was which party would be best placed to form either a minority or a coalition government. There was much discussion about the obligations of the president. Constitutional authorities agreed that he was not bound to call on the leader of the largest party if no party had an overall majority, but was obliged only to call on whoever he thought could command majority support in the *Lok Sabha*. Some authorities pointed to the precedent set in Britain in 1923 when King George V called on Ramsay MacDonald, the Labour leader, to form a government, even though Labour had won fewer seats than the Conservatives. The King had correctly anticipated that Stanley Baldwin's Conservative government would be defeated on the floor of the house by the combined votes of Labour and Liberals. The precedent could well have been held to apply to India since British precedents prevailing at the time of Independence have been held to apply to India.

The president's decision became easier when Congress made it clear that, despite having the most seats (193), they would not attempt to form a government. They accepted the fact that the Janata Dal (141), supported by the Bharatiya Janata Party (88) and the Communists and other leftists (51), had a better chance of forming a government, given the fact that these three groups had already enjoyed a loose alliance by their agreement not to contest against each other in many con-stituencies. Congress made no attempt to seek the support of any other party to help them form a government, but decided instead to accept defeat gracefully and to go into opposition. The decision was Rajiv's, though obviously he had the endorsement of senior Congress leaders.

The widely expected horse-trading, to induce elected members to change parties after being elected, did not take place, despite the facts that two well-known industrialists were sitting in Delhi hotels with cheque books at the ready, willing, it was said, to purchase support for Congress. The fact that this did not happen was due to Rajiv's anti-defection act which had effectively outlawed this practice by providing that any member changing his party would forfeit his seat, unless more than a third of elected party members changed sides. No newly elected MP would risk losing his seat in this way. So Rajiv offered his resignation, and broadcast to the nation: 'The people have given their verdict. In all humility, we respect their verdict.' It was as if he had looked back at the address his mother had given twelve years earlier on the only previous occasion that Congress had been defeated in a general election. Wanting to demonstrate that she continued to abide by the rules of democracy, even after the Emergency, she had said: 'My colleagues and I accept the verdict unreservedly, and in a spirit of humility.' Indira Gandhi in 1977 went on to offer her 'good wishes to the new government that will be formed'. So too did Rajiv in 1989. He said: 'A new government will be formed. We extend to them our good wishes, and offer them our constructive co-operation.' Rajiv pledged that Congress would re-dedicate itself to 'the cause of India's greatness', and expressed the hope that 'the basic pillars of our nationhood – democracy, socialism, secularism and non-alignment – would be maintained'.

Once Congress had accepted defeat, the focus of interest turned to the National Front to see if they could put together a government. Ideological differences ruled out the possibility of the Communists and the Bharatiya Janata party serving together in government, but both groups agreed to provide support from outside government to a minority National Front administration. The final hurdle was for the National Front to agree its leaders and candidate for prime minister. There was a challenge to V. P. Singh from at least one veteran politician, Mr Chandrashekar, who, as one columnist wrote, had spent more years being prime minister-in-waiting than most others had in politics. His candidacy was thwarted, though, after some nifty manoeuvring behind the scenes and V. P. Singh was appointed firstly by the Janata Dal and then by the National Front as leader. His decision to revive the post of deputy prime minister and to offer it to the Haryana chief minister, Devi Lal, owed more to the need for a balance of factions within the Front than anything else.

The swearing in of V. P. Singh was as graceful a transition of power as one could hope to witness. It took place under the glittering chandeliers and painted ceiling of the Ashoka Hall in the presidential palace, Rashtrapati Bhawan. Journalists outnumbered politicians, many of whom could not find seats. Rajiv Gandhi took his seat in the front row. When the prime minister-designate walked in, he made a bee-line for Rajiv, exchanging the clasped hands *'namastaye'* greeting with him. After President Venkataraman had administered the oaths of office to V.P. Singh and his appointed deputy, Devi Lal, in a ten-minute ceremony, Rajiv Gandhi was the first to offer the new leader his congratulations. It was as if he were saying 'no hard feelings' to this former friend and cabinet colleague, who had so strongly attacked Rajiv since being forced out of the government and out of the Congress Party two and a half years earlier.

The glamour of the occasion, with invited guests wearing their best apparel and the elegant presidential guard in turbans and red tunics, was a far cry from the sombre occasion five years one month and two days earlier when, in a hastily arranged ceremony, Rajiv Gandhi had been sworn in as prime minister a matter of hours after his mother's death. It marked the end of a politically-charged week which had seen the defeat of the Congress Party for only the second time in forty-two independent years. Speaking to journalists after the swearing in, an unrepentant Rajiv said he thought India had never had the sort of development and progress of the previous five years. This was one of the rare occasions on which representatives of the media had been able to speak to Rajiv since the Comptroller and Auditor General's report on the Bofors deal had appeared some months earlier. He had been cocooned by his aides throughout the election campaign. One journalist asked the former prime minister: 'Who got the Bofors money?' Noticing the editor of the *Hindu* in the circle of journalists, Rajiv replied: 'Why don't you ask N. Ram, he knows better than me?'

The new prime minister, V.P. Singh, scion of the small princely family of Manda in eastern Uttar Pradesh, is a very different man from Rajiv Gandhi. Despite his princely origins and university education, he has a better claim than Rajiv to be considered as a man of the people. He had cut his teeth in Uttar Pradesh state politics, rising to become chief minister, only to resign two years later after failing in his pledge to end banditry in the state. His strong principles, manifested in his determination as Rajiv's finance minister to crack down on corruption, bribery and other sorts of malpractice in public life, had both forced him out of Congress and won him popular support. This had also set him against Rajiv, and in Uttar Pradesh, from where both men draw their electoral support, the election was portrayed as a contest between Rajiv and 'the Rajah', as V.P. Singh is known.

Curiously Rajiv and V.P. Singh have at least two things in common.

Both received their secondary education in Dehra Dun; Rajiv attending the well known Doon School and V. P. Singh – Rajiv's senior by thirteen years – going to Colonel Brown's School. V. P. Singh still owns property in Dehra Dun, where he is regarded as a model landlord. Both Rajiv and V. P. Singh also regard the Uttar Pradesh city of Allahabad as their home town. All but one of India's seven prime ministers have come from Uttar Pradesh, but then three of the seven have come from the same family.

The day after resigning as prime minister, Rajiv was re-elected unopposed to lead the Congress party. There were many who believed Congress would dump him after the defeat. He owes his survival as party leader in the face of electoral defeat to two factors. First, the party's impressive showing in the four southern states, from where it won 103 of the 130 seats (more than half its total seats). It also recaptured control of the southern states of Andhra Pradesh and Karnataka in the simultaneous state assembly polls, some consolation for losing Uttar Pradesh. Congress was certainly not the losing party in south India, and the Congress MPs elected from there had reason to be grateful to Rajiv for the part he had played in their campaign. Unlike V. P. Singh, who confined his campaign to the north. Rajiv had campaigned extensively throughout the country.

The second factor that worked to Rajiv's advantage was the fact that all potential rivals for the Congress Party leadership – men like N. D. Tiwari of Uttar Pradesh, Jaganath Mishra of Bihar and Arjun Singh of Madhya Pradesh – found their power bases severely eroded by the election result. There were no clear contenders for leadership from the states where Congress remained strong, such as Maharashtra, Karnataka or Andhra Pradesh. Despite rumours that Rajiv already had a flight booked to Italy in the event of defeat, he made it clear he would continue to lead Congress, and repeated his pledge to bring democracy to the party. Sonia was said to have been strongly in favour of his remaining in politics.

Three months later, Rajiv suffered further setbacks when Congress fared badly at elections to eight more state assemblies. Only in Maharashtra and Arunachal Pradesh was Congress able to form governments. Rajiv had once again campaigned extensively, piloting himself in a light aircraft for much of the tour. He had greatly enjoyed the return to flying, but as far as the elections were concerned the results were, he said, 'very much as we had expected'. In other words, after losing the *Lok Sabha* elections, Congress had considerably reduced its expectations at the assembly polls.

By this time, Rajiv seemed to be enjoying Opposition, or at least had adjusted to his new role. In Parliament, Congress had not opposed some early measures by the V. P. Singh government, including the repeal of the notorious 59th amendment, which had provided for special emergency powers in Punjab. It also supported the constitutional amendment to extend President's Rule in Punjab. Rajiv had adjusted to a reduced level of security, which remained reasonably tight, had moved home a short distance to Janpath, one of New Delhi's elegant avenues, and had surrendered his much loved Mercedes and Range Rover to the government. They were the 'perks' of office that he had to leave behind. He also had to get used to travelling by public transport – scheduled flights and trains – except when Congress chartered the aircraft for his election tour. Till the state assembly polls were over, he was hardly less busy than he had been as prime minister, but was looking forward to spending more time with his family.

Shortly before the *Lok Sabha* elections, a music-loving friend from outside the political arena had put it to Rajiv: 'Suppose you lose the elections?' He replied: 'That would be peace for me. I shall just sit and listen to music with the children.' He was also hoping to take up old hobbies again; apart from the flying, he wanted to resume his interest in amateur radio. But remaining as Congress president, he also faced the tough task he had set himself four years earlier in Bombay of reforming the party, a task he said was still determined to carry out and which he thought would be easier to accomplish in opposition.

CHAPTER FOURTEEN

More Sinned Against than Sinning

When it seemed likely that Congress would not win the elections, a senior Delhi editor asked one of the prime minister's aides: 'Will Rajiv step down if he is defeated?' There seemed to be some doubt in his mind that Rajiv would accept the verdict of the people. The aide replied by pointing out that, as a 'Dosco' he would, of course, do the honourable thing. The editor understood, for both he and the aide were 'Doscos' too. The editor was Aroon Purie of *India Today,* a classmate of Rajiv's at Doon School. It was a vintage class of Doon School with, as the joke had it, both Rajiv and Aroon Purie running India today.

Behind that rather 'in' joke lies the truth that Doon School may not have provided Rajiv with the best preparation for the task of ruling India. Doon School boys benefited from some of the best teaching in India, but were, perhaps, not truly 'of India'. One of the main reasons Rajiv lost the 1989 election was because he was not seen to be a 'man of the people'. Five years earlier, that had not been an obstacle to his winning the largest majority ever won by any Indian prime minister; but different factors prevailed then. There had been the sympathy factor, the attraction of the political innocent, and there had been no clearly pre-eminent alternative. None of those facts was true any longer in 1989, when Rajiv was making a direct appeal to the people. He had promised to give power to the people, but the people – at least in northern India – were not impressed. Rajiv had become alienated from the people, who were more inclined to believe the Opposition when they promoted the notion that Rajiv, with his foreign wife, foreign tastes and excessive foreign travel, was himself a foreigner to the mass of Indians, for whom computers and the twenty-first century were as distant as another planet.

Rajiv found it more difficult than either his mother or his grandfather to transcend the hemispheres – to reconcile his Western education with the fact he was born an Indian. Both Nehru and Indira felt confident in the hurly burly of Indian political life; at the same time, they were at ease on the international stage. Rajiv often appeared to be more at ease abroad than at home. Nehru and Indira had both spoken better Hindi than Rajiv, and Nehru also spoke Urdu, the main language of India's Muslims. Rajiv's Hindi lacked finesse, or accuracy, and there are numerous stories of him choosing the wrong word, or pronouncing it in such a way that it sounded like the wrong word. A classic instance was his confusion of the Hindi words for independence, *swatantra,* and republic *ganatantra,* when he addressed the nation from Delhi's Red Fort on Independence Day, 15 August 1987, but repeatedly referred to it as Republic Day, India's other national day which falls on 26 January. A columnist asked: 'Does he really expect people to vote for a prime minister who doesn't know the difference between Independence Day and Republic Day?'

Rajiv knew his linguistic weakness, and took advice when preparing a broadcast, but that did not work when campaigning, or else he was too often given bad advice by others whose Hindi also left something to be desired. Rajiv also lacked a sense of history and often confused incidents from India's past; history and Hindi were never Rajiv's strong points at Doon School, where English is the teaching medium. It is notable that the elections demonstrated a ground swell of opinion against Congress throughout the Hindi-speaking states. Rajiv's deficiency in Hindi was not a problem in southern India, where Hindi is not widely used. There he addressed rallies in English, which was then translated into the regional language.

Corruption had become a key issue in the elections, largely at Rajiv's own behest. Rajiv had promised to change the system – to eliminate corruption and clean up public life. Far from having done so, it seemed to many he had let it become worse. One correspondent reported voters in one area as saying it was now impossible to complete any transaction, from getting a licence or permit to applying for a subsidised loan, without paying huge bribes. Even Rajiv himself had been tainted by charges of corruption, unjustifiably perhaps, although most people outside the major cities had little idea of the significance of the Bofors allegations. Even if they did, there was a tendency to say: 'So what? All politicians are thieves.' But corruption at the local level was another matter. In fact, the two were connected. There was an attitude of self-justification by the bribe taker saying: 'If the people at the top can do it, why can't I?'

The problems about the Bofors scandal for Rajiv was not so much the unproven suggestion that he had accepted commission money or bribes, as the way he continued to excuse their payment. He denied that commissions had been paid long after it was clear they had. Describing them as winding-up charges or payments for industrial espionage did not diminish the fact that commissions were paid. Then Rajiv repeatedly spoke of 'the feeling I get ... that we are not going to find any Indians', when asked who had received commissions. This contradicted the widespread belief that Indians had been the beneficiaries. These assertions combined to create an impression that Rajiv was not intent on getting to the bottom of the matter and identifying the beneficiaries. Rajiv's handling of the Bofors scandal allegations diminished his credibility as the incorruptible 'Mr Clean' of the Indian political establishment.

Yet, far from it being proven that Rajiv was corrupt, in many ways his weakness was that he had too much integrity to be a good politician. It was not so much a matter of taking or not taking bribes as the business of dispensing patronage. The circumstances of his coming to power – by inheritance rather than democracy in the first instance – prevented him from learning (as other politicians do) how the system worked. He had picked up a certain amount of experience of being prime minister by watching his grandfather and mother. But, unlike his mother, he had not picked up the technique of bestowing or denying patronage, which became so important after she concentrated party power in her own hands, or if he had he was unwilling to apply it. For Indira it had been a matter of survival, but Rajiv had never experienced the threat of political extinction, so had never been forced to play the survival game. Certainly, when Rajiv came to power he had brought friends into jobs around him, which is one form of political patronage, but he did not carry it further by, for example, rewarding political favours with election tickets or chief ministerships, whilst denying the same rewards to others who were not favoured.

One obvious test of Rajiv's integrity was his attitude to the Emergency, which most Indians had seen as an attempt to keep the Nehru–Gandhi dynasty in power. Rajiv had created an impression that he wanted to distance himself from the Emergency – the apology to the judge, a refusal to endorse the actions of his brother, Sanjay, even by moving his cremation away from Nehru's cremation site, and later by dispensing with Sanjay loyalists. Yet family loyalty would not allow a complete break with a policy that was as much his mother's as his brother's. It could have been another gaffe when he answered a question at his first prime ministerial press conference by saying that in certain circumstances it might be necessary 'to have another Emergency'. But it was not a gaffe, and he was not just being loyal. A few months later, he elaborated in an interview with the *Spectator*.[1] He said he had been against the proclamation of the Emergency at the beginning, and agreed with his interviewer that it had gone on too long: 'Six months would have been enough.' But he was not against emergency powers as such: 'There are situations when some powers are required by a government which it must use.' Later, he introduced the 59th amendment to ensure that his government had those powers ready to use in Punjab. As when he criticised his mother's government for not sending police into the Golden Temple earlier, his criticism of Indira's Emergency rule was one of degree rather than of the principle of assuming such powers.

Consistency was never Rajiv's strong point, which led to doubts about his motivation. He had, perhaps, failed to implement the Punjab accord because he subsequently realised it would do the Congress party no good. Similarly, he had second thoughts about his plans to reform the Congress party. It could have been a case of following the advice of the last person who offered it, or else of failing at first to comprehend fully the implications of what he was doing. All his domestic accords – Punjab, Assam, Mizoram – revealed a very noble desire to put national interests ahead of party interests. However, none completely worked; either because they were flawed from the start, or else because party interests prevailed – there were probably elements of both. Rajiv's attempts may have been naive but they had seemed to be well intentioned.

Rajiv badly wanted successes; probably he felt the need to prove himself as a politician. All his accords had been concluded at long, late-night negotiating sessions, though it can be questioned whether the right people were involved in the talks. Later, he was not above using accord politics as a means of distracting media attention from his political difficulties. For example, it has been claimed that Rajiv was over-hasty in rushing through the Sri Lanka accord because of

[1] *Spectator*, 12 October 1985: Rajiv Gandhi interviewed by Dhiren Bhagat.

fears that V. P. Singh was about to make a new revelation about the Bofors affair. Earlier, journalists had been flown to observe the air-drop over Jaffna as a diversion, it was claimed, from the publication the same day of the Swedish National Audit Bureau report into the Bofors deal.

Sanjay used, unkindly, to tell how the teenage Rajiv never could make up his mind whether to drink tea or coffee at breakfast, often changing his mind more than once before the servant had left the room. In power, too, he had a habit of changing his mind – on ministers, on party reform, on Muslim law, on the defamation bill, on R. K. Dhawan, on publishing the Thakkar report – even, famously in February 1986, on putting up the price of kerosene. Many of these *volte face* were the results of pressure, or uproar. He would have been better respected if he had done his homework first as to the likely impact of his measures, and then stuck by his decision. On party reform Rajiv admits it: 'I should have stuck to my guns.' On the Muslim law, and some of the other instances too, he later came to regret not following his first instincts. Such frequent changing of mind suggested an underlying lack of self-confidence, not a helpful trait in politics. Rajiv lacked the Durga-like power of his mother on such matters, but then he did not have the impetus, such as a threat from within the party, or from outside the country, to develop that power as she had done.

Rajiv's mother was, perhaps, his worst enemy. She had determined on dynastic succession, drafted him in as her heir, and yet failed to equip him fully for the task that was entrusted to him when she died. Rajiv insists he 'hadn't really thought of being prime minister at all'. Yet Indira's summoning of Rajiv into politics suggested she respected him so little as to disregard completely his clearly expressed wish to stick to his flying and the privacy of his family life, both of which meant a great deal to him. She may have needed him to fill the void left by Sanjay, for her own survival, but it was another thing to expect him to follow in her prime ministerial footsteps, as she clearly did. She was determined that the Nehru–Gandhis should continue to rule India. It was Indira who created the dilemma for Rajiv of having to choose between a son's duty to his mother and his own happiness. He chose the former, and in the process laid himself open to the charge of perpetuating a dynasty.

There had been a second 'drafting in' when Rajiv was persuaded to accept the job of prime minister. This time nobody's political survival was at stake. The deed had been done in the interests of national stability and party unity. Once again, Rajiv was left with little choice. At that crucial juncture, he truly was called to serve the nation. He talked about it with Sonia and 'finally decided to accept'. In such circumstances, could he have done anything else? The party had decided there was no alternative – it was a negative decision as much as a positive one. Recognising later how the party's self-serving interests had prevailed at that time of great difficulty, a senior Congress colleague of Rajiv's reflected: 'Rajiv really parachuted into the position of prime minister because of us. We got him down from the plane.' It had been an undisguised use of the Gandhi name to hold party and nation together.

The Nehru–Gandhi dynasty is referred to as if it were something unique in India. In terms of the way it has dominated the country since Independence, it is unique. But the family does not have a monopoly on dynastic succession. Two other former prime ministers – Lal Bahadur Shastri and Charan Singh – had sons who followed them into politics. In less prominent positions, there are many other political dynasties strewn around Bihar, Madhya Pradesh, Gujarat, Rajasthan and Haryana, to name just the states which seem to specialise in keeping politics within the family. The day that Rajiv stepped down as prime minister, the chief minister of Haryana, Devi Lal, stepped up to become deputy prime minister, bequeathing his old job to one of his sons, who was not even a member of the state assembly. Another son had been a rival for the job. Dynastic succession certainly did not end with the fall of Rajiv. The new government of V. P. Singh even included two members of the Nehru–Gandhi dynasty, Rajiv's second cousin, Arun Nehru, and his sister-in-law, Maneka Gandhi. Both were estranged from the politics of Congress, and estranged from Rajiv, but remained part of the dynasty.

Nor is dynastic succession unique to India. The subcontinent has seen Benazir Bhutto step into her father's shoes in Pakistan, something Sheikh Hasina Wajed would like to do in Bangladesh. Srimavo Bandaranaike stepped into her husband's shoes in Sri Lanka, and has both a son and a daughter who are rivals to succeed her. Further afield, Cory Aquino inherited her husband's mantle in the Philippines, and Aung San Suu Kyi is poised to inherit that of her father in Burma. The fact that, in most cases, the inheritance has been endorsed by an electorate does not change the fact that it is not only in monarchies that power has a habit of running in families.

In India, power has run in two families: the Nehru–Gandhi family as well as the great Congress family. For Rajiv, Congress could have been an even more valuable asset than his family name if, like his mother, he had used it to serve his own ends. Instead it became something of a millstone. It had been his mother who destroyed democracy within the Congress Party, making it her vehicle for wielding and holding onto power. It was a powerful vehicle which responded well to her own style of driving – appointing ministers, chief ministers and party office bearers and then removing them when they became too powerful. To manipulate the party in such a way required a close knowledge of its members. Political journalist Romesh Thapar likened Indira to 'a human computer' in this respect: 'She knew every Congressman, his relationships, his compromises in the past. She knew exactly how to place them, how they would vote.'[1] Rajiv did not have a close knowledge of the party or its senior members, even after being general secretary for more than three years, and prime minister and party president for five. He did not understand the rivalries between contending aspirants to chief ministerships, for example. It was as if Rajiv, who loved to drive all sorts of cars and aircraft, had finally come up against a vehicle that he could not drive because he could not understand what made it go. His solution was to drop his plans for change and reform, and send for his mother's former 'driver', R.K. Dhawan. In one of Rajiv's more blatant reversals, he acquitted Dhawan of four years' worth of post-assassination innuendo and gave him the key job of driving the Congress vehicle once more. This meant restoring to power those he had earlier castigated as 'self-seekers and spineless opportunists'. Business as usual had prevailed over reform and social transformation to bring back the party of his mother and brother.

When Rajiv's personal qualities were compared with those of Sanjay, Rajiv scored better in almost every respect. He lacked his late brother's political acumen, but that had made him seem at first like a refreshing alternative and given rise to new hope that the institutions his mother and brother had demolished would be reconstructed. Rajiv was 'a thoroughly decent chap' – everyone who knew him said so. He may have been a little lacking in imagination, but against that he is good-

---

[1] Quoted in *From Raj to Rajiv,* Tully and Masani.

looking, he is charming and he is affable. He has a warm personality and a sharp sense of humour. He is easy-going, hard-working and relaxed, if a little reserved. That reserve is something he acknowledges. Speaking in early 1984 in a BBC interview, he explained why he thought he would not make a good politician: 'I'm basically a very shy, introverted sort of person, so it would be difficult to come out openly.'

Rajiv has plenty of charisma. Furthermore, he is humble – not too proud to clean his own shoes, arrange his own books, drive his own car and stand up when a lady enters the room. Yet, in power he was accused of being arrogant, imperious, short-tempered with officials and politicians alike – traits which suggested insecurity. As an airline pilot he had not displayed these traits; colleagues from those days remember his modesty and humility. They developed after he had entered politics, and increased after he became prime minister. Probably it was a feeling of insecurity which gave Rajiv his tendency to talk down to officials, to tell them off or even sack them in public, like an autocrat from the Middle Ages. Some say Rajiv's main weakness was that he could not communicate with officials in a civilised manner. He was to regret his outbursts, especially when they did him harm. Of the humiliation of the foreign secretary he said: 'I didn't intend it that way, it just happened.' The victim believes it was a turning point: 'Until that day he could get away with abusing officials. Rajiv could do no wrong. After that it was different.'

Another wounding criticism was that Rajiv was out of touch. He did not find it easy to know what people were thinking – city people as well as rural people. As time went on, Rajiv became more and more insulated from public opinion. He was hindered, it is true, by a security apparatus which made it difficult for visitors to come in, and just as difficult for Rajiv to see out; hence the importance the aides assumed in granting access. They determined who saw Rajiv, and in that way determined what Rajiv saw. He was protected and isolated from much of India. Some of those who did manage to see Rajiv were not at all sure they had communicated with him, or he with them; there undoubtedly was a problem of communication. He seemed more amenable, more relaxed, with foreign visitors, or with members of the Indian intelligentsia. However, the Indian electorate do not appreciate aloofness on the part of their politicians, who are expected to be able to relate to the ordinary people. But then Rajiv had not wanted to be a politician and may have even despised politicians, just as he had once despised politics. Three years into his premiership, Rajiv admitted to a BBC interviewer that he still found politicking distasteful.

It may be Rajiv's aides who should be blamed for his failure to appreciate the extent to which there are two Indias. Those in a position to make comparisons between the two believe the gulf between them widened considerably under Rajiv. Much of what Rajiv stood for meant nothing to the India of the masses, who still do not earn enough to meet their daily needs and had yet to feel any benefits from economic liberalisation. Rajiv's appeal was essentially to India's middle classes to whom notions of modernity and of sweeping away the shibboleths of the past were attractive. The shining hope, the John F. Kennedy image, of the young technocrat who had promised to usher in clean and honest government was an attractive figure – until, that is, things began to go wrong and it became apparent that he could not deliver the goods. Over-ambitious plans led him to offer too much. He promised open government, but soon closed up again. He promised elections in the party, and *panchayat* elections in Punjab, but failed to meet the deadlines he himself set for holding them. The Punjab accord was to be implemented on Republic Day 1986, and the Sri Lanka accord was to bring peace almost immediately, and Indian troops home within about six months. Deadlines on both accords were wildly optimistic and the failure to meet them inevitably raised doubts as to whether Rajiv had ever intended to do so.

Indira had promised to eliminate poverty. The promise brought her re-election even if the task defeated her. Rajiv seemed less convincing when he made the equally-ambitious promise to eliminate unemployment and to give power to the people. Rajiv dreamed of a time when India was 'back in the leadership of human civilisation ... where poverty has been removed ... where there is social justice and every human being can live in dignity ... an India which is economically strong ... which has taken its rightful place in the world ... which sends out its message of tolerance and compassion ... to the whole world'. Much of Rajiv's dream was not particularly relevant to the mass of India's people, and even the parts which were barely came any nearer during his rule.

Many of those who criticised Rajiv used to claim he had been given bad advice – perhaps as a way of cushioning the impact of their criticism on Rajiv. Zail Singh, for example, blamed his alienation from the prime minister on those who had 'tried to create a rift' between them. Rajiv himself talked of his misjudgements in appointing ministers who were 'not up to the job'. But he had a free choice and could have chosen anyone he wanted, such was the power the mandate of the people had given him. In the last resort, he only can blame himself for his selections. Yet, in saying he misjudged their ability to 'cope with power', he may have been putting a brave face on the increasingly serious losses when one minister after another left him. These losses were more serious to his own standing than is appreciated. The loss of V. P. Singh, it can be argued, was fatal to his own survival in office. During mid-1987, Rajiv suspected there was a grand alliance against him involving V. P. Singh, Zail Singh and Arun Nehru among others. It nearly came about, but even in failure it induced a heightened sense of paranoia on Rajiv's part.

Rajiv Gandhi had come to power because of his family name and his immediate ancestry – he had no other qualification to be prime minister. His appointment was accompanied by the hope that he would hold together country and party. Later, he was returned to office by the electorate for similar reasons. He promised change and reform but in due course, Rajiv fell victim to the system he had inherited, a system he had difficulty understanding and making work in the way he wanted. He became frustrated by the obstacles that lay in his path. In the language of the piloting metaphor, to which Rajiv is addicted: 'There is so much free play in the controls that you can almost shake them at one end and nothing happens at the other end.' Had he succeeded in what he set out to do, he could have become a great prime minister.

Key Events Since Independence

15 August 1947	British India is partitioned into two new independent states, India and Pakistan, giving rise to communal violence between Hindus, Sikhs and Muslims; Jawaharlal Nehru becomes prime minister of India.
27 October 1947	The state of Jammu and Kashmir accedes to India, resulting in the first war between India and Pakistan for control of the state.
30 January 1948	The father figure of the independence movement, Mahatma Gandhi, is assassinated.
1 January 1949	A ceasefire comes into effect between India and Pakistan.
26 January 1950	Under its new constitution, India becomes a republic, but remains a member of the Commonwealth.
20 October 1962	War breaks out between India and China along their disputed frontier. Fighting ends a month later when China declares a unilateral ceasefire and withdraws.
27 May 1964	Jawaharlal Nehru dies; he is succeeded, after a brief interregnum, by Lal Bahadur Shastri.
5 August 1965	Breaches of the border and ceasefire line lead India and Pakistan into war for the second time.
11 January 1966	Lal Bahadur Shastri suffers a heart attack and dies a few hours after signing a peace treaty with his Pakistani counterpart in the Soviet city of Tashkent.
24 January 1966	Indira Gandhi is sworn in as India's third prime minister.
3 December 1971	A third war breaks out between India and Pakistan. This time, fighting is concentrated in the eastern wing of Pakistan, which emerges as the independent nation of Bangladesh after India vanquishes Pakistan.
2 July 1972	Indira Gandhi and President Zulfikar Ali Bhutto of

	Pakistan sign the Simla accord, marking the formal end of the Bangladesh war.
18 May 1974	India explodes what it describes as a peaceful nuclear device in the Rajasthan desert.
25 June 1975	Indira Gandhi declares an Emergency two weeks after the Allahabad High Court finds her guilty of corrupt electoral practices.
3 January 1976	Under the 42nd amendment to the constitution, India becomes a 'socialist secular' nation.
22 March 1977	After the sixth general election, Indira Gandhi resigns as prime minister, paving the way for the Janata Party, under Morarji Desai, to come to office; the Emergency is lifted.
19 December 1978	Parliament sentences Indira Gandhi to prison until the end of the session, a period of one week, for obstructing an enquiry into the Maruti car project.
28 July 1979	Charan Singh replaces Morarji Desai as prime minister after the latter is threatened with a parliamentary no-confidence motion.
14 January 1980	Indira Gandhi is sworn in as prime minister again after Congress triumphs in the seventh general election.
23 June 1980	Sanjay Gandhi is killed in a flying accident; ten days earlier he had been appointed a secretary general of the Congress Party.
15 June 1981	Rajiv Gandhi formally enters politics with his election to the *Lok Sabha* as MP for Amethi.
19 November 1982	Ninth Asian Games held in Delhi.
2 February 1983	Rajiv Gandhi is appointed a Congress Party general secretary.
5 June 1984	Indira Gandhi sends the Indian army into the Sikh Golden Temple at Amritsar in Operation Blue Star to flush out Sikh extremists; there is heavy loss of life.
31 October 1984	Indira Gandhi is assassinated by members of her bodyguard; Rajiv Gandhi is sworn in as India's sixth prime minister.

Bibliography

The following works were used extensively:

ABBAS, Khwaja Ahmad *Indira Gandhi: Return of the Red Rose* Bombay: Popular Prakashan, 1966.

AKBAR, M. J. *Nehru: The Making of India* Viking, pbk., 1988.

AKBAR, M. J. *Riot after Riot* Penguin, 1989.

ALI, Tariq *The Nehrus and the Gandhis: an Indian Dynasty* Picador, pbk., 1985.

GANDHI, Indira *My Truth by Indira Gandhi (as told to Emmanuel Pouchpadass)* New Delhi: Vision Books, 1981.

GUPTA, Bhabani Sen *Rajiv Gandhi: a Political Study* New Delhi, Konark, 1989.

GUPTE, Pranay *India The Challenge of Change* Mandarin, 1989.

HAZARIKA, Sanjoy *Bhopal: the Lessons of a Tragedy* Penguin, 1987.

MALHOTRA, Inder *Indira Gandhi: a Personal & Political Biography* Hodder & Stoughton, 1989.

MARTYN, Mady *Martin Sahib* New Delhi: Dass Media, 1985.

MASANI, Zareer *Indira Gandhi: a Biography* Hamish Hamilton, 1975.

RAM, Mohan *Sri Lanka: the Fractured Island* Penguin, 1989.

SHOURIE, Arun et al *The Assassination and After* New Delhi: Roli Books, 1985.

TULLY, Mark and JACOB, Satish *Amritsar: Mrs Gandhi's Last Battle* Jonathan Cape, hbk., 1985.

TULLY, Mark and MASANI, Zareer *From Raj to Rajiv: Forty Years of Indian Independence* BBC, 1988.

WOLPERT, Stanley *A New History of India* 3rd edn. New York: OUP, 1989.

Videocassette

GAREWAL, Simi *India's Rajiv* New Delhi: 1989.

Several newspapers and magazines were also used frequently, in particular the *Statesman, Hindu, Indian Post, India Today, Sunday,* the *Illustrated Weekly of India* and the twice-yearly *Perspectives on Current Affairs* (pub. Natraj, Dehra Dun).

Index